INTERNATIONAL ECONOMIC LAW SERIES

*Series Editors*

JOHN H JACKSON
ANDREW D MITCHELL
TANIA VOON

# Good Faith and International Economic Law

# Good Faith and International Economic Law

Edited by
ANDREW D MITCHELL
*Melbourne Law School, University of Melbourne, Australia*

M SORNARAJAH
*Faculty of Law, National University of Singapore*

TANIA VOON
*Melbourne Law School, University of Melbourne, Australia*

OXFORD
UNIVERSITY PRESS

OXFORD
UNIVERSITY PRESS

Great Clarendon Street, Oxford, OX2 6DP,
United Kingdom

Oxford University Press is a department of the University of Oxford. It furthers the University's objective of excellence in research, scholarship, and education by publishing worldwide. Oxford is a registered trade mark of Oxford University Press in the UK and in certain other countries



First Edition published in 2015



Published in the United States of America by Oxford University Press
198 Madison Avenue, New York, NY 10016, United States of America

British Library Cataloguing in Publication Data
Data available

Library of Congress Control Number: Data available

ISBN 978–0–19–873979–1

# *Acknowledgments*

This book was produced with generous support from the University of Melbourne and the National University of Singapore pursuant to an inaugural research partnership grant (2013–2014). Several of the chapters benefited from discussion at the Inaugural Symposium of the Global Economic Law Network held at the Melbourne School of Government on 2 May 2014 and the Symposium on Good Faith in International Law held at the Faculty of Law of the National University of Singapore on 3 October 2014, with funding from the Singapore Ministry of Education (Academic Research Fund Tier 1 Grant 2014).

The editors thank Alex Lee for his extensive editorial assistance in relation to numerous chapters. Valuable research assistance in the early stages was also provided by Elizabeth Sheargold pursuant to the Australian Research Council Discovery Project scheme (project ID DP130100838) and by Caroline Henckels. Finally, thanks go to Thijs de Jong for assistance in compiling the bibliography and to Jessica Casben and Irene Han for assistance at the final stages in proofreading and preparing the index and tables.

The opinions expressed in each chapter of this volume are those of the relevant authors and are not necessarily shared by the editors or any employer or other entity. The content of the chapters was drafted and finalized between April and October 2014.

# Contents

# Table of Cases

## INTERNATIONAL COURT OF JUSTICE

## PERMANENT COURT OF INTERNATIONAL JUSTICE

## WORLD TRADE ORGANIZATION

## INVESTMENT TREATY ARBITRATIONS

## OTHER INTER-STATE DISPUTES

# *Table of Treaties*

## BILATERAL AND REGIONAL INVESTMENT TREATIES

## PREFERENTIAL TRADE AGREEMENTS



## WORLD TRADE ORGANIZATION AGREEMENTS

## OTHER TREATIES

## DRAFT AND MODEL TREATIES

# *List of Contributors*

**Jorun Baumgartner** is currently a research and teaching assistant and PhD candidate at the Chair of Public International Law of the University of Lausanne. She is admitted to the bar in Germany and holds an LLM in European and International Economic and Commercial Law from the University of Lausanne and a Diploma of Advanced Studies in Mediation. Prior to pursuing her doctoral studies, she worked for several years as a legal advisor for the International Committee of the Red Cross in Geneva and as a lawyer in the private sector and private practice. Baumgarter is a contributing author to a *Commentary on the Swiss Penal Code* on crimes against humanity (2014). Her doctoral studies focus on international investment law.

**Heather L Bray** is a PhD Researcher at the University of Amsterdam for the Lex Mercatoria Publica Project directed by Professor Stephan Schill. She is also an SJD candidate in the International Trade and Business Law Program at the University of Arizona. Bray completed an Articling Placement in Ontario, Canada, with Dr Todd Weiler, in the area of international investment and commercial arbitration. She also was a Legal Research Associate with Juris Publishing, developing Arbitrationlaw.com, an online legal database dedicated to international arbitration. Bray completed a thesis-based LLM in Business Law and Taxation at the University of Western Ontario. She is a Barrister and Solicitor of the Law Society of Upper Canada. She holds an LLB from the University of New Brunswick and a BA in Justice Studies from Royal Roads University.

**Eric De Brabandere** is Associate Professor of International Law at the Grotius Centre for International Legal Studies at Leiden University, Visiting Professor at the Faculté Libre de Droit of the Université Catholique de Lille (France), editor-in-chief of the *Leiden Journal of International Law*, and a member of the board of editors of the *Journal of World Investment & Trade* and the *Revue belge de droit international*. He is also a member of the Brussels bar, practising in international law and international arbitration. He has published numerous articles and books on international investment law and arbitration, including *Investment Treaty Arbitration as Public International Law: Procedural Aspects and Implications* (Cambridge University Press 2014) and—as editor with Tarcisio Gazzini—*International Investment Law: The Sources of Rights and Obligations* (Martinus Nijhoff 2012) and *Foreign Investment in the Energy Sector: Balancing Private and Public Interests* (Martinus Nijhoff 2014).

**Andrew D Mitchell** is Professor at Melbourne Law School, Australian Research Council Future Fellow (2014-2018), Assistant Director Research at the Melbourne School of Government, Director of the Global Economic Law Network, and a member of both the Indicative List of Panellists to hear World Trade Organization disputes and the Energy Charter Roster of Panellists. In addition to his Melbourne teaching, Mitchell has taught law at Georgetown University, Bond University, Monash University, and the University of Western Ontario, and to Australian and overseas government officials for the Australian Attorney-General's Department and Department of Foreign Affairs and Trade, the International Development Law Organization, and the Canadian International Development Agency. Mitchell also consults for states, government departments, the private sector and international organizations. He has published over 100 academic books and journal articles on areas including the law of the World Trade Organization, international law, and international investment law. He is a series editor of the Oxford University Press International Economic Law Series, an editorial board member of the *Journal of International Economic Law*, and a general editor of the *Journal of International Dispute Settlement*. He has law degrees from Melbourne, Harvard and Cambridge.

**James Munro** is a PhD candidate at Melbourne Law School, The University of Melbourne. He has worked for a number of years in international trade law and international investment law as a Legal Officer in the Office of International Law of the Australian Attorney-General's Department. He has worked on a number of free trade agreement negotiations and on Australia's involvement in World Trade Organization disputes including as a third party, and he has provided general advice to government on World Trade Organization law and bilateral investment treaties. He has also spent time in the Office of International Climate Law, where he provided advice to government on legal issues relating to the *Kyoto Protocol to the United Nations Framework Convention on Climate Change*, international carbon markets, and various climate-related treaties under negotiation. Munro is currently undertaking graduate research into the consistency of the *Clean Energy Act 2012* with international trade law and international investment law.

**Martins Paparinskis** is Lecturer in Law at the University College London. He was previously a Junior Research Fellow at Merton College Oxford and a Hauser Research Scholar at New York University. He holds MJur, MPhil, and DPhil degrees from the University of Oxford. Paparinskis is a general international lawyer with a particular interest in international economic law and international dispute settlement. His publications on international economic law include articles in the *British Yearbook of International Law* and *European Journal of International Law; Basic Documents on International Investment Protection* (Hart Publications 2012); and a monograph, *The International Minimum Standard and Fair and Equitable Treatment* (Oxford University Press 2013). Paparinskis is a Member of the Council of Independent Experts in International and European Law for the Minister of Foreign Affairs of Latvia.

**Stephan W Schill** is Professor of International and Economic Law and Governance at the University of Amsterdam and Principal Investigator of the European Research Council-funded project on 'Transnational Public-Private Arbitration as Global Regulatory Governance'. He is admitted to the bar in Germany and New York and is a Member of the ICSID List of Conciliators. He is also the Editor-in-Chief of the *Journal* *of World Investment and Trade* and has published numerous articles and several books on international investment law, including *The Multilateralization of International Investment Law* (Cambridge University Press 2009) and, as editor, *International Investment Law and Comparative Public Law* (Oxford University Press 2010).

**M Sornarajah** LLB (Ceylon), LLM (Yale), LLM, PhD, LLD (London) is CJ Koh Professor at the Faculty of Law of the National University of Singapore. He was previously the Tunku Abdul Rahman Professor of International Law at the University of Malaya at Kuala Lumpur and Head of the Law School of the University of Tasmania, Australia. He is the author of *The Pursuit of Nationalized Property* (Martinus Nijhoff 1986), *International Commercial Arbitration* (Longman 1992), *The Law of International Joint Ventures* (Longman 1994), *The International Law on Foreign Investment* (Cambridge University Press 1996, 2nd ed 2004, 3rd ed 2010), and *The Settlement of Foreign Investment Disputes* (Kluwer 2001). He is joint editor of *China, India and the International Economic Order* (Cambridge University Press 2010). Sornarajah was the Director of the UNCTAD/WTO Programme on Investment Treaties, Pretoria and New Delhi. He is a Fellow of the Australian Centre for International Commercial Arbitration and is on the Regional Panel of the Singapore International Arbitration Centre. He has been arbitrator or counsel in several leading investment arbitrations. He has published extensively in the areas of international commercial arbitration, public international law and international investment law. He is an Advocate of the Supreme Court of Ceylon, an Advocate and Solicitor of the High Court of Singapore, and a Solicitor of the High Court of England and Wales. He is an Honorary Member of the Indian Society of International Law.

**Isabelle Van Damme** works as a legal secretary (référendaire) in the chambers of Advocate General Sharpston at the Court of Justice of the European Union and is a Visiting Lecturer at the Université Catholique de Louvain. She previously worked as an associate in Sidley Austin's Geneva office, with a practice focused on World Trade Organization law and its enforcement, and as a lecturer and the Turpin-Lipstein Fellow at Clare College, University of Cambridge. She has been a visiting researcher at Columbia University in New York, the Graduate Institute's Centre for Trade and Economic Integration in Geneva, and the Institute of International Economic Law in Washington DC. Her previous work experience also includes a legal internship at the Appellate Body Secretariat of the World Trade Organization and a Legal Liaison Officer position at the United Nations International Law Commission. She holds degrees from the Universiteit Gent, Georgetown University Law Center, and the University of Cambridge and is a member of the editorial boards of the *Revue belge de droit international* and the *Cambridge Journal of International and Comparative Law*. Her publications include a monograph on *Treaty Interpretation by the WTO Appellate Body* (Oxford University Press 2009).

**Tania Voon** is Professor and from 2012 to 2014 was Associate Dean (Research) at Melbourne Law School, The University of Melbourne. She is a former Legal Officer of the Appellate Body Secretariat of the World Trade Organization and has previously practised law with Mallesons Stephen Jaques and the Australian Government

Solicitor. She has taught law at Georgetown University, the University of Western Ontario, the Australian National University, Monash University, and Bond University. Voon undertook her LLM at Harvard Law School and her PhD in law at the University of Cambridge. She has published widely in the areas of public international law and international economic law. She is the author of *Cultural Products and the World Trade Organization* (Cambridge University Press 2007) and a member of the Indicative List of Governmental and Non-Governmental Panellists for resolving World Trade Organization disputes and the Roster of Panellists to assist in the resolution of trade disputes between parties to the Energy Charter Treaty. Voon has provided expert advice and training to entities such as the Australian Department of Foreign Affairs and Trade, the World Trade Organization, the World Health Organization, Telstra, and the McCabe Centre for Law and Cancer. In 2014 she was Senior Emile Noël Fellow at the Jean Monnet Center for International and Regional Economic Law & Justice, New York University School of Law.

**Andreas R Ziegler** studied economics, international relations and law at the Universities of St Gallen (BA, MA, BLaw, MLaw), Madrid (Escuela Diplomatica), Paris (SciencesPo), Florence (LLM, European University Institute), Oxford, and London (University of London, School of Oriental and African Studies (SOAS)). After obtaining his doctorate in St Gallen in 1995, he undertook post-doctoral research at Georgetown University Law Center (Washington DC) and the Max Planck Institute for Comparative Public Law and International Law in Heidelberg (Germany). He was a civil servant working for several Swiss Ministries as well as the European Free Trade Association (EFTA) Secretariat and the European Commission before being appointed full professor of law at the University of Lausanne in 2003. He is currently the Director of its LLM Program in International and European Economic and Commercial Law. Ziegler holds an adjunct professorship at the Law School of the University of New South Wales as well as permanent visiting appointments at the Universities of Saarbrücken, St Gallen and ETH Zürich. He has been invited to teach at many universities around the world, including Lund, Paris, Rome, Cyprus, Berlin, Chicago-Kent, Stetson College of Law, University of Technology, Sydney (UTS) and Pittsburgh. He has published widely on European law, public international law, international courts and tribunals, and trade and investment. He regularly consults for states, government departments, the private sector and international organizations and has represented clients in arbitral proceedings and before the European Court of Human Rights and is counsel with a Zürich-based law firm.

# 1

# Introduction

*M Sornarajah*

Good faith is a doctrine that is readily accepted in legal systems. Yet, its distinct meaning has always been elusive. Ideas such as justice and equity are omnipresent in the law. Good faith is counted among such ideas. Their function has been to provide a corrective approach in situations where the strict application of the law has unacceptable results. They are also used to support a decision-maker's conclusions on difficult issues where other solutions are equally possible. In these situations, good faith and similar ideas become rationalizations for the results arrived at. Defined or explained in this way, their existence in the law may be desirable. But put differently, these nebulous doctrines exist in the law to aid in finding subjective solutions to difficult issues, which may come to be justified through the use of such lofty notions. The latter conclusion immediately invites the criticism that the doctrine of good faith is capable of manipulation in order to justify a variety of inconsistent results. Critics argue that the subjectivity inherent in these concepts makes their use of doubtful significance. They have such a variable meaning that they could be used to support a variety of conclusions and befuddle the law in its search for certainty. Having in itself no power to lead to conclusions, the purpose of a concept such as good faith may be misguided: that of justifying conflicting solutions to difficult problems.

Yet the doctrine of good faith has been used so often in the law that it cannot be wished away on the basis that subjectivity needs to be eliminated. Clearly, its continuous use demonstrates that the application of good faith has extended beyond the criticisms relating to subjectivity. Other concepts of international law are equally nebulous but are not discarded for that reason. Indeed, natural lawyers found most rules of international law in concepts of justice and reasonableness. Specific instances of amorphous principles in international law are notions of necessity in state responsibility or equity in maritime delimitations. The law does have principles and values that loom over its rules to ensure that their application does not lead to unjust results.

The proper application of these principles has salutary results and aids in choosing between different solutions. Good faith is one such principle, which, though of uncertain content, guides the application of law by providing values, which in some cases do become reified into rules. An example is provided by estoppel, which originates in the notion of good faith, ensuring that a representation made by a state is binding on it when another state acting to its detriment in reliance on that representation seeks a remedy. Less concrete notions such as honesty, fidelity to agreements, reasonableness, and an expectation that corners are not cut so that the purpose of the law is defeated are all attributes of good faith. They abound in the common law relating to contracts and in administrative law relating the exercise of executive discretion. It is, however, not necessary to have recourse to good faith as a general principle of legal systems. It is sufficient to state that legal systems can function only when there is such a notion as good faith, which imposes fundamental values on international actors and ensures internal consistency in the law.

Since good faith prescribes normative values in international law, it may provide guidance in areas of international law that have become heavily contested. The international law on foreign investment—particularly that branch of it dealing with the application of rules in investment treaties by arbitral tribunals—is currently undergoing a crisis of legitimacy.[1] This area is replete with controversy, resulting from inconsistent awards relating to the same dispute or to the same or similar clauses in the various treaties. The reasoning adopted in the awards has also varied. It is sometimes alleged that expansionary interpretations are adopted in order to advance political or economic objectives unintended by the original parties to the treaty.[2] An allegation has recently gathered momentum that the law is made by a select group of identifiable arbitrators, who have directed the law on a particular course favouring investment protection over the regulatory interests of the state.[3]

These allegations have caused consternation in many areas of this branch of the law. Consequently, a question arises as to whether a review of the area through the normative prism of good faith may have a contribution to make in alleviating some of the harsher features of the crisis. This is one of the questions addressed in this book. None of the contributors set out with a vision that good faith offers solutions to the difficulties. In fact, it is the view

[1] See, eg, Susan Franck, 'The Legitimacy Crisis in Investment Treaty Arbitration: Privatizing Public International Law through Inconsistent Decisions' (2005) 73 Fordham L Rev 1521.

[2] See, eg, M Sornarajah, 'A Coming Crisis: Expansionary Trends in Investment Treaty Arbitration' in Karl Sauvant (ed), *Appeals Mechanism in International Investment Disputes* (OUP 2008) 39.

[3] See, eg, Gus Van Harten, *Investment Treaty Arbitration and Public Law* (OUP 2007) 167–75.

of some of the contributors that the significance of good faith to the controversies in the area is minimal. Nevertheless, the exercise is a useful one in that it indicates the extent to which good faith can play a role in difficult areas. The studies have a broader significance for international law in that they illustrate the manner in which good faith is relevant to treaty interpretation as well as to the solution of contested issues in international investment law.

In the context of international law, good faith may be relevant in many ways. Such relevance is explored in the early chapters of this work. As a doctrine that hovers above the law, good faith may have a corrective and harmonizing role to play that is essential in this field, given the inconsistencies that abound in the law as a result of conflicting awards. The legitimacy of the law depends on its internal coherence. This coherence is lacking in international investment law. Good faith may help in offering a test by which the inconsistent awards are to be judged. The difficulty with such a suggestion lies in reaching agreement on the overarching propositions. There are, however, essential ideas that good faith could provide, such as that dishonest resort to law should be avoided, or that the law should not be used to subvert the objectives of the host state's laws. The testing of the awards in the context of such good faith values may be a useful exercise in restoring legitimacy to the area. This suggestion presupposes that the inconsistencies are not due to entrenched attitudes within the subject area that would militate against the use of good faith in this fashion.

Good faith also has a role in restraining the decision-maker from wavering from an objective assessment of the fact situation or from an application of the law—determined through objective reasoning—to the facts. As already noted, one major criticism that has accumulated much force in the recent literature is that arbitrators are biased towards certain solutions that favour business over the public interest of the host state. The allegation is that arbitrators are drawn from a narrow circle[4] that is predisposed towards solutions that are favourable to big business. There is also the charge that arbitrators seek to build standards of transnational governance so that the doing of justice becomes secondary to the task of establishing such rules. Good faith may provide a corrective function in these instances, in that the arbitrator becomes tied to the purpose of making an analysis that is consistent with an objective doctrine. But, again, this proposed solution is open to the criticism that arbitrators inclined to give a pro-business award will be able to use good faith as an argument in their favour. The oft-repeated allegation is that arbitrators promote a neoliberal agenda that ensures that the law protecting

[4] See, eg, Anthea Roberts, 'Clash of Paradigms: Actors and Analogies Shaping the Investment Treaty System' (2013) 107 AJIL 45, 83.

business and investment interests are built up. Good faith, by providing a neutral touchstone, may provide a method of correction. But good faith may also be used as an argument to advance the neoliberal agenda, as the promotion of contractual sanctity or the protection of property are based on promises, the keeping of which can be consistent with good faith aims. Good faith may not provide a panacea in such situations.

A third situation in which good faith may be relevant in international investment law is at the procedural or jurisdictional stages of arbitration. The identification of the standing of the claimant is a pressing problem in investment arbitration, as the notion of corporate nationality can be manipulated to provide standing, as can be other rules, such as the obligation to accord most-favoured-nation treatment. The extent to which good faith is relevant to these issues is discussed in two chapters in this work (chapters 5 and 6). The conclusions that are arrived at are markedly different, revealing again the difficulties that arise from the use of good faith. But the promising fact is that both chapters agree on the relevance of good faith in at least some situations: where there is clear dishonesty involved in the use of potentially lawful doctrines to establish jurisdiction.

The assumption of good faith reduces transaction costs. Where parties to global transactions act with honesty and maintain commitments, mutual interest is furthered. The objectives of the transaction are achieved. Transparency and other values important to the functioning of business and investment are furthered. The making of rules that are favourable to establishing such a climate in which relationships take place are important. This is another reason why rules must be tested on the basis of whether or not they promote good faith.

Good faith also becomes relevant in establishing the substantive law. The allegation has been made that the substantive law of international investment has been developed in arbitral awards well beyond the original intention of the states parties to the relevant treaties. The tendency to develop a system of precedent in investment arbitration has led to the judicialization of the system.[5] With a select group of arbitrators dominating the course of developments in the law, the course the substantive law has taken has been unpredictable. States have tried, sometimes in vain, to check these tendencies. Many of the expansionist interpretations have related to the traditional substantive law of investment protection, such as expropriation or the international minimum standard for the treatment of aliens. These interpretations

[5] See Walter Mattli and Thomas Dietz, 'Mapping and Assessing the Rise of International Commercial Arbitration in the Globalization Era: An Introduction' in Walter Mattli and Thomas Dietz (eds), *International Arbitration and Global Governance* (OUP 2014) 1, 15.

have not attracted as much criticism as the adventures undertaken with the amorphous formula of 'fair and equitable treatment',[6] a phrase that remained dormant for over half a century of its use. Suddenly, the fair and equitable treatment standard has sprung to life. It has been given interpretations that had never before been thought possible. It has become the mainspring of modern investment arbitration, with a large number of awards pronouncing damages on the basis of its wide interpretation. One might attribute this tendency as the major underlying cause of the legitimacy crisis in investment arbitration. There could be much speculation as to why this phenomenon has taken place in the last few years. But the fact is that the law has been given new moorings simply through interpretation—a phenomenon that has caused much anxiety. The question is whether notions of good faith may offer any guidance in providing solutions to this anxiety—a question that is addressed in this work.

Good faith requires internal consistency of the law. One reason for the crisis is the absence of such internal consistency that results from contrary interpretations of the same clause in different treaties, or from the different solutions arrived at in disputes involving similar facts. The good faith doctrine is useful in requiring consistency that is arrived at without giving expression to subjective preferences for particular kinds of solutions. Unfortunately, discussions within the field have alleged that awards have been made based on the preferences of the handful of arbitrators who have dominated investment arbitration. Good faith mandates the ending of such a situation and the elimination of subjectivity.

This book demonstrates the range of scholarly views applicable to good faith in international investment law and the questions that remain to be answered. A summary of the remaining chapters of the book follows. In chapter 2, Andreas Ziegler and Jorun Baumgartner survey good faith in international law. This first chapter lays the foundation for later discussions. It addresses the fact that the doctrine of good faith is hazy and has no certain content. Good faith is, as the writers put it, like 'a Swiss army knife', a doctrine of utility that supports a wide variety of functions. Good faith has a role as a catalyser of values in international law, in unification and in law creation. In investment arbitration, Ziegler and Baumgartner point out that good faith acts to prevent an abuse of the system through concretizing concepts such as legitimate expectations, estoppel, acquiescence, abuse of rights, abuse of process, and clean hands. The chapter contains an analytical statement of the extent to which good faith has impacted international investment law in each

[6] See, eg, Martins Paparinskis, *The International Minimum Standard and Fair and Equitable Treatment* (OUP 2013) 251–56.

of these areas. While the risk of subjectivity exists, the writers conclude that good faith can help in clarifying and refining the content of specific obligations in the law.

Eric De Brabandere and Isabelle Van Damme deal with the use of good faith in treaty interpretation in chapter 3. Pointing out that the relevance of good faith in treaty interpretation cannot be denied,[7] the authors suggest that good faith has an objective function, in that the process of treaty interpretation must be clear. They advert also to the subjective function of good faith, which establishes that the interpreter must act reasonably. On this view, the criticism of subjectivity in good faith becomes limited by the notion of reasonableness. The authors consider some of the situations in international investment law and international trade law in which the good faith principle has figured in the interpretation of treaties. They indicate the manner in which the objective and subjective functions of good faith have guided interpretation. Their comparison of the WTO tribunals with investment treaty tribunals in the use of good faith in interpretation is particularly instructive.

Chapter 4, by Tania Voon, Andrew Mitchell and James Munro, further examines the roles played by the tribunals in international investment law and international trade law. This chapter considers the jurisdictional and substantive overlaps in trade and investment regimes that give rise to parallel disputes, and the normative considerations such as double remedies and conflicting outcomes that inform why parallel disputes may need to be proactively managed by adjudicatory bodies in certain circumstances. The principle of good faith has provided the conceptual framework for the development of a number of legal tools to manage parallel disputes including *lis pendens*, estoppel, and abuse of rights. This chapter evaluates the extent to which these tools may be deployed in trade and investment regimes. Although these tools are available to varying degrees *within* the trade and investment regimes, a margin of uncertainty exists in their scope and application, such that they are insufficient to manage disputes that originate *across* the two regimes.

The next three chapters deal with specific procedural and substantive areas of the law of international investment and the relevance of good faith in settling issues in these areas. These three chapters demonstrate the differences that are generated in the use of the good faith doctrine and how scholars may differ as to their use in specific areas. This is the problem that befuddles the whole field of investment arbitration and gives rise to inconsistency in the

[7] *Vienna Convention on the Law of Treaties*, opened for signature 23 May 1969, 1155 UNTS 331 (entered into force 27 January 1980) art 31(1) specifies that a 'treaty shall be interpreted in good faith in accordance with the ordinary meaning to be given to the terms of the treaty in their context and in the light of its object and purpose'.

awards. Reasonable lawyers arrive at entirely different conclusions through the use of perfectly logical processes of reasoning. Good faith does not provide a solution to the restoration of consistency, simply because of the subjectivities that are inherent in the doctrine.

Chapter 5, by Stephan Schill and Heather Bray, deals with issues that arise with protected investments and corporate restructuring. On numerous occasions, investment treaty tribunals have relied—and in some cases have refused to rely—on the principle of good faith to ensure that only *bona fide* investments and investors are protected under the relevant investment treaty. This chapter reviews the jurisprudence on illegal investments and corporate structuring and attempts to expose the purpose of the principle of good faith within this context. The chapter questions whether tribunals should rely on this principle to restrict the definition of investor and investment or whether the plain meaning of treaty provisions should prevail. Although there may be a small role for the principle of good faith in investment treaty arbitration, particularly where domestic regulation falls short of international standards, an expansive application of the principle should be rejected. Instead, the authors maintain that tribunals should focus on treaty language and respect domestic regulation in determining which investments and corporate structures the host state wishes to protect.

In chapter 6, I build on chapter 5 while focusing on the 'denial of benefits' provisions introduced in treaties as a direct consequence of investors attempting to invoke the protection of investment treaties through the device of incorporation of companies. The object of the treaty—being economic cooperation and promotion of investment flows between the two states parties—cannot be facilitated by 'post-box' companies. Therefore, states began in newer treaties to insert denial of benefits provisions, giving the host state the power to deny protection to companies it thought did not qualify for protection. Yet despite the common inclusion of such provisions, arbitral tribunals have shown continued reluctance to 'lift the veil' in order to find the true purpose of a given incorporation. Good faith principles may provide an answer that effectively accommodates the interests of investors as well as those of host states, in determining whether incorporation is used in a manner that satisfies the purposes behind the treaty.

Chapter 7, by Martins Paparinskis, deals with fair and equitable treatment. The fair and equitable treatment standard is one of the most important rules of international investment law, yet the vagueness of its textual expression causes considerable problems in interpretation and application. In the absence of clear textual guidance, tribunals and legal writers have sometimes turned to more general concepts such as good faith and abuse of rights to clarify the scope and meaning of fair and equitable treatment.

Good faith might certainly be relevant in informing established aspects of fair and equitable treatment, such as the more extreme cases of arbitrariness. At the same time, as Paparinskis makes clear, it would be misleading to equate fair and equitable treatment with an obligation to treat investors in good faith. Good faith is part of the interpretative process of fair and equitable treatment; it may inform the structure of certain elements of fair and equitable treatment, particularly in the early stages of development; still, there is no special normative relationship between fair and equitable treatment and good faith.

Overall, good faith is a relevant lens through which to look at the legitimacy crisis in international investment law. At the least, good faith highlights the issues, even if it does not provide solutions. An intermediate view is that good faith does provide solutions to identifiable facets of the developments that have taken place. At the most, one can argue that every facet of the present developments should be looked at through the prism of good faith and that such a view would provide suitable correctives to the crisis. All these different views are reflected in the chapters of this book.

# 2

# Good Faith as a General Principle of (International) Law

*Andreas R Ziegler and Jorun Baumgartner*

## 2.1 Introduction

Good faith permeates virtually every legal relationship, be it in the domestic or international law context. Without good faith, social relations would be doomed to fail, showing the importance of the principle for a peaceful coexistence of individuals and nations and its primordial social ordering function. In an ever more deeply integrated world economy, good faith also mandates a higher degree of cooperation and mutual confidence between the international actors involved, thus highlighting its stabilizing function. In international dispute settlement, good faith has a firm place as both a facilitating and a restraining agent: it helps, on the one hand, to infuse predictability and reasonableness into state behaviour, furthers due process, and serves as an interpretative tool for international courts and tribunals, while on the other hand it restrains legal formalism and arbitrariness.

With all these virtues incorporated in one principle, good faith could be characterized as the 'Swiss army knife' among international legal principles. Yet, at the same time, good faith is an inherently abstract notion, leaving a broad margin of discretion to the person deciding whether the principle of good faith has been respected. Unsurprisingly, then, international courts and tribunals, wary of their legitimacy and jurisdictional mandates, remain very careful to attach the principle only to more concrete particularizations.

To prepare the basis for more detailed discussions of specific issues related to the principle of good faith in subsequent chapters, this chapter will examine its various manifestations and provide an overview of their uses in general international law and international economic law. While the remainder of this introduction thus aims at giving shape to the content of the principle, part 2.2 looks at the still controversial question of whether the principle of good faith may be applied in an autonomous manner, ie even in the absence of a codified norm or concretizing principle. Part 2.3, finally, examines the various manifestations of the principle of good faith as applied and interpreted by international courts and tribunals.

### 2.1.1 Determining the content of good faith

There is little doubt that the principle of good faith can be considered both a general principle of law within the meaning of article 38(1)(c) of the *Statute of the International Court of Justice* (ICJ) and a general principle of international law.[1] Some commentators also consider the principle of good faith a principle of customary international law.[2] Moreover, good faith has sometimes been termed an 'essential'[3] or 'fundamental'[4] principle of international law, though the legal import of this terminology is not completely clear. However, whether the principle of good faith can also be considered a norm of *jus cogens* remains controversial.[5]

In accordance with the gap-filling function attached to general principles of law,[6] this classification means that the principle of good faith will usually be resorted to only where a dispute cannot be settled on grounds of its treaty or customary law-based concretizations. The difficulty lies thus not so much in the normative classification of the principle of good faith as in giving

[1] John O'Connor, *Good Faith in International Law* (Dartsmouth 1991) 119; Marion Panizzon, *Good Faith in the Jurisprudence of the WTO: The Protection of Legitimate Expectations, Good Faith Interpretation and Fair Dispute Settlement* (Hart Publishing 2006) 11; Ian Brownlie, *Principles of Public International Law* (7th edn, OUP 2008) 19; Appellate Body Report, *United States—Import Prohibition of Certain Shrimp and Shrimp Products,* WTO Doc WT/DS58/AB/R (adopted 6 November 1998) para 158; on the—not always clear—difference between a general principle of law and a general principle of international law, see, eg, Maurice Mendelson, 'The International Court of Justice and the Sources of International Law' in Vaughan Lowe and Malgosia Fitzmaurice (eds), *Fifty Years of the International Court of Justice: Essays in Honour of Sir Robert Jennings* (CUP 1996) 63, 79; Alain Pellet, 'Article 38' in Andreas Zimmermann, Christian Tomuschat and Karin Oellers-Frahm (eds), *The Statute of the International Court of Justice: A Commentary* (2nd edn, OUP 2012) paras 250, 260; Robert Kolb, *La Bonne Foi en Droit International Public* (Presses Universitaires de France 2000) 57.

[2] See, eg, Andrew Mitchell, 'Good Faith in WTO Dispute Settlement' (2006) 7 Melb J Intl L 339, 345.

[3] Bin Cheng, *General Principles of Law as Applied by International Courts and Tribunals* (Stevens and Sons 1953) 105.

[4] Brownlie (n 1) 19; O'Connor (n 1) 124; Elisabeth Zoller, *La Bonne Foi en Droit International Public* (Editions Pedone 1977) 12.

[5] Rejecting good faith as a *jus cogens* norm, see, eg, Panizzon (n 1) 11; Markus Kotzur, 'Good Faith (Bona fide)' in Rüdiger Wolfrum (ed), *Max Planck Encyclopedia of Public International Law* (OUP) <www.mpeil.com> accessed 29 July 2014, para 22; but see Kolb, *Bonne Foi* (n 1) 158–61.

[6] Pellet (n 1) para 278; Hersch Lauterpacht, *The Function of Law in the International Community* (Clarendon Press 1933) 115–18; Mendelson (n 1) 80; Kolb, *Bonne Foi* (n 1) 77.

shape to its content. First of all, a distinction is necessary between the legal and the 'extra-legal' elements of good faith, the latter of which can be seen as comprising a political and a moral meaning of good faith.[7] Most authors seem to agree that both legal and 'extra-legal' elements are inherent in the principle of good faith.[8]

As for the legal notion of good faith, scholars agree that in the absence of further particularization the principle remains an abstract and value-oriented notion that combines moral elements such as trust, honesty, fairness, loyalty or reasonableness with 'more precise legal contents, eg the principle of reciprocity [or] the objective and purpose-oriented method of interpretation'.[9] As long as it is not further particularized and thus rendered operational, its potential vagueness risks exposing the deciding tribunal to accusations of 'judicial activism'.[10]

As one commentator vividly explained:

> [G]ood faith plays ... a role in international law comparable to that of a catalyst in a chemical reaction. Alone, the catalyst is completely passive. It must be added to other elements for a reaction to occur; without it, nothing will happen, even if all the necessary components are present in sufficient quantities. It is a bit the same with good faith ... It is always related to specific behavior or declarations and it invests them with legal significance and legal effects ...[11]

The principle of good faith may thus find expression in various ways. As Cheng observed in 1953 in his seminal work on general principles of law, good faith plays an overarching role in treaty relations and 'governs treaties from the time of their formation to the time of their extinction',[12] thereby translating into general obligations (some of which are now codified in the *Vienna Convention on the Law of Treaties* (*VCLT*))[13] such as: to abstain from acts, pending ratification of a treaty, that would prejudice the rights of the other party; having ratified the treaty, to perform it in good faith and not to frustrate its object and purpose; to negotiate and settle disputes in good faith; to interpret treaties in good faith; and to exercise rights in good faith.[14] Other

[7] Kolb, *Bonne Foi* (n 1) 82–85; see also Kotzur, 'Good Faith' (n 5) para 22.

[8] *Contra* Zoller (n 4) 339, 345, for whom good faith is a purely psychological and thus non-legal notion.

[9] Kotzur, 'Good Faith' (n 5) para 22; O'Connor (n 1) 124.

[10] Kotzur, 'Good Faith' (n 5) para 26; Helge Elisabeth Zeitler, '"Good faith" in the WTO Jurisprudence, Necessary Balancing Element or an Open Door to Judicial Activism?' JIEL 8(3) 721, 753.

[11] Michel Virally, 'Notes and Comments: Review Essay: Good Faith in Public International Law' (1983) 77 AJIL 130, 133.

[12] Cheng (n 3) 106.

[13] Opened for signature 23 May 1969, 1155 UNTS 331 (entered into force 27 January 1980).

[14] Cheng (n 3) 106–20; Mitchell (n 2) 345.

authors emphasize the role of good faith in founding general duties of loyalty, cooperation, and information, which may also apply to unilateral acts.[15]

The principle of good faith thus conceived finds manifestation in related principles or concepts such as legitimate expectations, *pacta sunt servanda*, estoppel, acquiescence, equity, *abus de droit* and others, some of which may overlap with codified expressions and/or mutually reinforce each other. Some of these principles or concepts are sometimes considered to have further manifestations, most often in procedural terms, such as the abuse of process doctrine with respect to the prohibition of *abus de droit*, the procedural estoppel (*venire contra factum proprium*) with respect to the principle of estoppel, the clean hands doctrine, etc.[16] According to one author, the role of good faith is thus to found and nourish in substance different principles, institutions and norms that flow from it as its concretizations.[17]

## 2.1.2 Codifications of good faith

The principle of good faith finds manifold codified expression in public international law. The duty to fulfil one's obligations in good faith is, for example, most prominently found in article 2(2) of the *Charter of the United Nations*. The duty to settle disputes in good faith can be found in its article 33 as well as in paragraph 5 of the 1982 *Manila Declaration on the Peaceful Settlement of International Disputes*.[18] A duty of cooperation follows, for example, from article 86 of the *Rome Statute of the International Criminal Court*.[19] The 1970 *Declaration on Friendly Relations* contains several of the aforementioned duties.[20] For treaty relations specifically, articles 18, 26 and 31 of the *VCLT* prescribe various overarching good faith-related obligations, such as the obligation not to defeat the object and purpose of a treaty that has not yet been ratified, the rule of *pacta sunt servanda*, and the obligation to interpret a treaty provision in good faith. Articles 294 and 300 of the *UN Convention on the Law of the Sea* (*UNCLOS*)[21] contain the specific prohibitions of abuse

[15] Kotzur, 'Good Faith' (n 5) paras 23–24; Robert Kolb, 'General Principles of Procedural Law' in Andreas Zimmermann, Christian Tomuschat, and Karin Oellers-Frahm (eds), *The Statute of the International Court of Justice: A Commentary* (2nd edn, OUP 2012) 903–04, para 48.

[16] Kotzur, 'Good Faith' (n 5) paras 23–24, Kolb, 'General Principles' (n 15) 903–04.

[17] Kolb, *Bonne Foi* (n 1) 113.

[18] *Peaceful Settlement of Disputes Between States*, GA Res 37/10, UN GAOR, 37th sess, 68th plen mtg, Agenda Item 122, Annex, UN Doc A/RES/37/10 (15 November 1982).

[19] Opened for signature 17 July 1998, 2187 UNTS 90 (entered into force 7 January 2002).

[20] *Declaration on Principles of International Law Concerning Friendly Relations and Co-operation Among States in Accordance with the Charter of the United Nations*, GA Res 2625 (XXV), UN GAOR, 25th sess, 1883rd plen mtg, Agenda Item 85, UN Doc A/RES/2625 (24 October 1970) 124.

[21] Opened for signature 10 December 1982, 1833 UNTS 3 (entered into force 16 November 1994).

of rights and abuse of process. World trade law contains several expressions and elements of good faith, such as: the obligation to settle disputes in good faith in article 3.10 of the *Dispute Settlement Understanding* (*DSU*)[22] or to enter into consultations in good faith in article 4.3 of the *DSU*; the non-violation complaints in article XXIII:1(b) of the *General Agreement on Tariffs and Trade 1994* (*GATT*),[23] article XXIII:3 of the *General Agreement on Trade in Services* (*GATS*)[24] and article 26.1 of the *DSU* in their specific expression of the protection of legitimate expectations; and good faith-related duties in the *Agreement on Trade-Related Aspects of Intellectual Property Rights* (*TRIPS Agreement*),[25] such as articles 24, 48.2 and 58(c). Article 23 of the *Conciliation Rules*[26] of the International Centre for Settlement of Investment Disputes (ICSID) also provides for a duty of cooperation in good faith with the Conciliation Commission. Some institutional rules have also incorporated mechanisms to deal with abuses of process, eg rule 41(5) of the *ICSID Arbitration Rules*,[27] which gives a party the right to a preliminary objection and obliges the tribunal to examine whether the claim is manifestly without merits, such as in the case of frivolous claims. In a similar vein, article 3.7 of the *DSU* requires a member, before bringing a case, to 'exercise its judgment as to whether action under these procedures would be fruitful'.

### 2.1.3 Applicability to foreign investors

The principle of good faith and its manifestations are undoubtedly applicable in horizontal state-to-state relations. However, being endowed with (partial) international legal personality by virtue of most investment treaties, foreign investors must also comply with certain international law obligations, including the principle of good faith.[28] Many arbitral tribunals have thus in principle recognized the applicability of the principle of good faith—whether as a principle of national or international law—and its concretizations in investment treaty arbitration.[29]

[22] *Marrakesh Agreement Establishing the World Trade Organization, opened for signature 15 April 1994*, 1867 UNTS 3 (entered into force 1 January 1995), annex 2 (*Understanding on Rules and Procedures Governing the Settlement of Disputes*) 1869 UNTS 401.

[23] *Marrakesh Agreement Establishing the World Trade Organization* (n 22) annex 1A (*General Agreement on Tariffs and Trade 1994*) 1867 UNTS 187.

[24] *Marrakesh Agreement Establishing the World Trade Organization* (n 22) annex 1B (*General Agreement on Trade in Services*) 1869 UNTS 183.

[25] *Marrakesh Agreement Establishing the World Trade Organization* (n 22) annex 1C (*Agreement on Trade-Related Aspects of Intellectual Property Rights*) 1867 UNTS 299.

[26] *ICSID Rules of Procedure for Conciliation Proceedings* (April 2006).

[27] *ICSID Rules of Procedure for Arbitration Proceedings* (April 2006).

[28] Kotzur, 'Good Faith' (n 5) para 25.

[29] *Phoenix Action Ltd v Czech Republic (Award)* (ICSID Arbitral Tribunal, Case No ARB/06/5, 15 April 2009) para 107; *Europe Cement Investment & Trade v Turkey (Decision on Jurisdiction)*

## 2.2 Normative Autonomy of the Principle of Good Faith?

A question that remains highly controversial is whether in the absence of an expression in the form of a codified norm or a more specific rule or concept, the principle of good faith as general principle of law or rule of customary law can be applied in dispute settlement proceedings as an autonomous source of obligation.

### 2.2.1 General international law

For general international law, the ICJ has thus far denied any normative autonomy to the principle of good faith, as has been seen in its holdings in the *Nuclear Tests* and *Border and Transborder Armed Activities* cases.[30] However, this conception of the principle of good faith has been criticized by Kolb as being too narrow. Recalling that one of the essential functions of the general principle of good faith is to fill legal gaps where no treaty or customary rule has yet developed, thus giving clearer contours to specific obligations, Kolb considers it inevitable (and according to him implicitly accepted by the ICJ in the *Nuclear Tests Case*) that good faith has a certain law-making effect. Concluding that the principle of good faith can be directly applied as a normative legal basis, Kolb acknowledges however that there will rarely be a need for it in view of the ever increasing normative density in public international law.[31]

If the principle of good faith qualifies as customary international law or a general principle of law (as we contend it does), at least in theory, no objection can arise to the proposition that good faith has an independent normative basis. However, this conclusion does not help determine the normative content of good faith. In other words, the normative classification of good faith does not help in identifying the precise content of an independent good faith

(ICSID Arbitral Tribunal Case No ARB(AF)/07/2, 13 August 2009) para 171; *Mobil Corp, Venezuela Holdings BV v Venezuela (Decision on Jurisdiction)* (ICSID Arbitral Tribunal, Case No ARB/07/27, 10 June 2010) paras 169–85; *Abaclat v Argentina (Decision on Jurisdiction and Admissibility)* (ICSID Arbitral Tribunal, Case No ARB/07/5, 4 August 2011) para 646; Eric De Brabandere, 'Good Faith, Abuse of Process and the Initiation of Investment Treaty Claims' (2012) 3 JIDS 609, 619; but see John Gaffney, '"Abuse of Process" in Investment Treaty Arbitration' (2010) 11 JWIT 515, 523–24.

[30] *Nuclear Tests (Australia v France) (Merits)* [1974] ICJ Rep 253, 268–69; *Border and Transborder Armed Activities (Nicaragua/Honduras) (Jurisdiction and Admissibility)* [1988] ICJ Rep 69, 105; confirmed in *Land and Maritime Boundary between Cameroon and Nigeria (Cameroon v Nigeria) (Preliminary Objections)* [1998] ICJ Rep 275, 297.

[31] Kolb, *Bonne Foi* (n 1) 157–58.

obligation, which a state would have to respect under given circumstances. This content would depend on both the substantive obligations under interpretation—ie the applicable law—and the interpreting tribunal's mandate or its jurisdictional limitations. In particular, the latter would seem to explain the conservative position of most tribunals towards a normative autonomy of the principle of good faith, seeking to attach specific good faith content only to treaty-based obligations or one of the principle's particularizations. Thus, the gap-filling function (and thus law-making effect) that the principle of good faith has in theory remains in practice negligible.

### 2.2.2 WTO jurisprudence

Like the ICJ, the Appellate Body of the WTO has so far consistently rejected any normative autonomy of the principle of good faith in the absence of more specific manifestations of the principle in WTO law. Thus, in *US—Offset Act (Byrd Amendment)*,[32] though seemingly finding in general that 'there [was] a basis for a dispute settlement panel to determine, in an appropriate case, whether a Member has not acted in good faith',[33] the Appellate Body rejected the panel's finding that the United States had acted in bad faith on the evidence, holding:

> Nothing ... in the covered agreements supports the conclusion that simply because a WTO Member is found to have violated a substantive treaty provision, it has therefore not acted in good faith. In our view, it would be necessary to prove more than mere violation to support such a conclusion.[34]

Subsequent decisions of WTO panels and the Appellate Body, as adopted by the WTO's Dispute Settlement Body (DSB), have been equally sceptical towards the recognition of an independent good faith obligation adding to a substantive obligation contained in the covered agreements.[35] On the other hand, panels and the Appellate Body have more easily accepted the use of the principle of good faith to give shape to certain good faith obligations if embodied in more concrete manifestations or normative bases, such as article 26 of the VCLT, in particular if used for the purpose of interpreting a WTO

[32] Appellate Body Report, *United States—Continued Dumping and Subsidy Offset Act of 2000*, WTO Doc WT/DS217/AB/R, WT/DS234/AB/R (adopted 27 January 2003).

[33] ibid para 297.

[34] ibid para 298; for a critical discussion of the Appellate Body's treatment of the principle of good faith see Mitchell (n 2) 364–66.

[35] See, eg, Panel Report, *European Communities—Anti-Dumping Duties on Imports of Cotton-Type Bed Linen from India—Recourse to Art 21.5 DSU by India*, WTO Doc WT/DS141/RW (adopted 24 April 2003) paras 6.89–6.91; Panel Report, *Argentina—Definitive Anti-Dumping Duties on Poultry from Brazil*, WTO Doc WT/DS241/R (adopted 19 May 2003) paras 7.34–7.36.

agreement.[36] This approach seems in principle sound given the DSB's limited mandate 'not to add to or diminish the rights and obligations provided in the covered agreements'.[37] Moreover, as other scholars have pointed out, embracing an independent good faith obligation would risk blurring the separation between violation and non-violation complaints.[38]

### 2.2.3 Investment treaty jurisprudence

Investment tribunals do not appear ever to have explicitly discussed the question of a possible normative autonomy of the principle of good faith as have the ICJ and the WTO's DSB. Most investment tribunals have broached the principle of good faith through purpose-oriented interpretations of relevant provisions in the *Convention on the Settlement of Investment Disputes between States and Nationals of Other States* (*ICSID Convention*)[39] or bilateral investment treaties (BITs) aimed at preventing an abuse of the investment arbitration system, or through its (procedural or substantive) concretizations such as legitimate expectations, estoppel, abuse of rights or abuse of process. However, some arbitral tribunals seem to have assumed the applicability of an independent good faith obligation in particular with respect to the acquisition of an investment contrary to domestic laws or international public policy.[40]

Approaches taken by the arbitral tribunals have differed depending on whether they tackled the question of good faith and their manifestations as a matter of jurisdiction, admissibility or the merits.[41] This is more than a semantic distinction. As De Brabandere points out, if an arbitral tribunal dismisses jurisdiction, 'there is no possibility for the parties to re-submit the claim to the tribunal', while if the claim is found inadmissible, the claim can be resubmitted 'once the admissibility requirements are met'.[42] Particularly in the case of abuse of rights or abuse of process, arbitral tribunals have not

[36] See, eg, Panel Report, *Korea—Measures Affecting Government Procurement*, WTO Doc WT/DS163/R (adopted 19 June 2000) para 7.101; *United States—Certain Country of Origin Labelling (COOL) Requirements*, WTO Docs WT/DS384/R and WT/DS386/R (adopted 23 July 2012) para 7.605; see also below (n 57).

[37] *DSU* (n 22) arts 3.2, 19.2.

[38] Zeitler (n 10) 751–53.

[39] *Convention on the Settlement of Investment Disputes between States and Nationals of Other States*, opened for signature 18 March 1965 (entered into force 14 October 1966) (*ICSID Convention*).

[40] See chapter 5 of this volume.

[41] On the distinction and its practical significance see De Brabandere (n 29) 617–20. See also *Vannessa Ventures v Venezuela (Award)* (ICSID Arbitral Tribunal, Case No ARB(AF)/04/6, 16 January 2013) para 125.

[42] ibid 617.

always been clear and consistent as to whether this should be treated as a question of jurisdiction or admissibility.[43]

One can certainly wonder whether in view of the panoply of its different manifestations, recourse to an independent good faith obligation as a 'gap-filler' in investment arbitration is necessary at all. However, compared to the position of WTO panels and the Appellate Body, at least theoretically, an investment tribunal might have more room to explore the boundaries of an independent good faith obligation, given the normally relatively broad applicable law clauses,[44] the absence of adjudicatory limitations, and the limited annulment grounds. Yet, given its potential for subjective decision-making, an overly broad use of the principle of good faith may come at the expense of the quality of the legal reasoning of arbitral awards, leading to differing approaches and potentially inconsistent decisions. In a system already under suspicion of suffering a 'legitimacy crisis',[45] this concern must be taken seriously.

## 2.3 Concretizations of the Principle of Good Faith

### 2.3.1 Legitimate expectations

The protection of legitimate expectations takes a pre-eminent place in international relations in general. With good reason, the ICJ emphasized, for example in the *Nuclear Tests Case*, the fundamental role of mutual trust and confidence in promoting the stability of international relations.[46] The ECJ considers the principle of protection of legitimate expectations 'part of the Community legal order ... on which any economic operator to whom an institution has given justified hopes may rely'.[47]

International economic relations form no exception in this respect. World trade law provides for the protection of legitimate expectations of its participants through, for example, the possibility of non-violation complaints and

[43] See, eg, *Société Générale In respect of DR Energy Holdings Ltd and Empresa Distribuidora de Electricidad del Este v Dominican Republic (Award on Preliminary Objections to Jurisdiction)* (UNCITRAL, London Court of International Arbitration, Case No UN 7927, 19 September 2008) paras 110, 121; *Mobil v Venezuela* (n 29) para 206; *Pac Rim Cayman v El Salvador (Decision on the Respondent's Jurisdictional Objections)* (ICSID Arbitral Tribunal, Case No ARB/09/12, 1 June 2012) para 2.110.

[44] See, eg, *ICSID Convention* (n 39) art 42(1).

[45] See, eg, Susan Franck, 'The Legitimacy Crisis in Investment Treaty Arbitration: Privatizing Public International Law through Inconsistent Decisions' (2005) 73 Fordham L Rev 1521.

[46] *Nuclear Tests Case* (n 30) para 49.

[47] *Opel Austria v Council* (C-115/94) [1997] ECR-SC II-39, para 93.

the recognition, by WTO tribunals, of a 'de facto precedent' effect of their decisions. In international investment law, the protection of legitimate expectations has found a particularly important expression in the fair and equitable treatment standard, as will be seen more in detail in chapter 7 below. Further forms of the principle of protection of legitimate expectations are the principles or concepts of estoppel and acquiescence,[48] as will be elaborated on further below.

## 2.3.2 *Pacta sunt servanda*

### *2.3.2.1 Introduction to the rule*

The rule of *pacta sunt servanda* (PSS), with its origins in Roman law,[49] is today commonly considered a norm of both treaty and customary international law.[50] Whether it can also be considered a general principle of law seems unclear.[51] PSS is most prominently codified in article 26 of the VCLT, which stipulates that '[e]very treaty in force is binding upon the parties to it and must be performed by them in good faith'. Grotius recognized the importance of this rule to the stability of legal relations when he stated that '[t]o respect scrupulously the faith given is the foundation of States and of the grand community of nations'.[52] Similarly, Cheng, quoting the Venezuela–US Mixed Claims Commission, found that without this rule, '[i]nternational law as well as civil law would be a mere mockery'.[53]

The rule of PSS means that states cannot unilaterally modify, or free themselves from, the terms of a treaty as long as it is in force.[54] A treaty that is signed, but not yet ratified, thus creates only a 'limited' good faith obligation not to defeat its object and purpose, as can be seen in article 18 of the VCLT.[55]

As to the obligation to perform a treaty in good faith, the ICJ in the *Gabčíkovo-Nagymaros* case found that '[t]he principle of good faith obliges the Parties to apply it in a reasonable way and in such a manner that its purpose can be realized'.[56] The obligation to perform a treaty in good faith usually also includes the obligation to interpret a treaty provision in good faith, as codified in article 31(1) of the VCLT.[57]

[48] Kolb, *Bonne Foi* (n 1) 378.

[49] On the historical evolution of the principle see ibid 87–92.

[50] Panizzon (n 1) 27; Mitchell (n 2) 346.

[51] See Anthony Aust, 'Pacta Sunt Servanda' in Wolfrum (n 5) para 1; but see Jean Salmon, 'Article 26' in Olivier Corten and Pierre Klein (eds), *The Vienna Convention on the Law of Treaties: A Commentary*, vol I (OUP 2011) para 7.

[52] Hugo Grotius, *De Iure Belli ac Pacis* (1625) lib III cap XXV para 1, quoted in Kolb, *Bonne Foi* (n 1) 86.

[53] Cheng (n 3) 113. [54] ibid. [55] Aust (n 51) paras 4–8.

[56] *Gabčíkovo-Nagymaros Project (Hungary–Slovakia) (Merits)* [1997] ICJ Rep 7, 78–79.

[57] O'Connor (n 1) 109; but see Mitchell (n 2) 347. On good faith and treaty interpretation in more detail see chapter 3 of this volume.

The rule of PSS, as the Permanent Court of International Justice (PCIJ) and the ICJ have often confirmed,[58] entails a duty to negotiate in good faith, ie to negotiate in a 'meaningful' way, though it is controversial whether this duty goes as far as requiring the parties to arrive at specific results such as the conclusion of an agreement.[59] Various WTO tribunals have also derived from the rule of PSS a presumption that WTO members have acted in good faith in carrying out their WTO obligations.[60] Finally, it is generally now accepted that the rule of PSS applies not only to treaties, but more generally to any 'commitment to be legally bound which creates an agreement between subjects of law'.[61]

### *2.3.2.2 Relationship between good faith and PSS*

Although it has been uncontroversial that the rule of PSS is an expression of the principle of good faith, its exact relationship has been the subject of some doctrinal discussions. Whether one considers good faith the source of the PSS rule[62] or only a companion thereto,[63] the interplay between the principle of good faith and the rule of PSS is undeniable. As Kolb points out, in conventional law, good faith has a larger role to play than PSS, not only reinforcing the rule of PSS, but under certain circumstances also limiting it (such as in the case of the *clausula rebus sic stantibus*).[64] As has been seen in the ICJ's holding in the *Nuclear Tests Case*, good faith also plays an important role in the creation of obligations, thus not only at the moment of their execution.[65] Good faith may also preclude consideration of formal errors, as can be seen from the maxim *falsa demonstratio non nocet*.[66]

[58] *Railway Traffic between Lithuania and Poland (Advisory Opinion)* [1931] PCIJ (ser A/B) No 42, 116; *North Sea Continental Shelf (Germany v Denmark) (Merits)* [1969] ICJ Rep 3, 46–47; see also *Delimitation of the Maritime Boundary in the Gulf of Maine Area (Canada v United States) (Merits)* [1984] ICJ Rep 246, 292.

[59] See *Legality of the Threat or Use of Nuclear Weapons (Advisory Opinion)* [1996] ICJ Rep 226, 263–65; but see Panizzon (n 1) 74–75; Kolb, *Bonne Foi* (n 1) 201; Appellate Body Report, *United States—Import Prohibition of Certain Shrimp and Shrimp Products—Recourse to Article 21.5 by Malaysia*, WTO Doc WT/DS58/AB/RW (adopted 21 November 2001) para 123.

[60] See, eg, Appellate Body Report, *Chile—Taxes on Alcoholic Beverages*, WTO Docs WT/DS87/AB/R, WT/DS110/AB/R (adopted 12 January 2000) para 74; Appellate Body Report, *European Communities—Trade Description of Sardines*, WTO Doc WT/DS231/AB/R (adopted 23 October 2002) para 278; Appellate Body Report, *United States—Sunset Reviews of Anti-Dumping Measures on Oil Country Tubular Goods from Argentina*, WTO Doc WT/DS268/AB/R (adopted 17 December 2004) para 173.

[61] Salmon (n 51) paras 9–10; *Nuclear Tests* (n 30) 269; cf Aust (n 51) para 2.

[62] *Nuclear Tests* (n 30) 269; *Gabčíkovo-Nagymaros Project* (n 56) 78–79.

[63] Salmon (n 51) paras 27, 33.

[64] Kolb, *Bonne Foi* (n 1) 97–99.

[65] ibid.

[66] ibid.

### 2.3.3 Estoppel

The principle of estoppel flows from the principle of protection of legitimate expectations, which, as has been seen above, is itself a concretization of the principle of good faith.[67] Kolb therefore calls it the '*lex specialis* to the principle of protection of legitimate expectations'.[68] According to Cottier and Müller, one must distinguish between a restrictive and a more extensive conception of estoppel, the latter of which would include, for example, the maxims of *non licet venire contra factum proprium* or *allegans contraria non audiendus est*.[69] The restrictive conception of estoppel denotes a principle whereby a state is precluded from:

> contesting before the Court a situation contrary to a clear and unequivocal representation previously made by it to another State, either expressly or impliedly, on which representation the other State was, in the circumstances, entitled to rely and in fact did rely, and as a result that other State has been prejudiced or the State making it has secured some benefit or advantage for itself.[70]

Whether the principle of estoppel can be considered a general principle of law, a general principle of international law, or a rule of customary international law is controversial,[71] but probably irrelevant given its broad recognition in general international law by international courts and tribunals.

#### *2.3.3.1 Estoppel in general international law*

The PCIJ and the ICJ have primarily adopted a restrictive notion of estoppel, often (though not only) in cases involving the delimitation of land or maritime boundaries.[72] Perhaps due to this context, the PCIJ and ICJ have adopted a very cautious approach to the concept of estoppel.[73] Scholarship has also typically embraced a restrictive notion of estoppel, highlighting the

[67] Thomas Cottier and Jörg Müller, 'Estoppel' in Wolfrum (n 5) para 1; Panizzon (n 1) 24.

[68] Kolb, *Bonne Foi* (n 1) 378. [69] Cottier and Müller (n 67) 2.

[70] *Temple of Preah Vihear (Cambodia v Thailand) (Merits)* [1962] ICJ Rep 6, 143–44 (Spender J).

[71] Cheng (n 3) 141–49; Brownlie (n 1) 644; Panizzon (n 1) 24; Kolb, *Bonne Foi* (n 1) 378–79; Mitchell (n 2) 348; Cottier and Müller (n 67) paras 9–10.

[72] See, eg, *Payment of Various Serbian Loans Issued in France (France v Serbia) (Judgment)* [1929] PCIJ (ser A) No 20/21 6, 39; *Barcelona Traction, Light and Power Company (Belgium v Spain) (Preliminary Objections)* [1964] ICJ Rep 3, 24–25; *North Sea Continental Shelf Case* [1969] ICJ Rep 3, 26; *Gulf of Maine* (n 58) 308; *Military and Paramilitary Activities in and against Nicaragua (Nicaragua v United States) (Jurisdiction and Admissibility)* [1984] ICJ Rep 392, 414–15; *Gabčíkovo-Nagymaros Project* (n 56) 115–16 (Vice-President Weeramantry); *Land and Maritime Borders* (n 30) 303.

[73] Ian Sinclair, 'Estoppel and Acquiescence' in Vaughan Lowe and Malgosia Fitzmaurice (eds), *Fifty Years of the International Court of Justice: Essays in Honour of Sir Robert Jennings* (CUP 1996), 116.

particular role the protection of legitimate expectations plays for the predictability of law.[74]

### *2.3.3.2 Estoppel in WTO jurisprudence*

While various parties have pleaded the principle of estoppel in WTO proceedings, none has succeeded thus far.[75] In *Guatemala—Cement II*, the panel rejected Guatemala's contention that Mexico was estopped from alleging certain violations of the so-called *Anti-Dumping Agreement*,[76] finding estoppel to exist 'where one party has been induced to act in reliance on the assurances of another party, in such a way that it would be prejudiced were the other party to change its position, such a change is "estopped", that is precluded'.[77] In *Argentina—Poultry Anti-Dumping Duties*, the panel similarly embraced a narrow conception of the principle of estoppel in line with ICJ jurisprudence.[78]

The reluctance of the WTO Appellate Body to apply the principle of estoppel seems to be founded on similar motivations as its rejection of an autonomous good faith obligation as has been seen above.[79] This became particularly apparent in the *EC—Export Subsidies on Sugar* case, where both the panel and Appellate Body expressed hesitation regarding the applicability of the principle of estoppel in WTO law, though both ultimately found its conditions unfulfilled in the case at hand.[80] However, contrary to an autonomous good faith obligation, one can arguably read a procedural estoppel obligation into the obligation of WTO members, under article 3.10 of the *DSU*, to engage in the dispute settlement procedures in good faith.[81] The WTO Appellate Body may therefore have been overcautious in this regard.

[74] ibid 116; Cottier and Müller (n 67) para 3; Kolb, *Bonne Foi* (n 1) 392–93.

[75] Mitchell (n 2) 356.

[76] *Marrakesh Agreement Establishing the World Trade Organization* (n 22) annex 1A (*Agreement on Implementation of Article VI of the General Agreement on Tariffs and Trade 1994*) 1867 UNTS 187.

[77] Panel Report, *Guatemala—Definitive Anti-Dumping Measures on Grey Portland Cement from Mexico*, WTO Doc WT/DS156/R (adopted 17 November 2000) para 8.23.

[78] Panel Report, *Argentina—Poultry Anti-Dumping Duties* (n 35) paras 7.38–7.39; Mitchell (n 2) 357; Cottier and Müller (n 67) para 7.

[79] Mitchell (n 2) 360–61; see also Panizzon (n 1) 26.

[80] Panel Report, *European Communities—Export Subsidies on Sugar*, WTO Docs WT/DS265/R, WT/DS266/R, WT/DS283/R (adopted 19 May 2005) paras 7.63, 7.70; Appellate Body Report, *European Communities—Export Subsidies on Sugar*, WTO Docs WT/DS265/AB/R, WT/DS266/AB/R, WT/DS283/AB/R (adopted 19 May 2005) paras 310, 312; confirmed in Appellate Body Report, *European Communities—Regime for the Importation, Sale and Distribution of Bananas—Second Recourse to Article 21.5 of the DSU by Ecuador*, WTO Docs WT/DS27/AB/RW2/ECU, WT/DS27/AB/RW/USA (adopted 11 December 2008) para 228.

[81] Mitchell (n 2) 361–62.

### 2.3.3.3 *Estoppel in investment treaty jurisprudence*

Parties to investment claims have also pleaded the principle of estoppel several times, in particular with the aim of arguing that the other party was estopped from specific procedural steps or representations not made earlier. However, like WTO tribunals, investment arbitral tribunals have thus far—as far as publicly known—always rejected the estoppel principle on the facts of the case. Overall, though, the treatment by investment tribunals of the estoppel principle appears to attest to the recognition, in principle, of its applicability in investment treaty arbitration.

Thus, in the *Pope and Talbot v Canada* claim under the *North American Free Trade Agreement*,[82] related to the softwood lumber dispute between the United States and Canada, Canada argued that the claimant was estopped from bringing its claim due to alleged representations not to bring the claim. The tribunal, adopting a narrow conception of the principle of estoppel, rejected the claim on the facts of the case.[83] In another softwood lumber-related investment case, *Canfor Corp v US*, the tribunal also rejected the contention that the respondent was estopped from requesting the consolidation of the proceedings, based on a narrow conception of the principle of estoppel.[84] A narrow conception of the principle of estoppel was also espoused by the tribunal in *Cambodia Power Company v Cambodia*, rejecting the estoppel claim on the facts of the case.[85] The same was the case in *BP America Production Company v Argentina*[86] and in *Yukos v Russian Federation*.[87]

A broader notion of the principle of estoppel seems to have been adopted by the tribunal in *Duke Energy Peru v Peru*, where the tribunal equated the principle of estoppel with the *venire contra factum proprium* doctrine, apparently not requiring the element of prejudice or damage as part of the narrow conception of estoppel.[88]

[82] *North American Free Trade Agreement*, signed 17 December 1992 [1994] CTS 2 (entered into force 1 January 1994).

[83] See, eg, *Pope and Talbot Inc v Canada (Interim Award)* (UNCITRAL, 26 June 2000) paras 111–12.

[84] *Canfor Corp v United States (Order of the Consolidation Tribunal)* (UNCITRAL, 7 September 2005) paras 167–69.

[85] *Cambodia Power Company v Kingdom of Cambodia and Electricité du Cambodge LLC (Decision on Jurisdiction)* (ICSID Arbitral Tribunal, Case No ARB/09/18, 22 March 2011) para 261.

[86] *BP America Production Company v Argentina (Decision on Preliminary Objections)* (ICSID Arbitral Tribunal, Case No ARB/04/8, 27 July 2006) paras 159–60.

[87] *Yukos Universal Ltd (Isle of Man) v Russian Federation (Interim Award on Jurisdiction and Admissibility)* (Permanent Court of Arbitration, Case No AA 227, 30 November 2009) paras 286–88.

[88] *Duke Energy International Peru Investments v Peru (Award)* (ICSID Arbitral Tribunal, Case No ARB/03/28, 18 August 2008) paras 241–51, 320–23.

Other investment arbitral tribunals have also addressed estoppel claims, but without much theoretical underpinning. In *Eastern Sugar v Czech Republic*, for example, the tribunal rejected the Czech Republic's claim that the claimant was estopped from challenging administrative decisions that it failed to attack through internal Czech remedies, finding that 'the BIT [did] not provide for the exhaustion of local remedies as a pre-condition to a claim under the BIT'.[89] In *Quiborax v Bolivia*, the tribunal rejected the claimant's contention that Bolivia was estopped from contesting the legality of the investment because of prolonged settlement discussions.[90] In *Petrobart v Kyrgyz Republic*, the tribunal rejected the 'collateral estoppel' argument by the respondent on whether the failure to bring an objection in domestic proceedings precluded the investor from bringing the same objection in treaty arbitration, arguing that the BIT in question did not contain a fork-in-the-road clause.[91]

### 2.3.4 Acquiescence

The doctrine of acquiescence denotes a tacit and unilateral consent conveyed by a state 'through silence or inaction, in circumstances such that a response expressing disagreement or objection in relation to the conduct of another State would be called for'.[92] Based on the principle of good faith and equity, it is 'intended to prevent State from playing "fast and loose" with situations affecting other States'.[93]

The characteristic element of acquiescence is the 'qualified inaction' that is also expressed by its Latin adage, *qui tacet consentire videtur si loqui debuisset ac potuisset*. Not every kind of silence or inaction brings about the substantive legal consequences of acquiescence (ie the constitution, modification, disposal or termination of rights and duties);[94] acquiescence arises only when the passive state should and could have protested. This presupposes knowledge of the relevant facts:

> by the acquiescing State (notoriety), where such facts are of direct interest for the acquiescing State (interest), when these facts have existed for a significant period

[89] *Eastern Sugar BV (Netherlands) v Czech Republic (Partial Award)* (Stockholm Chamber of Commerce, Case No 088/2004, 27 March 2007) paras 140–41.

[90] *Quiborax SA, Non Metallic Minerals SA and Allan Fosk Kaplún v Bolivia (Decision on Jurisdiction)* (ICSID Arbitral Tribunal, Case No ARB/06/2, 27 September 2012) paras 257–58.

[91] *Petrobart Ltd v Kyrgyz Republic (Award)* (Stockholm Chamber of Commerce, Case No 126/2003, 29 March 2005) paras 363–68.

[92] Marques Antunes, 'Acquiescence' in Wolfrum (n 5) para 2.

[93] Müller and Cottier, 'Acquiescence' in Rudolf Bernhardt (ed), *Encyclopedia of Public International Law*, vol 1 (North-Holland Publishing Company 1992) 14.

[94] Antunes (n 92) para 11.

(lapse of time) without significant change of context and the meaning conveyed (consistency), and in cases in which the conduct is attributable to a relevant representative of the State (provenance).[95]

### *2.3.4.1 Distinction between estoppel and acquiescence*

Like estoppel, acquiescence is based on the principle of the protection of legitimate expectations.[96] However, although there is a close link between estoppel and acquiescence, a distinction does exist between these two concepts, as the ICJ acknowledged in the *Gulf of Maine* case:

> The Chamber observes that in any case the concepts of acquiescence and estoppel, irrespective of the status accorded to them by international law, both follow from the fundamental principles of good faith and equity. They are, however, based on different legal reasoning since acquiescence is equivalent to tacit recognition manifested by unilateral conduct which the other party may interpret as consent, while estoppel is linked to the idea of preclusion ... since the same facts are relevant to both acquiescence and estoppel, except as regards the existence of detriment, [the Chamber] is able to take the two concepts into consideration as different aspects of one and the same institution.[97]

A distinction between estoppel and acquiescence may thus become necessary, in particular when deciding whether the failure of a state to react or protest against a claim asserted or action taken by another state can result in a possible estoppel or be seen as evidence of acquiescence. Both scholars and international tribunals have in this regard attached prime importance to the period of time in which a silence has been maintained.[98] In the *Anglo-Norwegian Fisheries Case*, the ICJ found, for example, that the failure of various UK governments to protest over a period of more than 60 years resulted in the UK's acquiescence of Norway's fisheries practices.[99] The importance of the temporal aspect was also underlined by the ICJ in the *Gulf of Maine* case, where it stated that a 'brief silence' was not enough to attribute to the United States' conduct the precluding legal effect contended by Canada.[100] The court in the *Temple of Preah Vihear* case equally highlighted the failure of Thailand for some 50 years to object to the boundaries drawn on an official map assigning the contentious territory to French Indochina (later including relevant parts of Cambodia), concluding it had acquiesced to the boundary.[101]

[95] ibid para 20. [96] Kolb, *Bonne Foi* (n 1) 339. [97] *Gulf of Maine* (n 58) 305.
[98] See, eg, Sinclair (n 73) 112–15; Kolb, *Bonne Foi* (n 1) 342–45.
[99] *Fisheries Case (United Kingdom v Norway) (Merits)* [1951] ICJ Rep 116, 138–39.
[100] *Gulf of Maine* (n 58) 308. [101] *Temple of Preah Vihear* (n 70) 22–23.

#### *2.3.4.2 Acquiescence in general international law*

Compared to its cautious approach towards the principle of estoppel, the ICJ has been much more open in accepting the existence of acquiescence, in particular in boundary cases.[102] However, the distinguishing line between an estoppel and acquiescence has at times not always been clear.[103]

#### *2.3.4.3 Acquiescence in WTO jurisprudence*

The doctrine of acquiescence has been pleaded only very sparingly in WTO proceedings and has produced no significant holding or dictum by WTO dispute settlement bodies.[104] Thus, in *Guatemala—Cement I*, Guatemala pleaded acquiescence, but the Appellate Body did not elaborate on the argument on grounds of judicial economy.[105] Similarly, acquiescence was argued by Argentina (and rejected by the EU in its third party submission) in *Argentina—Textiles*, but not explicitly ruled on by the Appellate Body.[106]

#### *2.3.4.4 Acquiescence in investment treaty jurisprudence*

Acquiescence does not figure prominently in investment arbitration either. However, aside from the cases where the term acquiescence is referred to in a non-technical way, it often seems to carry a procedural content, as in the French doctrine of '*acquiescement*'.[107] Rule 44 of the *ICSID Arbitration Rules* provides, for example, that if a party makes a request for discontinuance of the proceedings and no objection is made in writing within the fixed time limit, the other party shall be deemed to have acquiesced in the discontinuance of the proceedings. This rule has been invoked by some claimants in the mass claim proceedings in *Ambiente Ufficio v Argentina*.[108]

Acquiescence is also sometimes associated with the legal figure of waiver. Thus, the tribunal in *Hochtief v Argentina* found that a respondent could 'accept or acquiesce' in the non-compliance of an 18-month waiting period foreseen by

[102] See, eg, *Fisheries Case* (n 99); *Temple of Preah Vihear* (n 70); *Land, Island and Maritime Frontier Dispute (El Salvador v Honduras) (Merits)* [1992] ICJ Rep 351, 408–09.

[103] See, eg, *Elettronica Sicula SpA (ELSI) (US v Italy) (Merits)* [1989] ICJ Rep 15, 44.

[104] See also Panizzon (n 1) 26.

[105] Appellate Body Report, *Guatemala—Anti-Dumping Investigation Regarding Portland Cement from Mexico*, WT-DS60/AB/R (adopted 25 November 1998) para 22.

[106] Appellate Body Report, *Argentina—Measures Affecting Imports of Footwear, Textiles, Apparel and Other Items*, WTO Doc WT/DS56/AB/R (adopted 22 April 1998) paras 13, 34.

[107] Müller and Cottier (n 67), 14.

[108] *Ambiente Ufficio SpA v Argentina (Decision on Jurisdiction and Admissibility)* (ICSID Arbitral Tribunal, Case No ARB/08/9, 8 February 2013) paras 339–46.

the BIT.[109] Similarly, the tribunal in *Tanzania Electric Power Supply v Independent Power Tanzania Ltd* equated waiver and 'estoppel by acquiescence'.[110]

In some decisions, parties to the arbitral proceedings have tried to attach a substantive legal effect to acquiescence. Thus, in *Siemens v Argentina*, Argentina argued that by failing to protest against the 2000 Emergency Legislation, Siemens waived its rights under the BIT to compensation.[111] However, the tribunal found Argentina's arguments on estoppel and acquiescence 'misplaced', arguing that 'acceptance of laws or regulations should not be held against a company which has accepted them by the Government that adopted them... to comply with the law is not an optional matter'.[112] The same argument was advanced by Argentina in *ICS Inspection and Control Services v Argentina*, but not decided by the tribunal because jurisdiction was rejected on grounds of most-favoured-nation arguments.[113] In *MCI Power Group and New Turbine v Ecuador*, however, the tribunal accepted—though without any discussion—that the claimants' local investment 'acquiesced in [the] cancellation of the [operating] permit by not seeking an administrative review of the decision'.[114]

## 2.3.5 Equity

### *2.3.5.1 Equity in general international law*

In general terms, equity in international law can be considered a concept or set of principles that has developed in order to infuse notions of fairness and reasonableness into the administration of justice, which may be necessary given the inherent abstraction, or lack of individualization, of legal norms.[115]

[109] *Hochtief AG v Argentina (Decision on Jurisdiction)* (ICSID Arbitral Tribunal, Case No ARB/07/31, 24 October 2011) paras 94–96; but see *Hochtief AG v Argentina (Decision on Jurisdiction)* (ICSID Case No ARB/07/31, 7 October 2011) paras 38–40 (Arb J Christopher Thomas).

[110] *Tanzania Electric Power Supply v Independent Power Tanzania Ltd (Decision on Tariffs and Other Remaining Issues)* (ICSID Arbitral Tribunal, Case No ARB/98/8, 22 June 2001) paras 158–60.

[111] *Siemens AG v Argentina (Award)* (ICSID Arbitral Tribunal, Case No ARB/02/8, 17 January 2007) paras 282–83.

[112] ibid para 306.

[113] *ICS Inspection and Control Services Ltd (United Kingdom) v Argentina (Award on Jurisdiction)* (UNCITRAL, Permanent Court of Arbitration, Case No 2010-9, 10 February 2012) paras 195–200, 327.

[114] *MCI Power Group LC and New Turbine v Ecuador (Award)* (ICSID Arbitral Tribunal, Case No ARB/03/6, 31 July 2007) paras 302–03.

[115] Francesco Francioni, 'Equity' in Wolfrum (n 5) para 8; Kolb, *Bonne Foi* (n 1) 100; Gillian White, 'The Principle of Good Faith' in Vaughan Lowe and Colin Warbrick (eds), *The United Nations and the Principles of International Law: Essays in Memory of Michael Akehurst* (Routledge 1994) 235–36; on the historical development of equity see Kolb, *Bonne Foi* (n 1) 101–05.

As concepts such as *pacta sunt servanda*, abuse of rights and *rebus sic stantibus* are sometimes considered equitable principles, the relationship with the principle of good faith is readily apparent. However, as Kolb notes, scholarship and international jurisprudence have often not sufficiently distinguished between these two notions, perhaps as a consequence of the variety of meanings and diversity of functions attributed to either term.[116] In a similar vein, the relationship between law, equity and justice has been pointed out by the ICJ in *North Sea Continental Shelf*,[117] though the exact distinguishing lines remain blurred.[118]

The question thus remains, what is equity? First, the use of equity as a general principle of law[119] must be set apart from the power to render a decision *ex aequo et bono*, as contained, for example, in article 38(2) of the ICJ Statute or article 42(3) of the *ICSID Convention*. In the latter case, the parties to the dispute must specifically authorize the judge to take a decision *ex aequo et bono*, ie a solution from outside the law.[120] The ICJ in the *North Sea Continental Shelf Case* described an equitable decision as opposed to a decision *ex aequo et bono* in the following terms:

> [W]hat is meant is that the decision finds its objective justification in considerations lying not outside but within the rules, and in this field it is precisely a rule of law that calls for the application of equitable principles. There is consequently no question in this case of any decision *ex aequo et bono* ...[121]

Second, international jurisprudence has distinguished between various meanings of equity. As the ICJ noted in several cases, equity *infra legem* denotes a method of interpretation, devoid of normative autonomy, in order to adapt the law to the specific circumstances of the case.[122] Equity *praeter legem*, on the other hand, is used as a means for filling the gaps of international law, equipping equity with the force of normative autonomy.[123] Thus, the ICJ in the *North Sea Continental Shelf Case* stated that it was not 'applying

[116] Kolb, *Bonne Foi* (n 1) 107–09.

[117] *North Sea Continental Shelf* (n 58) 48; see also *Continental Shelf (Tunisia/Libya) (Merits)* [1982] ICJ Rep 18, 60; *Continental Shelf (Libya/Malta) (Merits)* [1985] ICJ Rep 13, 39.

[118] Prosper Weil, 'L'Equité dans la Jurisprudence de la Cour Internationale de Justice' in Vaughan Lowe and Malgosia Fitzmaurice (eds), *Fifty Years of the International Court of Justice: Essays in Honour of Sir Robert Jennings* (CUP 1996) 122.

[119] *Diversion of Water from Meuse (Netherland v Belgium) (Judgment)* [1937] PCIJ (ser A/B) No 70, 76 (Hudson J) (*River Meuse*); Panizzon (n 1) 21; Francioni (n 115) para 5; but see Mendelson (n 1) 80.

[120] Kotzur, 'Ex Aequo et Bono' in Wolfrum (n 5) para 1.

[121] *North Sea Continental Shelf* (n 58) 48.

[122] *Frontier Dispute (Burkina Faso/Mali)* (*Merits*) [1986] ICJ Rep 554, 567–68, 633; *Continental Shelf (Tunisia/Libya)* [1982] ICJ 18, 60; Francioni (n 114) para 6; Pellet (n 1) para 135.

[123] Pellet (n 1) para 140; Francioni (n 114) para 12.

equity simply as a matter of abstract justice, but applying a rule of law which itself requires the application of equitable principles'.[124] In *Continental Shelf (Tunisia/Libya)*, the Court also highlighted the normative autonomy of equity *praeter legem*, finding that 'the legal concept of equity [was] a general principle directly applicable as law'.[125] Some have called into doubt the necessity of equity *praeter legem*, arguing that 'there will always be a rule or principle of law (as opposed to equity) which is capable of extension and application to the case at hand... [and thus] there need be "no gaps" which would need to be filled with equity *praeter legem*'.[126]

Finally, equity *contra legem* denotes the use of equity in derogation of the law, ie either outside the scope of or in antithesis to the law.[127] Here, the line distinguishing equity from a decision *ex aequo et bono* necessitating the parties' consent becomes particularly blurred, a situation that may be magnified by the absence of any 'precedent' *ex aequo et bono* decisions rendered by either the PCIJ or the ICJ.[128] First of all, it is unclear whether to situate equity *contra legem* as within the realm of international law, or outside it. Thus, while some consider equity *contra legem* as equity properly speaking,[129] others place it beyond *ex aequo et bono* decisions.[130] The difficulty in making this distinction has been highlighted by scholarship.[131] Equally problematic is the distinction between equity *praeter legem* and equity *contra legem*, 'the characterization of whether equity is contrary to the law essentially [depending] on the construction of the scope and of the evolutive dynamics of the relevant norms'.[132] These discussions clearly demonstrate concerns about the risk of subjectivism in the use of equity.[133]

### *2.3.5.2 Equity in WTO and investment treaty jurisprudence*

Unlike the law of the sea,[134] WTO law contains no textual references to equity.[135] As Francioni points out, 'more than as a criterion of adjudication,

[124] *North Sea Continental Shelf* (n 58) 46–47.

[125] *Continental Shelf (Tunisia/Libya)* (n 117) 60; confirmed in *Continental Shelf (Libya/Malta)* (n 117) 39.

[126] Vaughan Lowe, 'The Role of Equity' (1988–1989) 12 Aust YBIL 54, 61.

[127] Francioni (n 115) para 14; Lowe (n 126) 56.

[128] Kotzur, 'Ex Aequo et Bono' (n 120) para 7; Pellet (n 1) para 156.

[129] See, eg, Lowe (n 126) 56.

[130] Pellet (n 1) para 140; Kotzur, 'Ex Aequo et Bono' (n 120) para 13; see also *Frontier Dispute (Burkina Faso/Mali)* (n 12) 567–68.

[131] Weil (n 118) 131; Francioni (n 115) para 17.

[132] Francioni (n 115) para 18.

[133] Weil (n 118) 127; Francioni (n 115) para 11; Kotzur, 'Ex Aequo et Bono' (n 120) para 13.

[134] See, eg, *United Nations Convention on the Law of the Sea*, opened for signature 10 December 1982, 1833 UNTS 3 (entered into force 16 November 1994) arts 69, 70, 74, 82(4), 83, 140, 155(2), 160(2), 173(2).

[135] Panizzon (n 1) 21.

equity has played a role in the process of law formation and as a tool for the reconciliation of conflicting economic interests between developed and developing countries'.[136] In international investment law, equity has found its most pre-eminent place in the fair and equitable treatment standard included in virtually any investment treaty, as will be discussed in more detail in chapter 7 below.

### 2.3.6 Clean hands

The clean hands doctrine stems from Roman law maxims *ex dolo malo non oritur actio, nullus commodum capere potest de iniuria sua propria* and *ex iniuria ius non oritur* and is sometimes considered close to the abuse of rights doctrine or estoppel.[137] The clean hands doctrine has also been associated with the principle of equity, as Judge Hudson elaborated in the *River Meuse* case:

> It would seem to be an important principle of equity that where two parties have assumed an identical or reciprocal obligation, one party which is engaged in a continuing non-performance of that obligation should not be permitted to take advantage of a similar non-performance of that obligation by the other party.[138]

#### *2.3.6.1 Clean hands in general international law*

The status of the clean hands doctrine in general international law is unsettled. While some consider it a principle of contemporary international law[139] and states continue to plead it in inter-state proceedings,[140] a clear and unanimous doctrine has not crystallized, and international courts and tribunals, though often not outright rejecting it, remain sceptical as to its application.[141]

Thus, for example, the Permanent Court of Arbitration in the *Guyana v Surinam* award rejected the respondent's contentions of 'lack of good faith and clean hands', on the basis of both its scepticism as to the existence of the

136 Francioni (n 115) para 21.

137 Kolb, *Bonne Foi* (n 1) 569; Stephen Schwebel, 'Principle of Clean Hands' in Wolfrum (n 5) para 1.

138 *River Meuse* (n 119) 77 (Hudson J).

139 See, eg, Gerald Fitzmaurice, 'The General Principles of International Law, Considered from the Standpoint of the Rule of Law' (1957) 92(2) RdC 119; *Arrest Warrant of 11 April 2000 (Democratic Republic of the Congo v Belgium) (Merits)* [2002] ICJ Rep 3, 159–60 para 35 (Van den Wyngaert J); *Military and Paramilitary Activities in and against Nicaragua (Nicaragua v United States) (Merits)* [1986] ICJ Rep 14, 382–84, 392–94 (Schwebel J).

140 See, eg, *Oil Platforms (Iran v United States) (Merits)* [2003] ICJ Rep 161, 177; *Legal Consequences of the Construction of a Wall (Advisory Opinion)* [2004] ICJ Rep 136, 163–64.

141 Schwebel (n 137) paras 12–13.

clean hands doctrine in international law and on the facts of the case.[142] It did so on the basis of three criteria it had extracted from earlier jurisprudence (in particular Judge Hudson's dictum), namely that the violation must be ongoing, that the remedy sought must be directed at a discontinuation of that violation in the future rather than damages for past violations, and that there must be a reciprocity between the obligations concerned.[143]

#### *2.3.6.2 Clean hands in WTO and investment treaty jurisprudence*

While the clean hands doctrine has been referred to only once so far (and in a rather non-technical way) in WTO jurisprudence,[144] it has most recently been discussed by the investment tribunal in the case *Niko Resources Ltd v Bangladesh* with respect to allegations of corruption.[145] Bangladesh argued that jurisdiction should be denied because the claimant had engaged in acts of corruption. The tribunal referred extensively to both Judge Hudson's dictum in the *River Meuse* case and the *Guyana v Surinam* Permanent Court of Arbitration award.[146] Applying the three criteria extracted in the latter award, it rejected application of the clean hands doctrine on the facts of the case, holding that the violation, ie the act of corruption:

> [has] been completed long ago; the remedy which the Claimant seeks does not concern protection against this past violation; and there is no relation of reciprocity between the relief which the Claimant... seeks and the acts in the past which the Respondents characterize as involving unclean hands.[147]

### 2.3.7 *Abus de droit* (Abuse of rights)

Finally, an important particularization of the principle of good faith is the doctrine of *abus de droit* or abuse of rights. Known in civil law jurisdictions as the abuse of rights doctrine, properly speaking and in common law jurisdictions as a specific application of torts law,[148] scholarship and international jurisprudence seem to overwhelmingly accept it as a general principle

[142] *Guyana v Surinam* (Permanent Court of Arbitration, 17 September 2007) paras 417–22.

[143] ibid para 421.

[144] Panel Report, *European Communities and Certain Member States—Measures Affecting Trade in Large Civil Aircraft*, WTO Doc WT/DS316/R (adopted 1 June 2011) paras 7.1770–7.1771.

[145] *Niko Resources (Bangladesh) Ltd v Bangladesh, Bangladesh Petroleum Exploration & Production Company Ltd (Bapex), Bangladesh Oil Gas and Mineral Corp (Petrobangla) (Decision on Jurisdiction)* (ICSID Arbitral Tribunal, Case No ARB/10/18, 19 August 2013).

[146] *Guyana v Surinam* (n 142).

[147] ibid paras 476, 483.

[148] Mitchell (n 2) 349.

of law or as a part of customary international law.[149] This being so, its content also remains vague and thus needs further specification in order to become operational.[150]

Two important theoretical underpinnings seem noteworthy at the outset. First, no right is a priori absolute and in ever more closely interconnected legal relationships, rights and obligations of states have an increasing potential of restricting each other.[151] Second, when a right crystallizes, law, as a means of resolving social conflicts, incorporates an inherent bias in favour of the individual interest contained in the right as opposed to the general interest of the community. In the case of an anti-social use of the right, the abuse of rights doctrine helps in readjusting the balance of countervailing interests 'as soon as policy decides that it is socially more advantageous to restrict a right in favor of an interest which henceforth becomes a legal right'.[152]

This 'social ordering' function of the doctrine is particularly important in the absence of an authoritative world legislator, whereby international law is in need of a flexible tool to adapt the law to changed conditions.[153] The significance of the doctrine of abuse of rights thus increases to the extent that a given body of international law has not yet incorporated a mechanism for balancing interests or resolving normative conflicts.[154]

Some scholars have in the past questioned the necessity of an abuse of rights doctrine.[155] Byers, however, convincingly argues that abuse of rights is 'supplemental to the principle of good faith' in that 'it provides the threshold at which a lack of good faith gives rise to a violation of international law, with all the attendant consequences' and, contrary to the principle of good faith, 'one need not imply malice in order to establish that an abuse has occurred'.[156] Yet, even proponents of the doctrine such as Lauterpacht caution against its over-use for risk of equipping tribunals with too much power.[157] Panizzon

[149] Panizzon (n 1) 30; Kolb, *Bonne Foi* (n 1) 463; Lauterpacht, *Function of Law* (n 6) 298; Michael Byers, 'Abuse of rights: An Old Principle, A New Age' (2002) 47 McGill LJ 389, 397.

[150] Kolb, *Bonne Foi* (n 1) 463; Panizzon (n 1) 30.

[151] Kolb, *Bonne Foi* (n 1) 436–37; Cheng (n 3) 131.

[152] Lauterpacht, *Function of Law* (n 6) 296; see also Kolb, *Bonne Foi* (n 1) 438–39.

[153] Lauterpacht, *Function of Law* (n 6) 299–300; Panizzon (n 1) 32; Byers (n 149) 429.

[154] Byers (n 149) 417–18.

[155] See, eg, Anthony D'Amato, 'Good Faith' in Bernhardt (n 93) vol 2, 600; Jean-David Roulet, *Le Caractère Artificiel de la Théorie de l'Abus de Droit en Droit International Public* (Editions de la Baconnière 1958).

[156] Byers (n 149) 411–12.

[157] Hersch Lauterpacht, *The Development of International Law by the International Court* (Stevens and Sons 1958) 164.

also underlines the subsidiary character of the abuse of rights doctrine, which should be called upon only if treaty interpretation has been unsuccessful in finding the required balance of countervailing interests.[158]

### *2.3.7.1 Categories of abuse of rights*

Though categorizations may differ in minor details, scholarship and international jurisprudence overall distinguish the following categories of abuse of rights. First, a right being the legal protection of a legitimate interest, its malicious, arbitrary or fictitious exercise—ie for the sole purpose of causing injury to another or for the purpose of evading a rule of law or a contractual obligation, even without clearly violating another state's or person's right—cannot be considered worthy of protection and is thus prohibited as an abuse of rights.[159]

Second, rights and obligations being interdependent, where the exercise of a right would impinge on an obligation assumed, that right must be exercised reasonably and in good faith. Thus, the doctrine of abuse of rights, 'while protecting the legitimate interests of the owner of the right, imposes such limitations upon the right as will render its exercise compatible with that party's treaty obligations, or, in other words, with the legitimate interests of the other contracting party'.[160]

Third, the abuse of rights doctrine sanctions an abuse of discretion. Also known by the term '*détournement de pouvoir*', it commands that '[w]here the right confers upon its owner a discretionary power, this must be exercised honestly, sincerely, reasonably, in conformity with the spirit of the law and with due regard to the interests of others'.[161] In particular, abuse of rights in connection with discretion protects the finality of a norm against actions that would run counter to this finality.[162]

Finally, the abuse of rights doctrine is sometimes applied in respect of procedural irregularities. According to Kolb, abuse of process:

> consists of the use of procedural instruments or rights by one or more parties for purposes that are alien to those for which the procedural rights were established, especially for a fraudulent, procrastinatory or frivolous purpose, for the purpose of causing harm or obtaining an illegitimate advantage, for the purpose of reducing or removing the effectiveness of some other available process or for purposes of pure

[158] Panizzon (n 1) 34; see also Byers (n 149) 421–22.

[159] Cheng (n 3) 122–23; Mitchell (n 2) 350; Panizzon (n 1) 31; see also Kolb, *Bonne Foi* (n 1) 468–69.

[160] Cheng (n 3) 124, 129; see also Alexandre Kiss, 'Abuse of rights' in Wolfrum (n 5) para 4.

[161] Cheng (n 3) 130; Panizzon (n 1) 31.

[162] Kolb, *Bonne Foi* (n 1) 464–65; Kiss (n 160) para 5.

propaganda. To these situations, action with a malevolent intent or with bad faith can be added.[163]

### 2.3.7.2 *Abuse of rights or abuse of process in general international law*

States have often pleaded abuse of rights or abuse of process, but neither the PCIJ nor the ICJ has ever found the conditions for its application fulfilled.[164] However, this does not mean that these tribunals have rejected the concept as such. The PCIJ has explained that an abuse cannot be easily presumed,[165] showing the tribunals' awareness of the gravity of accusing a state of bad faith.

### 2.3.7.3 *Abuse of rights in WTO jurisprudence*

The WTO Appellate Body has referred to the abuse of rights doctrine in several decisions so far.[166] Most prominently, the Appellate Body found in *US—Shrimp* that the 'chapeau of Article XX is ... but one expression of the principle of good faith', one application of which is the prohibition of *abus de droit*.[167] Recognizing that the function of the abuse of rights doctrine is to prevent the 'abusive exercise by a Member of its own treaty right thus [resulting] in a breach of the treaty rights of the other Members and, as well, a violation of the treaty obligation of the Member so acting',[168] the Appellate Body interpreted the language of the chapeau with the aim of:

> locating and marking out a line of equilibrium between the right of a Member to invoke an exception under Article XX and the rights of the other Members under varying substantive provisions (eg, Article XI) of the GATT 1994, so that neither of the competing rights will cancel out the other and thereby distort and nullify or impair the balance of rights and obligations constructed by the Members themselves in that Agreement.[169]

[163] Kolb, *General Principles* (n 15) 904 para 49; see also Gaffney (n 29) 518.

[164] See, eg, *Oscar Chinn Case (United Kingdom v Belgium) (Judgment)* [1934] PCIJ (ser A/B) No 63, 86; *Free Zones of Upper Savoy and District of Gex (France v Switzerland) (Judgment)* [1932] PCIJ (ser A/B) No 46, 167; *Certain German Interests in Polish Upper Silesia (Germany v Poland) (Judgment)* [1926] PCIJ (ser A) No 7, 30; *Trail Smelter Arbitration (United States v Canada) (Award II)* (1941) 3 UNRIAA 1905, 1965; *Barcelona Traction* (n 72) 24–25; *Avena and Other Mexican Nationals (Mexico v United States) (Judgment)* [2004] ICJ Rep 12, 37–38.

[165] *Free Zones* (n 164) 167; *German Interests* (n 164) 30.

[166] See, eg, Appellate Body Report, *US—Shrimp* (n 1); Appellate Body Report, *United States—Transitional Safeguard Measure on Combed Cotton Yarn from Pakistan*, WTO Doc WT/DS192/AB/R (adopted 5 November 2001); Appellate Body Report, *United States—Measures Affecting the Cross-Border Supply of Gambling and Betting Services*, WTO Doc WT/DS285/AB/R (adopted 20 April 2005).

[167] Appellate Body Report, *US—Shrimp* (n 1) para 158.

[168] ibid.

[169] ibid para 159.

Within the meaning of the chapeau of article XX, the prohibition of abuse of rights thus translates into a requirement of absence of protectionism and discrimination, extending as far as basic fairness and due process requirements.[170] However, once again the Appellate Body has been very cautious not to apply the abuse of rights doctrine (as an expression of the principle of good faith) autonomously, but rather to attach it to the wording of the *GATT*.[171]

### *2.3.7.4 Abuse of rights in investment treaty jurisprudence*

The abuse of rights or abuse of process doctrine has seen an incremental use in investment arbitration over past years, in particular in relation to the question whether (and under which conditions) corporate (re-)structuring, also known as treaty shopping, should be considered unlawful.[172] The question has also been posed whether the bringing of multiple proceedings for what is in essence the same claim constitutes an abuse of rights or abuse of process.[173]

Approaches of investment tribunals have been heterogenic, showing however an overall reluctance to assume an abuse too lightly. Examining a possible lack of good faith through its various forms or purpose-oriented interpretations, some tribunals have questioned whether the putative investor–claimant had, for natural persons, another 'more genuine' nationality[174] or whether, for legal persons, the 'corporate veil should be pierced'.[175] Others have inquired into whether the 'sole purpose' of the transaction in question was to obtain access to ICSID jurisdiction where none would otherwise exist. As motivations are traditionally difficult to establish, a line of jurisprudence has started to increasingly emphasise the timing of the corporate transaction, asking whether at that moment a dispute existed or not and if not, if the

[170] Appellate Body Report, *US—Shrimp* (n 1) para 181; Panizzon (n 1) 90–91.

[171] Mitchell (n 2) 368; Panizzon (n 1) 32–33.

[172] See also chapter 5 of this volume.

[173] On parallel proceedings see also chapter 4 of this volume.

[174] See, eg, *Soufraki v United Arab Emirates (Award)* (ICSID Arbitral Tribunal, Case No ARB/02/7, 7 July 2004); *Ioan Micula, Viorel Micula, SC European Food SA, SC Starmill SRL and SC Multipack SRL v Romania (Decision on Jurisdiction and Admissibility)* (ICSID Arbitral Tribunal, Case No ARB/05/20, 24 September 2008); *Champion Trading Company, Ameritrade International Inc v Egypt (Decision on Jurisdiction)* (ICSID Arbitral Tribunal, Case No ARB/02/9, 21 October 2003).

[175] See, eg, *Tokios Tokelès v Ukraine (Decision on Jurisdiction)* (ICSID Arbitral Tribunal, Case No ARB/02/18, 28 April 2004); *Rompetrol Group NV v Romania (Decision on Respondent's Preliminary Objections on Jurisdiction and Admissibility)* (ICSID Arbitral Tribunal, Case No ARB/06/3, 18 April 2008); *ADC Affiliate Ltd and ADC & ADMC Management Ltd v Hungary (Award)* (ICSID Arbitral Tribunal, Case No ARB/03/16, 2 October 2006); *Saluka Investments BV v Czech Republic (Partial Award)* (Permanent Court of Arbitration, 17 March 2006).

dispute was foreseeable.[176] The former in reality being a question of whether jurisdiction *ratione temporis* is established,[177] some tribunals have reserved the abuse of rights or abuse of process doctrine to the (highly fact-sensitive) question of whether a future dispute was foreseeable. Abuse of rights or abuse of process findings have thus been rare, probably in part due to the slightly differing foreseeability tests applied by arbitral tribunals.[178]

Whether the bringing of multiple proceedings in relation to the same measure by investors that are formally different but belong to the same corporate structure can also constitute an abuse of process seems to remain unsettled. The tribunals in the *CME* and *Lauder Cases* rejected the respondents' submissions that the bringing of parallel proceedings was an abuse of process.[179] However, some scholars have criticized this conclusion.[180] This issue is addressed further below in chapter 4.

## 2.4 Conclusion

The principle of good faith, both a general principle of law and a general principle of international law, continues to play an eminent role in international treaty relations in general and in international economic relations in particular. Its manifold expressions and concretizations thus remain in principle highly significant in international adjudication. However, to determine the exact content of good faith constitutes a formidable task and must necessarily be context-specific. In particular, the ICJ and the WTO Appellate Body have thus far shown themselves extremely cautious in attaching a possible lack of

[176] *Société Générale v Dominican Republic* (n 43) paras 105–10; *Phoenix Action Ltd v Israel* (n 29) para 92; *Cementownia 'Nowa Huta' SA v Turkey (Award)* (ICSID Arbitral Tribunal, Case No ARB(AF)/06/2, 17 September 2009) para 117; *Europe Cement v Turkey* (n 29) para 175; *Mobil v Venezuela* (n 29) paras 204–05; *Pac Rim Cayman v El Salvador* (n 43) para 2.99; *Tidewater Inc v Venezuela (Decision on Jurisdiction)* (ICSID Arbitral Tribunal, Case No ARB/10/5, 8 February 2013) paras 148, 184; *Lao Holdings NV v Lao People's Democratic Republic (Decision on Jurisdiction)* (ICSID Arbitral Tribunal, Case No ARB(AF)/12/6, 21 February 2014) paras 68–83.

[177] See also chapter 5 of this volume.

[178] See *Pac Rim Cayman v El Salvador* (n 43) para 2.99; *Tidewater v Venezuela* (n 176) para 193; *Lao Holdings v Lao* (n 176) para 76.

[179] *CME Czech Republic BV v Czech Republic (Partial Award)* (UNCITRAL, 13 September 2001) para 412; *Lauder v Czech Republic (Award)* (UNCITRAL, 3 September 2001) paras 174, 177.

[180] Yuval Shany, *The Competing Jurisdictions of International Courts and Tribunals* (OUP 2003) 258–60; Hanno Wehland, *The Coordination of Multiple Proceedings in Investment Treaty Arbitration* (OUP 2013) 218–25; Chester Brown, 'The Relevance of the Doctrine of Abuse of Process in International Arbitration' (2011) 8(2) TDM 1 <transnational-dispute-management.com>.

good faith only to specific good faith norms or concepts, while investment tribunals have shown somewhat less restraint, probably due to differing adjudicatory mandates. Yet even in the absence of limitations on the adjudicatory mandate, tribunals should be careful not to engage in an overly broad use of the principle of good faith, which could negatively impact the quality of the legal reasoning and thus the legitimacy of the arbitral process. Thus checked in its risk of subjectivity, the principle of good faith can make valuable contributions to clarifying and refining the content of specific obligations under international law.

# 3

# Good Faith in Treaty Interpretation

*Eric De Brabandere and Isabelle Van Damme*

## 3.1 Introduction

The principle of good faith in treaty interpretation is difficult to define. In essence, good faith in treaty interpretation corresponds with the idea that contracts should be interpreted in good faith.[1] Whilst statements that a rule of international law is based on the principle of good faith are not uncommon in state practice and decisions of international courts and tribunals, explanations of the principle in its raw form are rare, particularly in connection with treaty interpretation. In any event, just as with other principles of treaty interpretation, theoretical or isolated explanations of good faith do not necessarily contribute to a better understanding of how to interpret a particular treaty or a treaty term. Therefore, this chapter focuses on the functions of the principle of good faith as reflected in the practice of treaty interpretation.

The existence of the principle of good faith in treaty interpretation in itself is not open to question. However, the function of the principle and its relationship with other principles of treaty interpretation remain the subject of debate. The interpretative practices of international courts and tribunals contain few references to the principle of good faith as a stand-alone principle. Rather, good faith is usually applied together with other principles that might be based on the notion of good faith or substantive treaty provisions that are allegedly infringed. As well as assisting in finding the meaning of a treaty, good faith can contribute to the accountability of treaty interpreters.[2]

[1] See Hersch Lauterpacht, 'Restrictive Interpretation and the Principle of Effectiveness in the Interpretation of Treaties' (1949) 26 BYBIL 48, 56; *Affaire relative à la concession des phares de l'Empire ottoman (Grèce, France) (Sentence Arbitrale)* (Permanent Court of Arbitration, 24/27 July 1956) XII UNRIAA 155, 226–27.

[2] On the dual function of the principle, see, eg, *Inceysa Vallisoletana SL v El Salvador (Award)* (ICSID Arbitral Tribunal, Case No ARB/03/26, 2 August 2006) para 179.

This chapter covers both functions of good faith: as an interpretative aid and as a mechanism of accountability of the treaty interpreter. First, the chapter sets out the sequence of elements to consider in an interpretative analysis. Some of these elements are codified in articles 31 to 33 of the *Vienna Convention on the Law of Treaties* (*VCLT*).[3] Others are not. Whether the latter are accepted as forming part of a good faith interpretation or an otherwise acceptable treaty interpretation under international law is not always clear. In forming the basis for treaty interpretation, good faith serves an objective function, that is, a function relating to the process of interpretation. Second, the chapter considers good faith's establishment of a general standard of behaviour for treaty interpreters by requiring that they act reasonably and fairly. In that sense, the principle of good faith has a subjective function, that is, one relating to the interpreter.

In describing and distinguishing these two functions of the principle of good faith, this chapter draws on the case law of investment treaty tribunals and the World Trade Organization (WTO) dispute settlement system, as well as historical materials recording the relevant debates in the International Law Commission (ILC) (and elsewhere) leading to the conclusion of the *VCLT*. This chapter offers a general background for other chapters that focus on distinct elements of good faith in the context of international investment law and international trade law.

## 3.2 Good Faith and Treaty Interpretation

The principle of good faith applies to the creation and performance of legal obligations assumed by means of treaty.[4] The focus here is on its functions under international law in interpreting treaties. Performing a treaty in good faith presupposes its interpretation in good faith.[5] According to article 31(1) of the *VCLT*, a 'treaty shall be interpreted in good faith in accordance with the ordinary meaning to be given to the terms of the treaty in their context and in the light of its object and purpose'. That provision of the *VCLT* applies

[3] *Vienna Convention on the Law of Treaties*, opened for signature 23 May 1969, 1155 UNTS 331 (entered into force 27 January 1980) (*VCLT*). The wording of *VCLT* arts 31 to 33 corresponds with that of arts 31 to 33 of the *Vienna Convention on the Law of Treaties between States and International Organizations or between International Organizations*, UN Doc A/CONF.129/15, concluded 21 March 1986, 25 ILM 543 (not yet in force).

[4] *Nuclear Tests (Australia v France) (Judgment)* [1974] ICJ 253, para 46. See also Bin Cheng, *General Principles of Law as Applied by International Courts and Tribunals* (CUP 1953, reissued 2006) 106 (noting that it 'governs treaties from the time of their formation to the time of their extinction').

[5] See, eg, Humphrey Waldock, Special Rapporteur, 'Third Report on the Law of Treaties' [1964] II Yearbook ILC 5, 8.

together with the principle stated in article 26 that every treaty must be performed in good faith by the parties to it. Moreover, if a treaty has not yet entered into force, article 18 sets out the circumstances in which a state must refrain from acts that would defeat its object and purpose. That too is an expression of the principle of good faith.[6]

At a basic level, a good faith interpretation is an interpretation in accordance with law, which thus includes in principle international law governing interpretation and the rules governing the competence of treaty interpreters. That definition presupposes that the methods of treaty interpretation are settled and that the rules of treaty interpretation are clear. However, the drafting of the rules of treaty interpretation in the *VCLT* suggests that they are based on and determined by the principle of good faith itself. The rules of treaty interpretation are thus closely interwoven with the principle of good faith.

Sir Humphrey Waldock wrote in his 'Third Report on the Law of Treaties' that principles of interpretation 'are, for the most part, principles of logic and good sense valuable only as guides to assist in appreciating the meaning which the parties may have intended to attach to the expressions which they employed in a document' and are principles of which the 'suitability for use in any given case hinges on a variety of considerations which have first to be appreciated by the interpreter of the document [such as] the particular arrangement of the words and sentences, their relation to each other and to other parts of the document, the general nature and subject matter of the document, the circumstances in which it was drawn up'.[7] That remains an appropriate description of how principles of interpretation are to be used. The principle of good faith interacts in different ways with the elements of this description.

The principle of good faith is difficult to define in positive terms. It is easier to explain what might not be a good faith interpretation of a treaty: an interpretation that is arbitrary, unreasonable, illogical, unfair, dishonest, deceptive, abusive or excessive. Thus, the Appellate Body in *US—Anti-Dumping and Countervailing Duties (China)* explained that one meaning of good faith interpretation is that 'terms of a treaty are *not* to be interpreted based on the assumption that one party is seeking to evade its obligations and will exercise its rights so as to cause injury to the other party'.[8] Despite the apparently

[6] See, eg, Markus Kotzur, 'Good Faith (Bona fide)' in Rüdiger Wolfrüm (ed), *Max Planck Encyclopedia of Public International Law* (OUP) <www.mpepil.com> accessed 29 July 2014, para 19; *Maritime Delimitation and Territorial Questions between Qatar and Bahrain (Qatar v Bahrain) (Jurisdiction and Admissibility)* [1995] ICJ Rep 6, 36 (Vice-President Schwebel).

[7] Waldock (n 5) 54.

[8] Appellate Body Report, *United States—Definitive Anti-Dumping and Countervailing Duties on Certain Products from China*, WTO Doc WT/DS379/AB/R (adopted 25 March 2011) para 326 (emphasis added).

elusive character of the principle,[9] acting contrary to it while being in accordance with international law appears to be excluded because it is not possible to depart from the principle of good faith in accordance with international (treaty) law.

## 3.3 Status of Good Faith Treaty Interpretation under International Law

As explained in chapter 1 of this volume, the principle of good faith has been described as both a general principle of law and a principle of customary international law. Thus, the Appellate Body has identified good faith as 'at once a general principle of law and a principle of general international law'.[10] In the specific context of treaty interpretation, the principle is often treated as forming part of customary international law rather than as a general principle of law, because it is reflected in several provisions of the *VCLT* that are regarded as having attained the status of customary international law.[11] In the context of the case law of the International Court of Justice (ICJ) to that

[9] See, for example, Andrew Mitchell, 'Good Faith in WTO Dispute Settlement' (2006) 7 Melb J Intl L 339.

[10] Appellate Body Report, *United States—Tax Treatment for 'Foreign Sales Corporations'*, WTO Doc WT/DS108/AB/R (adopted 20 March 2000) para 166.

[11] See, eg, *Oil Platforms (Iran v USA) (Preliminary Objections)* [1996] ICJ Rep 812, para 23. In the WTO (as regards *VCLT* (n 3) arts 31, 32), see, eg, Appellate Body Report, *United States—Standards for Reformulated and Conventional Gasoline*, WTO Doc WT/DS2/AB/R (adopted 20 May 1996) 16–17; Appellate Body Report, *Japan—Taxes on Alcoholic Beverages*, WTO Docs WT/DS8/AB/R, WT/DS10/AB/R, WT/DS11/AB/R (adopted 1 November 1996) 104. See also Appellate Body Report, *European Communities—Customs Classification of Certain Computer Equipment*, WTO Docs WT/DS62/AB/R, WT/DS67/AB/R, WT/DS68/AB/R (adopted 22 June 1998) para 84; Appellate Body Report, *United States—Import Prohibition of Certain Shrimp and Shrimp Products*, WTO Doc WT/DS58/AB/R (adopted 6 November 1998) para 114; Appellate Body Report, *Korea—Definitive Safeguard Measure on Imports of Certain Dairy Products*, WTO Doc WT/DS98/AB/R (adopted 12 January 2000) para 81; Appellate Body Report, *India—Patent Protection for Pharmaceutical and Agricultural Chemical Products*, WTO Doc WT/DS50/AB/R (adopted 16 January 1998) para 46. As regards investment law, see, for example, *Tokios Tokelés v Ukraine (Decision on Jurisdiction)* (ICSID Arbitral Tribunal, Case No ARB/02/18, 29 April 2004) para 27; *Salini Costruttori SpA and Italstrade SpA v Hashemite Kingdom of Jordan (Decision on Jurisdiction)* (ICSID Arbitral Tribunal, Case No ARB/02/13, 29 November 2004) para 75; *Sempra Energy International v Argentina* (*Decision on Objections to Jurisdiction*) (ICSID Arbitral Tribunal, Case No ARB/02/16, 11 May 2005) para 141; *Noble Ventures Inc v Romania (Award)* (ICSID Arbitral Tribunal, Case No ARB/01/11, 12 October 2005) para 50; *Aguas del Tunari SA v Bolivia (Decision on Respondent's Objections to Jurisdiction)* (ICSID Arbitral Tribunal, Case No ARB/02/3, 21 October 2005) para 88; *Churchill Mining PLC and Planet Mining Pty Ltd v Indonesia (Decision on Jurisdiction)* (ICSID Arbitral Tribunal, Case No ARB/12/14 and 12/40, 24 February 2014) para 149.

effect, one explanation offered is that the ICJ is reluctant to resort to general principles of law if it can rely on treaty law or customary international law.[12] However, the ICJ has accepted that the obligation to act in accordance with good faith is a general principle of law.[13] In WTO dispute settlement, that characterization can be explained on the basis of the text of article 3.2 of the *Understanding on Rules and Procedures Governing the Settlement of Disputes* (*Dispute Settlement Understanding* or *DSU*),[14] which states that the dispute settlement system 'serves ... to clarify the existing provisions of [the covered] agreements in accordance with customary rules of interpretation of public international law'. This provision authorizes WTO panels and the Appellate Body to use the principle of good faith in interpreting the WTO covered agreements (though the inclusion of this phrase in article 3.2 has historical origins specific to the WTO, and customary principles of treaty interpretation were used before the establishment of the WTO).[15]

Investment treaty tribunals have also considered the principle of good faith to be part of customary international law and a general principle of law. However, such tribunals are often reluctant to apply general principles of law.[16] This reluctance is not necessarily due to the common references in applicable law clauses in investment treaties and the *Convention on the Settlement of Investment Disputes between States and Nationals of Other States* (*ICSID Convention*)[17] to 'rules of international law as may be applicable'[18] or the fact that such agreements leave open the question of what rules of international law apply. The main reason for the reluctance of investment treaty tribunals to use general principles of law is that they are often regarded as unimportant and 'weak sources' of international law.[19] This is not to say that general principles are not applied in practice; their role is mostly to fill gaps

[12] See Hugh Thirlway, *The Sources of International Law* (OUP 2014) 101.

[13] *Certain Norwegian Loans (France v Norway) (Jurisdiction)* [1957] ICJ Rep 9, 53.

[14] *Marrakesh Agreement Establishing the World Trade Organization*, opened for signature 15 April 1994, 1867 UNTS 3 (entered into force 1 January 1995), annex 2 (*Understanding on Rules and Procedures Governing the Settlement of Disputes*) (*DSU*).

[15] See also Isabelle Van Damme, *Treaty Interpretation by the WTO Appellate Body* (OUP 2008) 357–66.

[16] From a quantitative perspective, in very few cases have general principles of law been relied upon as a separate legal basis. See further Ole Kristian Fauchald, 'The Legal Reasoning of ICSID Tribunals—An Empirical Analysis' (2008) 19(2) EJIL 301, 312.

[17] Opened for signature 18 March 1965, entered into force 14 October 1966.

[18] ibid art 42.

[19] M Sornarajah, *The International Law on Foreign Investment* (3rd edn, CUP 2010) 418. For a discussion, see Stephan Schill, 'General Principles of Law and International Investment Law' in Tarcisio Gazzini and Eric De Brabandere (eds), *International Investment Law: The Sources of Rights and Obligations* (Martinus Nijhoff 2012) 139–47.

left by the treaty and customary international law.[20] Thus, investment treaty tribunals usually prefer to rely on either treaty law or customary international law. References to good faith as a general principle of law are occasionally found in investment treaty decisions outside the context of treaty interpretation (for instance in relation to acquisitions of investments or the existence of a protected investment).[21]

## 3.4 Objective Function: Giving Meaning to a Treaty Text

### 3.4.1 Good faith and interpretation within and beyond the *Vienna Convention*

Principles of treaty interpretation assist in giving meaning to texts with authority as law by establishing potentially relevant factors and a sequence of analytical steps, although debate may exist on the applicable sequence. The introductory part of article 31(1) of the *VCLT* informs the remaining parts of articles 31 to 33,[22] which can be read as a guide to interpreting treaties in good faith. The principle of good faith can help to justify choices in applying articles 31 to 33 of the *VCLT*. For example, whilst the use of preparatory work is a supplementary means of interpretation pursuant to article 32, in the absence of a definition of preparatory work in the text of that provision, good faith can be used to justify the selection of relevant preparatory work. Good faith also can be used to justify the use of other supplementary means of interpretation not explicitly mentioned in article 32.

Such an approach was adopted by the tribunal in *HICEE BV v Slovakia*. In that case, the claimant and respondent had put forward opposing interpretations of the phrase 'directly or through an investor of a third State' in article 1(a) of the Netherlands–Czechoslovakia Bilateral Investment Treaty (BIT).[23] The tribunal relied on supplementary means of interpretation[24]—in

[20] For a list of examples of general principles referred to in the practice of ICSID tribunals, see 'Article 42' in Christoph Schreuer with Loretta Malintoppi, August Reinisch and Anthony Sinclair, *The ICSID Convention: A Commentary* (2nd edn, CUP 2009) para 180.

[21] See, eg, *Inceysa* (n 2) paras 230–39; *Phoenix Action Ltd v Czech Republic (Award)* (ICSID Arbitral Tribunal, Case No ARB/06/5, 15 April 2009) paras 106–13.

[22] See also Richard Gardiner, *Treaty Interpretation* (OUP 2008) 148.

[23] *Agreement on encouragement and reciprocal protection of investments between the Kingdom of the Netherlands and the Czech and Slovak Federal Republic*, signed 29 April 1991 (entered into force 1 October 1992).

[24] *HICEE BV v Slovak Republic (Partial Award)* (UNCITRAL, Permanent Court of Arbitration, Case No 2009-11, 23 May 2011) paras 122–47.

particular, unilaterally drafted documents (explanatory notes) submitted by the Dutch Minister of Foreign Affairs to the Dutch Parliament during the domestic BIT ratification process—in concluding (by majority) that the phrase did not cover investments made by wholly-owned subsidiaries in the Slovak Republic.[25] The tribunal justified its decision to rely on these documents on the basis of the need to interpret treaties in good faith: ignoring the documents would 'fly in the face of logic and good sense' and would not 'be reconcilable with the requirement that a treaty is to be interpreted in good faith'.[26] However, such justification may well be specific to the interpretation of *bilateral* treaties. Use of this type of supplementary means of interpretation is more difficult to justify when interpreting multilateral treaties.

The principle of good faith is sometimes regarded as a meta-norm underlying all forms and methods of treaty interpretation and their use in practice. The principle in this guise is a legitimate source for identifying other tools, principles or even values that can be taken into account in interpreting treaties, despite the absence of any express reference to them in the *VCLT*.[27] The principle of good faith is then both constitutive of principles of treaty interpretation under international law and complementary to the application of those principles, and it can be difficult to identify a stand-alone application of good faith in treaty interpretation.[28] Yet, that point is separate from the idea that the principle of good faith in itself is not a source of obligation where none would otherwise exist,[29] which relates to the substantive standard of the good faith *application* of a treaty, as stated in article 26 of the *VCLT*.

In any event, even if it is possible to catalogue some of the tools, principles and values that are accepted in a good faith interpretation, their purpose and appeal often depend on a range of contextual elements, including the specificity of the treaty text being interpreted, the object and purpose of the treaty, and the relevant institutional context. These different factors make it difficult

[25] ibid para 116. [26] ibid para 136.

[27] For example, the principle of effectiveness, which is discussed in the next sub-section of this chapter.

[28] See, eg, Gardiner (n 22) 148; Martin Dawidowicz, 'The Effect of the Passage of Time on the Interpretation of Treaties: Some Reflections on *Costa Rica v Nicaragua*' (2011) 24(1) LJIL 201, 212.

[29] See, eg, *Border and Transborder Armed Actions (Nicaragua v Honduras) (Jurisdiction and Admissibility)* [1988] ICJ Rep 105, para 94. For example, the principle of good faith cannot be a stand-alone source of an obligation under international law for states to inform other states parties to the *Statute of the International Court of Justice* that they intend to subscribe or have subscribed to the optional clause. See also *Land and Maritime Boundary between Cameroon and Nigeria (Cameroon v Nigeria) (Preliminary Objections)* [1998] ICJ Rep 275, para 39; Appellate Body Report, *United States—Continued Dumping and Subsidy Offset Act of 2000*, WTO Doc WT/DS217/AB/R, WT/DS234/AB/R (adopted 27 January 2003) para 298; Panel Report, *Argentina—Definitive Anti-Dumping Duties on Poultry from Brazil*, WTO Doc WT/DS241/R (adopted 19 May 2003) para 7.36.

to theorize in a generally applicable manner about the criteria determining the use of one principle of interpretation over another and the manner of its application. The same may be said of the content of articles 31 to 33 of the *VCLT*, as illustrated by more recent work of the ILC on the meaning of articles 31(3)(a)–(b) (on subsequent agreements and subsequent practice)[30] and 31(3)(c) (on any relevant rules of international law applicable in the relations between the parties).[31]

### 3.4.2 The principle of effectiveness

The principle of effectiveness provides a useful illustration of good faith as a meta-norm that is both constitutive of principles of treaty interpretation and complements their application. According to the principle of effectiveness, the preferred interpretation is that which enables the treaty to have appropriate effects. Whilst that principle is not expressly stated in articles 31 to 33 of the *VCLT*, it is a specific articulation of the principle of good faith and the consideration that a treaty is to be interpreted in accordance with its object and purpose.[32] The principle of effectiveness is, as the ILC put it, implied in the general rule on interpretation.[33] Proposals were submitted to codify the principle of effectiveness in order to distinguish it from the notion of an extensive or teleological interpretation[34] and to ensure the effectiveness of the principle of *pacta sunt servanda*.[35] However, the ILC finally decided not to do so because the principle of effectiveness is part of the general rule that a treaty is to be interpreted in good faith in accordance with the ordinary meaning to be given to its terms in the context of that treaty and in the light of its object and purpose. The application of the general rule means that if 'a treaty is

[30] *Report of the International Law Commission on the work of its sixty-fourth session (7 May–1 June and 2 July–3 August 2012)*, UN GAOR, 67th sess, Supp No 10, UN Doc A/67/10 (2012) paras 222–24.

[31] ibid.

[32] See, eg, Waldock (n 5) 61; 'Draft Articles on the Law of Treaties with Commentaries' [1966] II Yearbook ILC para 6.

[33] 'Report of the International Law Commission on the Work of Its Sixteenth Session, 11 July 1964, Official Records of the General Assembly—Nineteenth Session' [1964] II Yearbook ILC 201.

[34] Waldock (n 5) 60–61. The proposed art 72, entitled 'Effective interpretation of the terms (ut res magis valeat quam pereat)', read: 'In the application of articles 70 and 71 a term of a treaty shall be so interpreted as to give it the fullest weight and effect consistent—(a) with its natural and ordinary meaning and that of the other terms of the treaty; and (b) with the objects and purposes of the treaty'.

[35] Waldock (n 5) 61, para 29: 'If the principle of effective interpretation may be said to be implicit in the requirement of good faith, there are, it is thought, two reasons which may make it desirable to formulate it in a separate article. The first is that the principle has special significance as the basis upon which it is justifiable to imply terms in a treaty for the purpose of giving efficacy to an intention necessarily to be inferred from the express provisions of the treaty'.

open to two interpretations one of which does and the other does not enable the treaty to have appropriate effects, good faith and the objects and purposes of the treaty demand that the former interpretation should be adopted'.[36]

### 3.4.3 Restrictive interpretation, *in dubio mitius* and strict interpretation of exceptions

The notion of restrictive interpretation is often used interchangeably with the principle of *in dubio mitius*, but the former can also be used to refer to other methods of interpretation, such as the interpretation of exceptions. According to the principle of *in dubio mitius*, 'if the meaning of a term is ambiguous, that meaning is to be preferred which is less onerous to the party assuming an obligation, or which interferes less with the territorial and personal supremacy of a party, or involves less general restrictions upon the parties'.[37] Treaty language is not to be interpreted so as to limit state sovereignty or a state's 'personal and territorial supremacy', 'even though these stipulations do not conflict with such interpretation'.[38] If the language on the existence or scope of an obligation is unclear, the *in dubio mitius* principle supports the proposition that no or only a minimal obligation should be applied. The application of the principle essentially results in an interpretation in deference to the sovereignty of one specific signatory, the party assuming an obligation (in practice, this is often the respondent state).

Such an interpretation is supposed to protect the sovereignty of the parties to a treaty.[39] But most treaty law restricts sovereignty, albeit through the exercise of state sovereignty. The Permanent Court of International Justice (PCIJ) initially formulated the *in dubio mitius* principle as applicable 'when, in spite of all pertinent considerations, the intention of the Parties still remains doubtful'[40] and unless its application would lead to an interpretation 'contrary to the plain terms ... and would destroy what has been

[36] 'Report of the International Law Commission on the Work of Its Eighteenth Session (4 May–19 July 1966)' [1966] II Yearbook ILC 219.

[37] Appellate Body Report, *EC Measures Concerning Meat and Meat Products (Hormones)*, WTO Docs WT/DS26/AB/R, WT/DS48/AB/R (adopted 13 February 1998) para 165, n 154. See also *Article 3, Paragraph 2 of the Treaty of Lausanne (Frontier between Turkey and Iraq)* [1925] PCIJ (ser B) No 12, 25.

[38] *SS Wimbledon (Judgment of 17 August 1923)* [1923] PCIJ (ser A) No 1, 35, 37 (Anzilotti and Huber JJ); Lord McNair, *The Law of Treaties* (reissued 1961 edn, Clarendon Press 1986) 466.

[39] Lauterpacht, 'Restrictive Interpretation' (n 1) 58. Furthermore, the PCIJ in *Lotus* concluded that '[r]estrictions upon the independence of States cannot ... be presumed': *SS 'Lotus' (France v Turkey) (Judgment)* [1927] PCIJ (ser A) No 10, 18. For early examples, see McNair (n 38) 211–16.

[40] *Territorial Jurisdiction of the International Commission of the River Oder (United Kingdom, Czechoslovakia, Denmark, France, Germany, Sweden v Poland) (Judgment)* [1929] PCIJ (ser A) No 23, 26.

clearly granted'.[41] The principle is not codified in the *VCLT* and is unlikely to qualify as a general principle of law or part of customary international law.[42] The validity of applying the principle has also been denied where the language in different authentic versions of a treaty conflicts and the conflict cannot be resolved through the general principles of interpretation.[43] The use of the principle appears to have received more support from scholars than from international courts and tribunals.[44]

Although the PCIJ cited the notion of restrictive interpretation (meaning, in this context, the principle of *in dubio mitius*) in several cases, it relied upon it only as a last resort[45] and always emphasized its limits. The starting point of interpretation remains the terms of the treaty, not the interests of those who drafted the treaty in exercise of their sovereignty with the effect of transferring parts of that sovereignty.[46] In the *Wimbledon* case, the PCIJ found that a restrictive interpretation stops 'at the point where [it] would be contrary to the plain terms of the article and would destroy what has been clearly granted'.[47] In the *Nuclear Tests* case, the ICJ applied a restrictive interpretation to unilateral statements limiting a state's freedom of action, followed by an extensive approach to whether a commitment existed.[48]

[41] *Wimbledon* (n 38) 24; see also *Japan—Alcoholic Beverages II* (n 11) 108: 'The WTO Agreement is a treaty—the international equivalent of a contract. It is self-evident that in an exercise of their sovereignty, and in pursuit of their own respective national interests, the Members of the WTO have made a bargain. In exchange for the benefits they expect to derive as Members of the WTO, they have agreed to exercise their sovereignty according to the commitments they have made in the WTO Agreement'.

[42] See Hersch Lauterpacht, *The Development of International Law by the International Court* (rev edn, Stevens & Sons Ltd 1958) 338; Lauterpacht, 'Restrictive Interpretation' (n 1) 59.

[43] Waldock (n 5) 65.

[44] See Lauterpacht, 'Restrictive Interpretation' (n 1) 48; Lauterpacht, *Development of International Law* (n 42) 305–06; Ian Brownlie, *Principles of Public International Law* (6th edn, OUP 2003) 606; Robert Hudec, 'The New WTO Dispute Settlement Procedure: An Overview of the First Three Years' (1999) 8(1) Minn J Global Trade 1, 1; Petros Mavroidis, 'Highway XVI re-visited: The Road from Non-Discrimination to Market Access in GATS' (2007) 6(1) World TR 1, 11; Richard Steinberg, 'Judicial Lawmaking at the WTO: Discursive, Constitutional, and Political Restraints' (2004) 98(2) AJIL 247, 258; Gene Grossman and Petros Mavroidis, 'United States—Countervailing Duties on Certain Corrosion-Resistant Carbon Steel Flat Products from Germany (WTO Doc WT/DS213/AB/R): The Sound of Silence' in Henrik Horn and Petros Mavroidis (eds), *The WTO Case Law of 2002* (CUP 2005) 71.

[45] *Lotus* (n 39) 18; *Wimbledon* (n 38) 24–25; *Polish Postal Service in Danzig (Advisory Opinion)* [1925] PCIJ (ser B) No 11, 40; *River Oder* (n 40) 26; *Free Zones of Upper Savoy and the District of Gex* [1932] PCIJ (ser A/B) No 46, 167. Lauterpacht noted the *jurisprudence constante* of the PCIJ in rejecting the application of the principle of restrictive interpretation but criticized it for not being sufficiently consequential: Lauterpacht, *Development of International Law* (n 42) 302–03.

[46] *Competence of the International Labour Organization in regard to International Regulation of the Conditions of Labour of Persons Employed in Agriculture (Advisory Opinion)* [1922] PCIJ (ser B) No 2, 23.

[47] *Wimbledon* (n 38) 24.

[48] *Nuclear Tests* (n 4) 267.

The Appellate Body has applied the principle of *in dubio mitius* as a non-codified customary principle of interpretation, but only once. In *EC—Hormones*, the Appellate Body embraced the principle of *in dubio mitius* as a supplementary means to interpret WTO members' obligations under the *Agreement on the Application of Sanitary and Phytosanitary Measures*.[49] The Appellate Body judged, not entirely correctly, that *in dubio mitius* was 'widely recognized in international law as a "supplementary means of interpretation"' in legal writing and decisions of the ICJ, the PCIJ, arbitration tribunals, and conciliation commissions.[50] The Appellate Body cited only the *Nuclear Tests* case in support of *in dubio mitius*, and it did not rely on the principle as a last resort, as the PCIJ had suggested. After examining the text and the object and purpose of article 3.1 of the *DSU*, the Appellate Body immediately turned to the principle of *in dubio mitius* without looking at subsequent practice and agreements, relevant rules of international law, or other supplementary means of interpretation. In subsequent disputes, disputants or third parties have relied on the principle in their submissions but the Appellate Body has not followed those arguments. In fact, recent case law suggests that the Appellate Body has doubts about the relevance of the principle in WTO dispute settlement.[51]

Certain investment tribunals have similarly applied the principle of *in dubio mitius* as the 'appropriate interpretative approach' and have even relied explicitly on the Appellate Body's report in *EC—Hormones*.[52] Nonetheless, the application of the principle in investment law remains contentious, in particular as regards dispute settlement clauses in BITs, 'umbrella clauses', definitions of investment, and thus of the consent of states to arbitration more generally.[53] The principle of *in dubio mitius* has received little support in the practice of tribunals and a 'restrictive approach' in interpreting

[49] *Marrakesh Agreement Establishing the World Trade Organization* (n 14) annex 1A (*Agreement on the Application of Sanitary and Phytosanitary Measures*).

[50] *EC—Hormones* (n 37) para 165, n 154.

[51] See Appellate Body Report, *China—Measures Affecting Trading Rights and Distribution Services for Certain Publications and Audiovisual Entertainment Products*, WTO Doc WT/DS363/AB/R (adopted 19 January 2010) para 411.

[52] See, eg, *SGS Société Générale de Surveillance SA v Pakistan (Decision of the Tribunal on Objections to Jurisdiction)* (ICSID Arbitral Tribunal, Case No ARB/01/13, 6 August 2003) para 171: 'We believe, for the foregoing considerations, that Article 11 of the BIT would have to be considerably more specifically worded before it can reasonably be read in the extraordinarily expansive manner submitted by the claimant. The appropriate interpretative approach is the prudential one summed up in the literature as *in dubio pars mitior est sequenda*, or more tersely, *in dubio mitius*'.

[53] Thomas Wälde, 'Interpreting Investment Treaties: Experiences and Examples' in Christina Binder, Ursula Kriebaum, August Reinisch and Stephan Wittich (eds), *International Investment Law for the 21st Century: Essays in Honour of Christoph Schreuer* (OUP 2009) 724, 733–36.

investment treaties has been criticized.[54] However, a criticism of an allegedly restrictive interpretation can sometimes be a criticism of the *result* or *effect* of the interpretation of the provision—for instance when the interpretation results in a tribunal declining jurisdiction, which is considered 'restrictive' compared to an allegedly more 'effective' result, which would entail upholding jurisdiction. This criticism has little to do with the interpretative process or method in itself.[55]

'Restrictive interpretation' is sometimes used to refer to a strict interpretation of exceptions to obligations assumed under a treaty (and the implications for corresponding rights). It is doubtful whether that is an accepted method of interpretation and, when used in isolation, it can be part of a good faith interpretation. A close reading of the cases where that method was allegedly applied reveals that investment tribunals (in interpreting the applicable treaty) in fact do not apply a strict or restrictive interpretation method. Rather, they apply the often invoked principle that exceptions—in particular clauses containing consent to arbitration—must be interpreted according to, as the tribunal in *Plama v Bulgaria* put it, the 'well-established principle, both in domestic and international law, that [an agreement to arbitrate] should be clear and unambiguous'.[56] In the absence of any clear evidence in the text itself or other proof to the contrary, one cannot presume that a state has accepted an agreement to arbitrate.[57] The relationship between that approach and the principles of interpretation set out in the *VCLT* was described by the tribunal in *Noble Ventures v Romania*, which stated:

> [A]n umbrella clause ... introduces an exception to the general separation of States['] obligations under municipal and under international law ... [T]he identification of a provision as an 'umbrella clause' can as a consequence proceed only from a strict, if not indeed restrictive, interpretation of its terms and, more generally, in accordance with the well known customary rules codified under Article 31 of the [*VCLT*].[58]

The tribunal then proceeded to analyse the terms of the umbrella clause at issue[59] and suggested that an interpretation not 'exclusively in favour of

[54] See Ian Laird, 'Interpretation in International Investment Arbitration—Through the Looking Glass' in Jacques Werner and Arif Hyder Ali (eds), *A Liber Amicorum: Thomas Wälde—Law Beyond Conventional Thought* (Cameron May 2009) 151, 156.

[55] See generally Charles de Visscher, *Problèmes d'interprétation judiciaire en droit international public* (Pedone 1963) 87–88.

[56] *Plama Consortium Ltd v Bulgaria (Decision on Jurisdiction)* (ICSID Arbitral Tribunal, Case No ARB/03/24, 8 February 2005) para 198.

[57] See also Lauterpacht, 'Restrictive Interpretation' (n 1) 59. See also *Elettronica Sicula SpA (ELSI) (United States v Italy) (Judgment)* [1989] ICJ Rep 1989 15, para 50.

[58] *Noble Ventures* (n 11) para 55.

[59] ibid para 56.

investors' would 'deprive Art. II (2)(c) of practical content' and that 'reference has necessarily to be made to the principle of effectiveness'.[60]

The approach of interpreting exceptions strictly, in the sense of not presuming an exception in the absence of a clear and ambiguous text, has no stand-alone function. Investment tribunals, when apparently adopting that approach, in fact look at the exact terms of a treaty provision (though the practice of different tribunals does not appear to be entirely uniform on this matter, in particular in the context of the interpretation of dispute settlement clauses.)[61] This is nothing more than an application of article 31 of the *VCLT*. The practice of the WTO dispute settlement organs also confirms that position.[62]

### 3.4.4 Legitimate expectations

The results of a good faith interpretation can also depend on more general considerations about the purpose of treaty interpretation. Thus, for example, in the context of the WTO, some panels and the Appellate Body disagree on the relevance of legitimate expectations in interpreting the WTO covered agreements. The Appellate Body has been reluctant to apply legitimate expectations as a basis for interpretation.[63] Some panels have been more receptive to such an approach.[64]

[60] ibid para 52. See also *El Paso Energy International Co v Argentina (Decision on Jurisdiction)* (ICSID Arbitral Tribunal, Case No ARB/03/15, 27 April 2006). In that case, the tribunal, while criticizing *Noble Ventures* for failing to interpret exceptions restrictively ('as exceptions should be interpreted'), also analysed the wording of the clause and applied the principle of effectiveness in view of the object and purpose of the treaty at issue (para 77).

[61] See Laird (n 54) 155–56. See, also, eg, *Amco Asia Corp v Indonesia (Decision on Jurisdiction)* (ICSID Arbitral Tribunal, Case No ARB/81/1, 25 September 1983) para 14: 'a convention to arbitrate is not to be construed *restrictively*, nor, as a matter of fact, *broadly* or *liberally*. It is to be construed in a way which leads to find out and to respect the common will of the parties: such a method of interpretation is but the application of the fundamental principle *pacta sunt servanda*, a principle common, indeed, to all systems of internal law and to international law. Moreover—and this is again a general principle of law—any convention, including conventions to arbitrate, should be construed in good faith, that is to say by taking into account the consequences of their commitments the parties may be considered as having reasonably and legitimately envisaged' (emphasis in original). See also, eg, *Ethyl Corp v Canada (Award on Jurisdiction)* (UNCITRAL, NAFTA, 24 June 1998) para 55; *Methanex Corp v United States (Partial Award)* (UNCITRAL, NAFTA, 7 August 2002) para 105; *El Paso* (n 60) para 70; *Inceysa* (n 2) para 177; *Phoenix Action* (n 21) paras 106–08; *Churchill Mining* (n 11) para 151. See also Schreuer (n 20) 251, para 587.

[62] See, eg, Appellate Body Report, *European Communities—Conditions for the Granting of Tariff Preferences to Developing Countries*, WTO Doc WT/DS246/AB/R (adopted 7 April 2004) para 98.

[63] *India—Patents (US)* (n 11) paras 45, 46; *EC—Computer Equipment* (n 11) para 84.

[64] See Panel Report, *United States—Restrictions on Imports of Cotton and Man-made Fibre Underwear*, WTO Doc WT/DS24/R (adopted 25 February 1997) para 7.20; Panel Report, *India—Patent Protection for Pharmaceutical and Agricultural Chemical Products, Complaint by the United States*, WTO Doc WT/DS50/R (adopted 16 January 1998) para 7.18; Panel Report,

The panel in *US—Underwear* established the link between the principle of good faith and the protection of legitimate expectations. Referring to the need for a good faith interpretation, the panel found that:

> based upon the wording, the context and the overall purpose of the [*Agreement on Textiles and Clothing*],[65] exporting Members can legitimately expect that transitional safeguards ... would only be applied sparingly in order to serve the narrow purpose of protecting domestic producers of like and/or directly competitive products.[66]

In *India—Patents (US)*, the Appellate Body found that '[t]he legitimate expectations of the parties to a treaty are reflected in the language of the treaty itself'.[67] In its view, the recognition of the protection of legitimate expectations as a stand-alone principle conflicts with the *VCLT* because 'these principles of interpretation neither require nor condone the imputation into a treaty of words that are not there or the importation into a treaty of concepts that were not intended'.[68] The Appellate Body criticized the panel in that case for having 'created its own interpretative principle, which is consistent with neither the customary rules of interpretation of public international law nor established GATT/WTO practice'.[69] The panel had also confused two concepts that apply in different contexts, one being non-violation complaints and the other being violation complaints.[70]

The Appellate Body was more outspoken on legitimate expectations in *EC—Computer Equipment*, where it remarked:

> The purpose of treaty interpretation under Article 31 of the [*VCLT*] is to ascertain the *common* intentions of the parties. These *common* intentions cannot be ascertained on the basis of the subjective and unilaterally determined 'expectations' of *one* of the parties to a treaty.[71]

Thus, the Appellate Body has not accepted the protection of legitimate expectations as a principle of good faith interpretation. The Appellate Body may suspect that such an equivocal principle could easily drift towards a principle of substantive law extraneous to the covered agreements. The protection of legitimate expectations could then become a separate basis for a claim and part of the applicable law.

*European Communities—Customs Classification of Certain Computer Equipment*, WTO Docs WT/DS62/R, WT/DS67/R, WT/DS68/R (adopted 22 June 1998) para 8.25.

[65] *Marrakesh Agreement Establishing the World Trade Organization* (n 14) annex 1A (*Agreement on Textiles and Clothing*).

[66] *US—Underwear* (n 64) para 7.20. For a discussion of the WTO case law on legitimate expectations, see also Marion Panizzon, *Good Faith in the Jurisprudence of the WTO: The Protection of Legitimate Expectations, Good Faith Interpretation and Fair Dispute Settlement* (Hart 2006) 236–44.

[67] *India—Patents (US)* (n 11) para 45. [68] ibid. [69] ibid para 46.

[70] ibid para 42. [71] *EC—Computer Equipment* (n 11) para 84 (emphasis in original).

In investment law, there is debate about whether the legitimate expectations of the foreign investor form a key element of the fair and equitable treatment (FET) standard.[72] Yet, with respect to broadly formulated or 'unqualified' FET treaty provisions, tribunals appear to interpret that standard as including respect for foreign investors' legitimate expectations. This interpretation of an FET clause is not necessarily inconsistent with the treaty language.[73]

The protection of legitimate expectations of foreign investors functions differently from legitimate expectations in the WTO. In the context of investment law, the legitimate expectations of the parties to the treaty are not at issue because the investor is alien to its formation. Instead, the legitimate expectations of foreign investors form part of the substantive content of states' obligation to provide fair and equitable treatment to foreign investors. Put differently, the legitimate expectations of foreign investors form part of the primary norms imposed upon states. When used by investment treaty tribunals, the protection of legitimate expectations is not used as a principle of treaty interpretation: the FET norm requires states to take into account the legitimate expectations of foreign investors, but the legitimate expectations of foreign investors are not used to interpret that obligation under the treaty.

The relevance of legitimate expectations in conjunction with good faith in international trade law and international investment law is examined further in chapter 7 of this volume.

[72] For a discussion of the practice of investment tribunals, see: Andrew Newcombe and Lluís Paradell, *Law and Practice of Investment Treaties: Standards of Treatment* (Kluwer Law International 2009) 279; Roland Kläger, *'Fair and Equitable Treatment' in International Investment Law* (CUP 2011) 164. For a critical discussion of the use of 'legitimate expectations' of foreign investors as part of the FET standard, see: *Suez, Sociedad General de Aguas de Barcelona SA and Vivendi Universal SA v Argentina (Decision on Liability)* (ICSID Arbitral Tribunal, Case No ARB/03/19, 30 July 2010) (Separate Opinion of Arbitrator Pedro Nikken) para 19; *AWG Group Ltd v Argentina (Decision on Liability)* (ICSID Arbitral Tribunal, Case No ARB/03/19, 30 July 2010) (Separate Opinion of Arbitrator Pedro Nikken) para 19.

[73] See generally Patrick Dumberry, 'The Protection of Investors' Legitimate Expectations and the Fair and Equitable Treatment Standard under NAFTA Article' (2014) 31 J Intl Arb 47; Michele Potestà, 'Legitimate Expectations in Investment Treaty Law: Understanding the Roots and the Limits of a Controversial Concept' (2013) 28 ICSID Rev 88. 'Unqualified' FET clauses contain no reference to international law or the minimum standards of treatment. An example is art 2(2) of the *Bilateral Investment Treaty between the Government of Great Britain and Northern Ireland and the Government of Romania for the Promotion and Reciprocal Protection of Investments*, signed 13 July 1995 (entered into force 10 January 1996): 'Investments of nationals or companies of each contracting party shall at all times be accorded fair and equitable treatment'. This clause has been interpreted to encompass the legitimate expectations of investors, characterized as 'one of the major components of the fair and equitable treatment standard': *EDF (Services) Ltd v Romania (Award)* (ICSID Arbitral Tribunal, Case No ARB/05/13, 8 October 2009) para 216.

### 3.4.5 Harmonious interpretation and use of international law

Another understanding of good faith interpretation is that a treaty can be interpreted in the light of relevant treaties, general principles of law and customary international law. In this context, a good faith interpretation requires reference to other international law, as foreseen in article 31(3)(c) of the *VCLT* and consistent with the notion of harmonious interpretation.

The need to interpret a treaty in good faith applies also to treaty obligations concerning good faith. That is so, for example, where WTO panels and the Appellate Body interpret article 3.10 of the *DSU*, which states that 'if a dispute arises, all Members will engage in these procedures in good faith in an effort to resolve the dispute'.[74] Other parts of the *DSU* can be interpreted in the context of article 3.10 without necessarily resorting to the principle of good faith or article 31(3)(c) of the *VCLT*.

Article 31(3)(c) of the *VCLT* explains that, in interpreting treaties, account should be given to the context and 'any relevant rules of international law applicable in the relations between the parties'. This provision explains that other rules should be taken into account, but not *which* rules,[75] nor, more importantly, *how* these different rules should be 'integrated'.[76] This provision thus simply tends to require taking into account the normative environment in which the relevant treaty and its provisions exist, without predefining how rules can be applied together or how one rule is relevant to the interpretation of another.[77] An example of the use of the principle of good faith in the interpretation of treaty provisions taking into account the broader rules of international law is the decision of the WTO Appellate Body in *US—Shrimp*,[78] in which the Appellate Body referred to the principle of good faith in applying

[74] See, eg, *US—FSC* (n 10) para 166; Appellate Body Report, *United States—Measures Affecting the Cross-Border Supply of Gambling and Betting Services*, WTO Doc WT/DS285/AB/R (adopted 20 April 2005) para 269. Another example is art 4.3 of the *DSU*, according to which a respondent is to enter into consultations in good faith.

[75] Although it might not be contested that art 31(3)(c) of the *VCLT* (n 3) includes all sources of international law (see, eg, Anne van Aaken, 'Defragmentation of Public International Law Through Interpretation: A Methodological Proposal' (2009) 16(2) Ind J Global Legal Studies 483, 497), debate remains as to which treaties can be relied upon on the basis of that provision.

[76] ibid 501.

[77] ILC, *Fragmentation of International Law: Difficulties Arising from the Diversification and Expansion of International Law—Report of the Study Group of the International Law Commission*, UN Doc A/CN.4/L.682 (4 April 2006) para 419.

[78] *US—Shrimp* (n 11) paras 158, 159. See Campbell McLachlan, 'The Principle of Systemic Integration and Article 31(3)(c) of the Vienna Convention' (2005) 54(2) ICLQ 279, 303, 313; Lorand Bartels, 'The chapeau of Article XX GATT: a new interpretation' (Cambridge Legal Studies Research Paper Series, Paper No 40/2014, July 2014).

(in the form of the doctrine of *abus de droit*) and interpreting the chapeau of article XX of the *General Agreement on Tariffs and Trade*.[79]

However, a good faith interpretation does not necessarily depend on whether a treaty is interpreted in accordance with other rules and principles of international law. The principle of good faith does not itself function as a basis for interpreting a treaty in the light of all surrounding relevant rules of international law, whatever their source. Interpreting a treaty in such a manner can be one element of a good faith interpretation but is not a prerequisite for it.

Moreover, the use of good faith as a principle of treaty interpretation must be distinguished from its application to the performance of a treaty. For example, a treaty provision may embody good faith, which therefore informs the content of the obligation to be performed under the treaty. Whilst such conceptual distinctions can be made in concrete circumstances, the principle according to which treaties are to be applied in good faith logically also embodies the principle of good faith interpretation because, as already noted, application presupposes interpretation.[80] Or, as the ILC put it, the interpretation of treaties in good faith is essential to the effect of the principle of *pacta sunt servanda*.[81] That is also apparent from the ICJ case law. For example, in *Gabčíkovo-Nagymaros*, the ICJ explained that the duty to perform treaties in good faith in article 26 of the *VCLT*:

> implies that, in this case, it is the purpose of the Treaty, and the intentions of the parties in concluding it, which should prevail over its literal application. The principle of good faith obliges the Parties to apply it in a reasonable way and in such a manner that its purpose can be realized.[82]

However, there are circumstances in which interpretation and application, which are in principle distinct processes in judicial reasoning, are difficult to separate, because treaties are not complete.[83] Nothing is decided comprehensively in advance. In addition to the instances in which treaties provide for good faith as a treaty obligation, the principle of good faith can be used in interpreting silences in treaties. When used for that purpose, the principle

[79] *Marrakesh Agreement Establishing the World Trade Organization* (n 14) annex 1A (*General Agreement on Tariffs and Trade*).

[80] See, eg, Gardiner (n 22) 27–29; ILC (n 77) para 423; *Second report on subsequent agreements and subsequent practice in relation to the interpretation of treaties by Georg Nolte, Special Rapporteur*, UN Doc A/CN.4/671 (26 March 2014) para 4.

[81] 'Report of the International Law Commission on the Work of Its Eighteenth Session (4 May–19 July 1966)' [1966] II Yearbook ILC 219.

[82] *Gabčíkovo-Nagymaros Project (Hungary/Slovakia) (Judgment)* [1997] ICJ Rep 7, para 142.

[83] See also Van Damme (n 15) ch 4.

can justify completing the treaties with content that is not expressly stated and possibly with norms of customary international law or general principles of law, including the principle of good faith itself. As Lauterpacht put it, many examples of interpretation of silence are no more than interpretations 'by reference to common sense and the canons of good faith'.[84]

The significance of good faith in interpreting treaty 'silence' is visible in the WTO dispute settlement system, in particular as regards silences in the WTO covered agreements on procedural matters. The Appellate Body has supplemented both the *DSU* and other covered agreements by applying the principle of good faith and its different incarnations in international law. For example, article 3.7 of the *DSU* prescribes that, 'before bringing a case, a Member shall exercise its judgment as to whether action under these procedures would be fruitful'. The mandatory language of 'shall' establishes an obligation on WTO members. Article 3.7 thus constitutes a good faith obligation 'not [to] frivolously set in motion the procedures contemplated in the DSU'.[85] When submitting a request for the establishment of a panel, a member is presumed to act in good faith, 'having duly exercised its judgment as to whether recourse to that panel would be "fruitful"'.[86] The Appellate Body has added that article 3.7 of the *DSU* imposes an obligation on WTO members but does not deal with the power of panels 'to look behind that Member's decision and to question its exercise of judgment'. As a result, a panel can examine issues of good faith on its own initiative. Even if a Member, in complying with the obligation under article 3.7, is expected to be 'largely self-regulating',[87] the provision would lose its effectiveness without a corresponding power of panels and the Appellate Body to sanction or monitor non-compliance.

In investment treaty arbitration, good faith is also used in interpreting treaty silence, notably in cases dealing with access to arbitration.[88] In that

[84] Lauterpacht, *Development of International Law* (n 42) 167.

[85] Appellate Body Report, *Mexico—Anti Dumping Investigation of High Fructose Corn Syrup (HFCS) from the United States—Recourse to Article 21.5 of the DSU by the United States*, WTO Doc WT/DS132/AB/RW (adopted 21 November 2001) para 73.

[86] ibid para 74.

[87] Appellate Body Report, *European Communities—Regime for the Importation, Sale and Distribution of Bananas*, WTO Doc WT/DS27/AB/R (adopted 25 September 1997) para 135, n 20; cited in *Mexico—Corn Syrup (Article 21.5—US)* (n 85) para 74; Appellate Body Reports, *European Communities—Regime for the Importation, Sale and Distribution of Bananas—Second Recourse to Article 21.5 of the DSU by Ecuador*, WTO Doc WT/DS27/AB/RW2/ECU (adopted 11 December 2008) and Corr.1/*European Communities—Regime for the Importation, Sale and Distribution of Bananas—Recourse to Article 21.5 of the DSU by the United States*, WTO Doc WT/DS27/AB/RW/USA and Corr 1 (adopted 22 December 2008) para 211.

[88] See generally E De Brabandere, '"Good Faith", "Abuse of Process" and the Initiation of Investment Treaty Claims' (2012) 3(3) JIDS 609.

context, the principle of good faith has been used as a justification for completing an applicable treaty with norms of customary international law or general principles of law that are not expressly stated, in particular the principle of good faith itself. For example, the tribunal in *Phoenix Action Ltd v Czech Republic*,[89] which concerned questions of corporate restructuring and access to arbitration, engaged in a broad discussion of the application and role of good faith in interpreting and applying international investment law. Although neither the *ICSID Convention* nor the applicable BIT required investments to have been made in good faith, the tribunal supplemented these treaties by applying the principle of good faith as a condition for an 'investment to benefit from the international protection of ICSID'[90] and as a requirement to benefit from the protection of the BIT, which the tribunal considered to be 'implicit even when not expressly stated in the relevant BIT'.[91] In this case also, the dividing line between using good faith for the purposes of interpretation or application is difficult to draw, because the application of the principle of good faith results from both interpreting treaty provisions and supplementing them with the application of good faith as a general principle of law.

## 3.5 Subjective Function: Assessing Behaviour of Interpreters

The application of articles 31 to 33 of the *VCLT* does not guarantee uniform interpretation of treaty terms. Indeed, those provisions leave considerable discretion to the interpreting authority. Interpretation—being a subjective process (despite the 'objective' rules in the *VCLT*)—may yield different results.[92] A failure to apply (properly) the principle of good faith in treaty

[89] *Phoenix Action* (n 21). See also *Plama Consortium Ltd v Bulgaria (Award)* (ICSID Arbitral Tribunal, Case No ARB/03/24, 27 August 2008); *Europe Cement Investment & Trade SA v Turkey (Award)* (ICSID Arbitral Tribunal, Case No ARB(AF)/07/2, 13 August 2009) and *Cementownia 'Nowa Huta' SA v Turkey (Award)* (ICSID Arbitral Tribunal, Case No ARB(AF)/06/2, 17 September 2009). But see *Saba Fakes v Turkey (Award)* (ICSID Arbitral Tribunal, Case No ARB/07/20, 14 July 2010) para 112: 'the principles of good faith and legality cannot be incorporated into the definition of Article 25(1) of the ICSID Convention without doing violence to the language of the ICSID Convention: an investment might be 'legal or "illegal", made in "good faith" or not, it nonetheless remains an investment. The expressions "legal investment" or "investment made in good faith" are not pleonasms, and the expressions "illegal investment" or "investment made in bad faith" are not oxymorons'.

[90] *Phoenix Action* (n 21) para 106.

[91] ibid para 101.

[92] On the argument that the commercial arbitration or the public international law background of arbitrators in investment law influences the interpretation, see Wälde (n 53) 725–26.

interpretation or other principles of interpretation rarely indicates a bad faith interpretation. A prohibition of interpretation in bad faith must thus be distinguished from the prescription of interpretation in good faith. The latter does not depend on demonstrating bad faith in the sense of the intention or state of mind of the interpreter. Rather, the need for interpretation in good faith functions as a limit on the exercise of discretion, which any interpretative analysis involves. Other rules (such as the obligation to ensure due process) may have similar functions.

Treaty interpreters are bound to apply principles of treaty interpretation under international law in the performance of their duties and observance of international law. States and international courts and tribunals are the main interpreters of treaties. National courts, in so far as their jurisdiction foresees the interpretation of treaties, may also form an important category of interpreter.[93] Good faith governs the conduct of these treaty interpreters rather than the intention of the parties to the treaty,[94] limiting the exercise of powers of interpretation.

Findings that states have failed to interpret treaties in good faith are more common than similar assessments of the conduct of international courts and tribunals. The jurisdiction of courts and tribunals includes control of the states' interpretation of relevant treaties to which they are a party. Thus, for example, article 3.2 of the *DSU* provides that the WTO dispute settlement system 'is a central element in providing security and predictability to the multilateral trading system' and 'serves ... to clarify the existing provisions of [the covered] agreements in accordance with customary rules of interpretation of public international law'. At the same time, article 3.2 explicitly limits the exercise of the interpretative powers of the WTO dispute settlement bodies, which 'cannot add to or diminish the rights and obligations provided in the covered agreements'. A tension between the vague standard of good faith and the objectives of security and predictability may exist,[95] but the practice of interpretation shows that detailed specific language can be as uncertain as the meaning of a general principle when applied in a specific context.

[93] On the application of the principle of good faith in treaty interpretation in national contexts, see, eg, Michael Van Alstine, 'The Death of Good Faith in Treaty Jurisprudence and a Call for Resurrection' (2005) 93 Georgetown LJ 1885; for the European Union context, see, eg, Koen Lenaerts and José Gutiérrez-Fons, 'To Say What the Law of the EU Is: Methods of Interpretation and the European Court of Justice' (European University Institute Working Papers, Academy of European Law, AEL 2013/9).

[94] See, eg, Antoine Favre, 'L'interpretation objectiviste des traits internationaux' (1960) XVII *Annuaire suisse de droit international* 75, 80.

[95] See Andrew Mitchell and David Heaton, 'Book Review: Good Faith in the Jurisprudence of the WTO, by Marion Panizzon' (2009) 36(3) L Issues Eco Integration 273, 273.

The description of the jurisdiction of investment tribunals typically refers to the application of domestic law and the applicable rules of international law, as for instance in article 42 of the *ICSID Convention*,[96] which applies to ICSID arbitrations unless the parties provide otherwise.[97] Certain clauses on the applicable law such as those contained in the 2012 US Model BIT and the 2004 Canada Model FIPA refer to international law generally *and* the investment treaty in particular.[98] No specific mention is usually made of the rules applicable to interpretation, but these are covered by the relevant clauses' reference to applicable rules of international law.

Due to the nature of the judicial function and the jurisdiction of international courts and tribunals, allegations that these types of body have failed to interpret the relevant treaty law in good faith are rare. Exceptionally, such statements may arise as a form of autocriticism to the extent allowed under a judicial system. For example, in the broader context of public international law, Vice-President Schwebel wrote in his dissenting opinion in the case before the International Court of Justice (ICJ) on *Maritime Delimitation and Territorial Questions between Qatar and Bahrain* that the ICJ's interpretation did 'not comport with a good faith interpretation of the treaty's terms' and that its failure to resort to preparatory work resulted 'if not in an unreasonable interpretation of the treaty itself, in an interpretation of the preparatory work which is "manifestly… unreasonable"…'.[99]

In performing its subjective function, the focus of good faith is on whether or not a treaty interpreter properly applied the relevant principles of interpretation and whether its interpretative reasoning is based on valid substantive arguments.[100] In this context, too, something beyond the mere failure to apply properly the principles of interpretation (which allow for considerable discretion) is needed in order to establish bad faith or a lack of good faith.

[96] *ICSID Convention* (n 18) art 42.

[97] Many investment treaties in fact do not contain applicable law clauses: see, eg, the Model BITs of France and Germany <http://www.italaw.com/investment-treaties> accessed 31 May 2014.

[98] 2012 United States Model BIT art 30(1) mentions that the tribunal will 'decide the issues in dispute in accordance with this Treaty and applicable rules of international law': <www.state.gov/e/eb/ifd/bit/index.htm> accessed 31 May 2014. 2004 Canada Model BIT art 40 requires tribunals to 'decide the issues in dispute in accordance with this Agreement and applicable rules of international law': <italaw.com/documents/Canadian2004-FIPA-model-en.pdf> accessed 31 May 2014. See also *Accord entre l'Union économique belgo-luxembourgeoise et le Gouvernement de la République de Bolivie concernant l'encouragement et la protection réciproques des investissements*, signed 25 April 1990 (entered into force 10 January 2004) art 11(5); Netherlands–Czechoslovakia BIT (n 23) art 8(6).

[99] *Qatar v Bahrain* (n 6) 36 (Vice-President Schwebel).

[100] See, eg, *Arbitration on the Delimitation of the Maritime Boundary between Guinea and Guinea-Bissau (Decision)* (14 February 1985) XIX UNRIAA 149, para 46.

For example, the principle of good faith has been invoked in order to denounce 'selective' applications of the *VCLT*, or what some authors have called investment tribunals' 'cavalier attitude towards treaty interpretation'.[101] In *Garanti Koza v Turkmenistan*, Arbitrator Laurence Boisson de Chazournes issued a dissenting opinion, in which she essentially argued that the excessive focus by the majority on the 'meaning' of a treaty term in isolation to the other provisions was contrary to the rules of the *VCLT*, and although not stated explicitly as such, would not take account of the primary rule of interpretation in article 31(1) *VCLT*.[102]

Another example of good faith being used in challenging a treaty interpreter's approach is *Hrvatska Elektroprivreda v Slovenia*, where the tribunal dealt extensively with 'good faith', even though its analysis only confirmed the interpretation that the tribunal had already made.[103] Arbitrator Jan Paulsson issued an 'individual opinion' in which he refuted the majority's 'good faith' interpretation on the basis that the:

> majority's natural desire to reach a result that they consider fair and reasonable leads them to imply terms that are not in the Treaty, to ignore terms that are in the Treaty, and to give retroactive effect to a Treaty when neither its express terms nor its object require retroactivity.[104]

Paulsson argued that the tribunal had misused the principle of 'good faith' because the majority had proceeded from the view that 'instruments are … to be read starting from one's perception of their object and purpose and requirements of good faith, and the express terms are secondary'.[105] Thus, he denounced the use of the principle of 'good faith' to confirm a preconceived outcome. In his view, 'the text of the Treaty' could not '*plausibly* be read to establish the obligation that the majority' imposed on Slovenia.[106]

[101] Michael Waibel, 'International Investment Law and Treaty Interpretation' in Rainer Hofmann and Christian Tams (eds), *From Clinical Isolation to Systemic Integration* (Nomos 2011) 29, 29, 40. See also the concurring and dissenting opinions of Arbitrator Holtzmann in *Gibbs and Hill Inc v Iran Power Generation and Transmission Company (TAVANIR) of the Ministry of Energy of the Government of Iran (Interlocutory Award) Award No ITL 1-6-FT* (5 November 1982) 1 Iran–US CTR 236, 248.

[102] *Garanti Koza LLP v Turkmenistan (Decision on the Objection to Jurisdiction for Lack of Consent)* (ICSID Arbitral Tribunal, Case No ARB/11/20, 2 July 2013) 11–12 (Arbitrator Laurence Boisson de Chazournes).

[103] *Hrvatska Elektroprivreda v Slovenia (Decision on the Treaty Interpretation Issue)* (ICSID Arbitral Tribunal, Case No ARB/05/24, 12 June 2009) paras 191–94.

[104] ibid Individual Opinion of Arbitrator Jan Paulsson para 5 (see also paras 40–48).

[105] ibid Individual Opinion of Arbitrator Jan Paulsson para 48.

[106] ibid Individual Opinion of Arbitrator Jan Paulsson para 39 (emphasis added).

## 3.6 Conclusion

Treaty interpretation in accordance with international law must be conducted in compliance with the principle of good faith, which enables and limits the exercise of interpretative power. The meaning of the principle of good faith is not exact, as with most other principles of treaty interpretation. This chapter has argued that the requirement to interpret treaties in good faith in article 31 of the *VCLT* (as an overarching principle and corresponding to the idea that contracts should be interpreted in good faith) functions in two ways. First, the objective function of good faith is in identifying how to interpret treaties. Second, good faith serves a subjective function in providing a general standard of behaviour for the interpreter, requiring the latter to act reasonably and properly. The case law of the WTO dispute settlement system and investment tribunals illustrates both functions.

Although it is rare to find explanations of the application of the principle of good faith in treaty interpretation, the case law shows that in essence the principle requires interpretation in accordance with international law in order to arrive at the meaning of a treaty. Good faith may thus be used to justify: the use of certain principles of treaty interpretation above others; the use of other tools, principles or values that can be taken into account in interpreting treaties (such as the principle of effectiveness); the choice of what preparatory work to use in relying on supplementary means of treaty interpretation; or reliance on other (relevant) rules of international law. Good faith can also justify completing treaties with content that is not expressly stated and complementing treaties with norms of customary international law or general principles of law, including the principle of good faith itself.

The principle of good faith equally functions as a limit on the exercise of discretion that any interpretative analysis involves and thus the exercise of judicial or judicial-like powers. As a consequence, an evaluation of the interpretative process with reference to good faith has been undertaken to denounce selective applications of articles 31 to 33 of the *VCLT.* In that sense, good faith is a principle that contributes to the accountability of interpreters in conformity with the applicable rules of international law and when evaluating *ex post facto* the interpretative process.

# 4

# Good Faith in Parallel Trade and Investment Disputes

*Tania Voon, Andrew D Mitchell and James Munro**

## 4.1 Introduction

International trade law and international investment law form two distinct but overlapping bodies of rules. In some circumstances, a discriminatory measure that violates a state's obligations under international trade law may also appear inconsistent with its obligations under international investment agreements (IIAs), or vice versa. In a number of disputes to date, an aggrieved investor has brought a claim against a financial or regulatory measure imposed by the host state of its investment pursuant to an investor–state dispute settlement mechanism under an IIA, while the investor's home state has challenged the same measure within the dispute settlement system of the World Trade Organization (WTO).[1] Other forms of 'parallel' disputes

* The research and writing for this chapter was supported by funds provided for independent research by the Australian National Preventive Health Agency (Grant ID 203MIT2011) and the Australian Research Council pursuant to the Linkage Project scheme (project number LP120200028). The views expressed here are those of the authors and do not necessarily reflect those of any other entity or employer. The content of this chapter was largely finalized in May 2014.

[1] See, eg, the WTO and investment treaty claims relating to Australia's 'plain' tobacco packaging measure: *Australia—Certain Measures Concerning Trademarks and Other Plain Packaging Requirements Applicable to Tobacco Products and Packaging: Request for the Establishment of a Panel by Ukraine*, WTO Doc WT/DS434/11 (17 August 2012); *Australia—Certain Measures Concerning Trademarks, Geographical Indications and Other Plain Packaging Requirements Applicable to Tobacco Products and Packaging: Request for the Establishment of a Panel by Honduras*, WTO Doc WT/DS435/16 (17 October 2012); *Australia—Certain Measures Concerning Trademarks, Geographical Indications and Other Plain Packaging Requirements Applicable to Tobacco Products and Packaging: Request for the Establishment of a Panel by the Dominican Republic*, WTO Doc WT/DS441/15 (13 November 2012); *Australia—Certain Measures Concerning Trademarks, Geographical Indications and Other Plain Packaging Requirements Applicable to Tobacco Products and Packaging: Request for the Establishment of a Panel by Indonesia*, WTO Doc WT/DS467/15 (6 March 2014); *Australia—Certain Measures Concerning Trademarks, Geographical Indications and Other Plain Packaging Requirements*

in international economic law may arise where a given investor brings claims against the same host state under different IIAs,[2] or a home state challenges a host state under both an IIA—or another preferential trade agreement (PTA)—and WTO law.[3] This chapter examines the role of the principle of good faith in managing such disputes, focusing on WTO disputes as an exemplar of disputes under international trade law.

In part 4.2, we explain the areas of jurisdictional and substantive overlap between WTO and investment law that give rise to the potential for parallel disputes across the two spheres of law, using as an illustration the ongoing challenges against Australia regarding its tobacco packaging laws. Part 4.3 outlines the core issues arising from the relationship between good faith and parallel disputes in international trade and investment law, including the normative foundations of a good faith defence to a parallel dispute and the specific legal doctrines that have developed on the basis of these foundations. Part 4.4 analyses how international trade law and international investment law have addressed parallel disputes to date, including by reference to the principle of good faith.

*Applicable to Tobacco Products and Packaging: Request for the Establishment of a Panel by Cuba*, WTO Doc WT/DS458/14 (14 April 2014); Notice of Arbitration by Philip Morris Asia Ltd to the Commonwealth of Australia pursuant to Agreement between the Government of Hong Kong and the Government of Australia for the Promotion and Protection of Investments (21 November 2011) para 1.6. See also the WTO and investment treaty claims relating to Mexican taxes on sweeteners: *Cargill, Incorporated v Mexico (Award)* (ICSID Arbitral Tribunal, Case No ARB(AF)/05/2, 13 August 2009); *Corn Products International v Mexico (Decision on Responsibility)* (ICSID Arbitral Tribunal, Case No ARB(AF)/04/1, 15 January 2009); *Archer Daniels Midland Company and Tate & Lyle Ingredients Americas v Mexico (Award)* (ICSID Arbitral Tribunal, Case No ARB(AF)/04/5, 21 November 2007); Appellate Body Report, *Mexico—Tax Measures on Soft Drinks and Other Beverages*, WTO Doc WT/DS308/AB/R (adopted 24 March 2006). See also the WTO and investment treaty claims regarding United States measures on lumber: *Canfor Corp v United States (Order of the Consolidation Tribunal)* (UNCITRAL, 7 September 2005); Appellate Body Report, *United States—Final Countervailing Duty Determination with Respect to Certain Softwood Lumber from Canada*, WTO Doc WT/DS257/AB/R (adopted 17 February 2004).

[2] See, eg, *Lauder v Czech Republic (Award)* (Ad Hoc Tribunal, UNCITRAL, 3 September 2001); *CME v Czech Republic (Partial Award)* (Ad Hoc Tribunal, UNCITRAL, 13 September 2001). See generally Hanno Wehland, *The Coordination of Multiple Proceedings in Investment Treaty Arbitration* (OUP 2013), which also discusses simultaneous proceedings in domestic courts and other international fora.

[3] See, eg, Panel Report, *Argentina—Definitive Anti-Dumping Duties on Poultry from Brazil*, WTO Doc WT/DS241/R (adopted 19 May 2003) (Brazil first challenged an Argentinian measure before a MERCOSUR tribunal and lost. Not content with that outcome, it then relitigated the same matter before a WTO panel and won). See also Joost Pauwelyn, 'Adding Sweeteners to Softwood Lumber: The WTO–NAFTA "Spaghetti Bowl" Is Cooking' (2006) 9(1) JIEL 197; Leonila Guglya, 'The Dispute Settlement Architecture of the Softwood Lumber Agreement 2006: the Interplay of Dispute Resolution Mechanisms in the Late Phases of Softwood Lumber Controversy' (2011) 8(3) TDM 1, 7–30 <transnational-dispute-management.com>.

In conclusion, we evaluate the extent to which a dispute settlement tribunal under international trade law or international investment law may use good faith-based tools to respond to parallel proceedings brought in another forum (whether an IIA, PTA or the WTO). Although the pursuit of parallel claims in trade and investment law may appear to be simply a vexatious litigation strategy, several scenarios may justify such an approach: for example, to the extent that the two fora encompass different substantive obligations, procedural aspects (such as who has standing to bring a claim), or remedies. Accordingly, good faith may have only a limited role to play in mitigating difficulties arising from parallel disputes in international trade and investment law.

## 4.2 Substantive and Jurisdictional Overlap in WTO and Investment Disputes

The potential for parallel litigation under the WTO dispute settlement system and one or more IIAs stems from their regulation of similar matters and their application of similar norms. For convenience, we discuss these issues within the broad classifications of 'jurisdictional' and 'substantive' overlaps below.

### 4.2.1 Jurisdictional overlap and divergence

#### *4.2.1.1 Coverage of WTO law and IIAs*

IIAs and the WTO agreements are somewhat aligned in the objects and subject matter they regulate. WTO law regulates trade in goods pursuant to the *General Agreement on Tariffs and Trade 1994* (*GATT*)[4] and related agreements, including the *Agreement on Trade-Related Investment Measures* (*TRIMS Agreement*)[5]—which covers investment measures related to trade in goods—and the *Agreement on Technical Barriers to Trade* (*TBT Agreement*),[6] which covers such matters as product packaging, labelling, and ingredients. WTO law also regulates measures affecting trade in services, through the *General Agreement on Trade in Services* (*GATS*),[7] including services

[4] *Marrakesh Agreement Establishing the World Trade Organization*, opened for signature 15 April 1994, 1867 UNTS 3 (entered into force 1 January 1995), annex 1A (*General Agreement on Tariffs and Trade*) (*GATT*).

[5] *Marrakesh Agreement Establishing the World Trade Organization* (n 4) annex 1A (*Agreement on Trade-Related Investment Measures*) (*TRIMS Agreement*).

[6] *Marrakesh Agreement Establishing the World Trade Organization* (n 4) annex 1A (*Agreement on Technical Barriers to Trade*) (*TBT Agreement*).

[7] *Marrakesh Agreement Establishing the World Trade Organization* (n 4) annex 1B (*General Agreement on Trade in Services*) (*GATS*).

supplied through the commercial presence of enterprises of other WTO members. Finally, WTO law regulates the most common forms of intellectual property—such as patents, trademarks, and copyright—through the *Agreement on Trade-Related Intellectual Property* (*TRIPS Agreement*).[8]

IIAs regulate 'investments' made by investors of one state party to the IIA within the territory of the other state party to the IIA.[9] Intellectual property is typically included within the definition of an 'investment', thus generating an overlap with the *TRIPS Agreement* in the regulation of intellectual property.[10] IIAs also typically include 'enterprises' within the definition of an 'investment', which leads to an overlap with *GATS* in relation to the regulation of foreign enterprises engaged in the supply of a service through commercial presence.[11] The usual inclusion of 'property' within the definition of 'investment'[12] likewise leads to a conceivable overlap with *GATT* in terms of the objects regulated, since 'goods' are usually a form of moveable property.[13]

The coverage of the WTO agreements on goods and the coverage of IIAs in respect of goods are not identical. A good *itself* (as opposed to, for example, a right to produce that good) does not ordinarily constitute the 'investment' that is the subject of an investment treaty claim,[14] because investments must generally be made *in the territory* of the host state in order to qualify for protection under an IIA. Since interstate trade in goods occurs *between* countries, rather than representing an economic activity *within* the host state, it

[8] *Marrakesh Agreement Establishing the World Trade Organization* (n 4) annex 1C (*Agreement on Trade-Related Aspects of Intellectual Property Rights*) (*TRIPS Agreement*).

[9] United Nations Conference on Trade and Development, *Scope and Definition* (United Nations 2011) xi; Catherine Yannaca-Small, *International Investment Law: Understanding Concepts and Tracking Innovations* (OECD 2008) 8.

[10] Andrew Mitchell, Tania Voon and James Munro, 'Intellectual Property Rights in International Investment Agreements: Striving for Coherence in National and International Law' in Bryan Mercurio and Chin Lim (eds), *International Economic Law After the Global Crisis: A Tale of Fragmented Disciplines* (CUP forthcoming 2015).

[11] Martin Molinuevo, *Protecting Investment in Services: Investor–State Arbitration versus WTO Dispute Settlement* (Kluwer Law International 2011) 77–78.

[12] See, eg, 2004 Canada Model BIT art 1 <italaw.com/documents/Canadian2004-FIPA-model-en.pdf> accessed 16 January 2014; 2012 US Model Bilateral Investment Treaty art 1 <www.state.gov/e/eb/ifd/bit/index.htm> accessed 16 January 2014; 2008 German Model BIT art 1.1(a) <http://italaw.com/sites/default/files/archive/ita1025.pdf> accessed 16 January 2014; Indian Model Text of Bilateral Investment Promotion and Protection Agreement art 1(b)(i) <http://finmin.nic.in/the_ministry/dept_eco_affairs/icsection/Indian%20Model%20Text%20BIPA.asp> accessed 16 January 2014; *Agreement between the Swiss Federal Council and the Government of the People's Republic of China on the Promotion and Reciprocal Protection of Investments*, signed 27 January 2009 (entered into force 1 April 2010) art 1.1(a).

[13] Appellate Body Report, *US—Softwood Lumber IV*, WTO Doc WT/DS257/AB/R (adopted 17 February 2004) para 59.

[14] But see, eg, *Middle East Cement Shipping and Handling Co SA v Egypt (Jurisdiction and Liability)* (ICSID Arbitral Tribunal, Case No ARB/99/6, 12 April 2002) paras 135–36.

is not ordinarily covered as an investment.[15] Some IIAs even expressly clarify that interstate trade in goods is excluded from the term 'investment'.[16] Nevertheless, to the extent that an investor sets up a commercial presence such as a company in another country to manufacture or market and distribute goods, that company will likely qualify as an 'investment' and thus be covered under IIAs.[17] Host state measures that hinder the ability of the company to engage in interstate trade in goods (for example, by importing and distributing goods in the host state, or manufacturing goods in the host state for export) could adversely affect this investment and would thus be protected under an applicable IIA.[18]

As an example of how the overlapping coverage of WTO law and IIAs can lead to parallel disputes, investment and trade litigation is continuing in relation to Australia's standardized (so-called plain) packaging measures in respect of tobacco products.[19] Cuba, the Dominican Republic, Honduras, Indonesia and Ukraine have initiated disputes against Australia in the WTO arguing, inter alia, that the measures violate the protection of trademarks under the *TRIPS Agreement*. At the same time, Philip Morris Asia has initiated a dispute against Australia under the Australia–Hong Kong Bilateral Investment Treaty (Australia–Hong Kong BIT),[20] arguing that the measure expropriates its trademarks and violates a number of other investment obligations. This case demonstrates how both rule sets can apply to the same subject matter or object, in this case intellectual property.

#### *4.2.1.2 Standing to claim*

Within the WTO, only WTO members have access to dispute settlement procedures and hence the ability to pursue violations of WTO law.[21] This means that a private company aggrieved by a given measure must convince

[15] *Canadian Cattlemen for Free Trade v United States (Award on Jurisdiction)* (Ad Hoc Arbitral Tribunal, UNCITRAL, 28 January 2008) para 144; *Apotex v United States (Award on Jurisdiction and Admissibility)* (Ad Hoc Arbitral Tribunal, UNCITRAL, 14 June 2013) para 233.

[16] See, eg, 2004 Canada Model BIT (n 12) art 1.

[17] *Pope & Talbot v Canada (Interim Award)* (Ad Hoc Arbitral Tribunal, UNCITRAL, 26 June 2000) paras 87–98.

[18] See, eg, *SD Myers v Canada (Partial Award)* (Ad Hoc Arbitral Tribunal, UNCITRAL, 13 November 2000) paras 289–97; *Pope & Talbot v Canada (Claimant's Motion for Interim Measures)* (Ad Hoc Arbitral Tribunal, UNCITRAL, 7 August 2000) paras 19–26.

[19] See above sources (n 1).

[20] *Agreement between the Government of Hong Kong and the Government of Australia for the Promotion and Protection of Investments*, signed 15 September 1993, 1748 UNTS 385 (entered into force 15 October 1993).

[21] *Marrakesh Agreement Establishing the World Trade Organization* (n 4) annex 2 (*Understanding on Rules and Procedures Governing the Settlement of Disputes*) (*DSU*) art 1.1.

one WTO member to initiate a legal dispute against another WTO member on its behalf, otherwise known as providing 'diplomatic protection'.[22] Beyond lobbying governments to bring a dispute, companies are powerless to seek redress in respect of measures alleged to violate WTO law.

International investment law takes a very different approach. Most IIAs give private actors direct access to international tribunals to remedy breaches of applicable IIAs, through the mechanism known as investor–state arbitration or investor–state dispute settlement. This is unusual in public international law, which traditionally does not confer direct rights on individuals, and hence does not usually allow private claims before international judicial bodies.[23] States can also initiate disputes against other states under international investment law for breaches of IIAs but this ability is normally curtailed once an investor has initiated a dispute in respect of the same matter.[24]

In the plain packaging disputes, Philip Morris has no standing to bring a claim within the WTO. Equally, the WTO members challenging Australia's measures within the WTO have no standing under the Australia–Hong Kong BIT.

#### *4.2.1.3 Remedies*

Remedies available under international investment law usually depend on the IIA in question. Some specify that the only remedy available is monetary compensation for damages, thereby excluding specific performance.[25] Others are silent as to available remedies, potentially allowing for specific performance.[26] However, the overwhelming majority of tribunals issue awards for monetary damages, which are essentially retrospective in nature.[27]

By contrast, the remedies available within the WTO dispute settlement system are generally prospective, requiring a WTO member that has been found to be in breach of an obligation to bring its laws into conformity.[28] As

[22] John Dugard, 'Diplomatic Protection' in Rüdiger Wolfrum (ed), *Max Planck Encyclopedia of Public International Law* (OUP) <www.mpepil.com> accessed 16 January 2014.

[23] Simone Gorski, 'Individuals in International Law' in Wolfrum (n 22).

[24] *Convention on the Settlement of Investment Disputes between States and Nationals of Other States*, concluded 18 March 1965, 575 UNTS 159 (entered into force 14 October 1966) art 27; *AES Corp v Argentina (Decision on Jurisdiction)* (ICSID Arbitral Tribunal, Case No ARB/02/17, 26 April 2005) para 99.

[25] Thomas Sebastian and Anthony Sinclair, 'Remedies in WTO Dispute Settlement and Investor-State Arbitration: Contrasts and Lessons' in Jorge Huerta-Goldman, Antoine Romanetti and Frank Stirnimann (eds), *WTO Litigation, Investment Arbitration, and Commercial Arbitration, Global Trade Law Series Volume 43* (Kluwer Law International 2013) 280–85; Molinuevo (n 11) 222–26.

[26] Sebastian and Sinclair (n 25) 280–85; Molinuevo (n 11) 222–26.

[27] Sebastian and Sinclair (n 25) 282.

[28] *DSU* (n 21) art 3.7.

a last resort, on a temporary basis in the absence of compliance, the recommendations and rulings of the WTO's Dispute Settlement Body may be de facto 'enforced' through the complainant's suspension of trade concessions against the breaching member.[29] This suspension or retaliation is available only in respect of the period following the expiry of the 'reasonable period time' for compliance,[30] which may be some months after the relevant panel or Appellate Body report is adopted.[31] Unlike in international investment law, damages are not awarded for retrospective harm.

In the plain packaging disputes, whereas Philip Morris seeks both suspension of the measures and retrospective compensation for loss from the date they came into force,[32] the WTO members initiating challenges within the WTO must, at first instance, seek the rescission of the measures with prospective effect.[33]

### 4.2.2 Substantive overlap and divergence

#### *4.2.2.1 Non-discrimination and market access*

The norms applied by many IIAs overlap with those under the WTO agreements. For instance, non-discrimination is a core tenet in the WTO, which includes disciplines on national treatment and most-favoured-nation treatment.[34] Similarly, many IIAs include non-discrimination rules.[35] Important differences exist between the legal standards for non-discrimination employed under some IIAs and the WTO agreements, and some investment tribunals have expressly eschewed WTO jurisprudence on non-discrimination.[36] However, others have expressly endorsed WTO approaches.[37] At a broad level of abstraction, Molinuevo concludes that the WTO (specifically, *GATS*) and IIAs 'provide essentially equivalent levels of investment protection' in relation to non-discrimination, with their respective national

[29] ibid art 22.1. [30] ibid art 22.2. [31] ibid art 23.1.

[32] Notice of Arbitration by Philip Morris Asia Ltd to the Commonwealth of Australia (n 1) para 8.2.

[33] *DSU* (n 21) arts 3.7, 22.

[34] See, eg, *GATT* (n 4) arts I, III; *GATS* (n 7) arts II, XIV; *TRIPS Agreement* (n 8) arts 3, 4.

[35] Andrew Newcombe and Lluís Paradell, *Law and Practice of Investment Treaties* (Kluwer Law International 2009) 155, 193.

[36] See, eg, *Cargill* (n 1) para 193; *Methanex Corp v United States (Final Award)* (Ad Hoc Arbitral Tribunal, UNCITRAL, 3 August 2005) paras 29–34; Jürgen Kurtz, 'The Use and Abuse of WTO Law in Investor–State Arbitration: Competition and its Discontents' (2009) 20 EJIL 749, 759–69; José Alvarez and Tegan Brink, 'Revisiting the Necessity Defense' in Karl Sauvant (ed), *Yearbook on International Investment Law & Policy 2011-2012* (OUP 2013) 319, 369–72.

[37] See, eg, *Feldman v Mexico (Award)* (ICSID Arbitral Tribunal, Case No ARB(AF)/99/1, 16 December 2002) para 165.

treatment and most-favoured-nation principles constituting 'essentially identical instruments'.[38]

As another example of overlapping norms, WTO law and an increasing number of modern IIAs contain comparable disciplines on market access. These include domestic content requirements, which are prohibited in relation to investment measures for trade in goods in the WTO[39] and are similarly proscribed by certain IIAs, such as the United States Model IIA,[40] the Energy Charter Treaty,[41] and the Canadian Model IIA.[42] In relation to services, to the extent that a WTO member has made commitments in a given sector, *GATS* generally prohibits quantitative restrictions (for example, on the number of service suppliers, the total value of service transactions and the total quantity of service output) and prohibits measures requiring joint ventures or limiting the participation of foreign capital in a given service-oriented investment.[43] Certain modern IIAs contain similar prohibitions on quantitative measures in respect of investments, including in the services sector.[44]

#### *4.2.2.2 Fair and equitable treatment*

Another further potential area of overlap between international trade law and international investment law relates to transparency, due process and procedural fairness, good faith, and refraining from arbitrary and discriminatory conduct. These matters tend to be protected in IIAs through guarantees of 'fair and equitable treatment', as discussed further in chapter 7.[45] While the precise scope and coverage of fair and equitable treatment is a matter of ongoing controversy in international investment law,[46] it will usually cover those minimum standards of treatment.

Although WTO law contains no overarching concept of 'fair and equitable treatment',[47] it protects much of the content of that standard through a collection of separate provisions. For example, WTO law requires that all relevant laws, regulations, judicial decisions and administrative rulings of general application be promptly published in such a way that interested parties can become acquainted with them, prohibiting such measures from

[38] Molinuevo (n 11) 114, 116. [39] *TRIMS Agreement* (n 5) art 2.1.

[40] 2012 United States Model BIT art 8 <www.state.gov/e/eb/ifd/bit/index.htm> accessed 16 January 2014.

[41] *Energy Charter Treaty*, signed 17 December 1994, 2080 UNTS 95 (entered into force 16 April 1998) art 5.

[42] 2004 Canada Model BIT (n 12) art 7. [43] *GATS* (n 7) art XVI.

[44] See, eg, 2012 United States Model BIT (n 40) art 8.

[45] Newcombe and Paradell (n 35) 278–89.

[46] See, eg, Newcombe and Paradell (n 35) 262–71.

[47] Note that this concept does arise in specific instances, for example *TRIPS Agreement* (n 8) art 41.2 and *GATT* (n 4) art XVII.2.

being enforced until publication.[48] *GATT* and *GATS* also require the reasonable, objective, uniform, and impartial administration of measures of general application falling within their respective scopes.[49] This means, in the words of the panel in *EC—Selected Customs Matters*, that private actors are treated 'fairly and consistently' in their economic operations.[50] While little trade law jurisprudence exists on these requirements, they do seem to relate to the prohibition on arbitrary and discriminatory conduct in the fair and equitable treatment standard. Further, *GATT, GATS* and the *TRIPS Agreement* all require access to courts or quasi-judicial tribunals that provide avenues of review in respect of relevant administrative decisions and actions.[51] According to the jurisprudence, these tribunals should be independent and impartial and afford procedural fairness and due process.[52]

The different foci of these bodies of law—the WTO on the macro project of trade liberalization, and investment law on the protection of specific investments—lead to important differences in the application of these kinds of provisions. The WTO is more concerned with the administration of *general* laws, whereas investment law is directed at the circumstances of *individual* investors and investments. Nevertheless, some similarities can be discerned in the context of fair and equitable treatment, which is discussed further in chapter 7 in relation to international investment law.

#### *4.2.2.3 Expropriation and umbrella clauses*

Important differences exist between the norms covered under international trade and investment law. Whereas almost all IIAs contain disciplines relating to the expropriation of protected investments, the prohibition on unlawful expropriation is absent from the WTO.[53] Similarly, whereas many IIAs include 'umbrella clauses', which bring obligations or undertakings that have been made by a host state *outside* the IIA (for example, a specific investment authorization or contract with a particular investor) within the ambit of its actionable protections, the WTO treaty contains no such provisions.

The key area of normative overlap in the plain packaging disputes relates to Philip Morris' invocation of the umbrella clause in the Australia–Hong Kong BIT, which it asserted provides it with an enforceable and compensable

[48] *GATT* (n 4) art X; *GATS* (n 7) art III; *TRIPS Agreement* (n 8) art 63.

[49] *GATT* (n 4) art X; *GATS* (n 7) art VI.

[50] Panel Report, *European Communities—Selected Customs Matters*, WTO Doc WT/DS315/R (adopted 11 December 2006) para 7.108.

[51] *GATT* (n 4) art X.3(b); *GATS* (n 7) art VI.2(a); *TRIPS Agreement* (n 8) art 42.

[52] Appellate Body Report, *Thailand—Customs and Fiscal Measures on Cigarettes from the Philippines*, WTO Doc WT/DS371/AB/R (adopted 15 July 2011) para 203.

[53] See Molinuevo (n 11) 199.

guarantee that Australia will observe its international trade treaty obligations in respect of its investment.[54] In practical terms, Philip Morris argued that the umbrella clause effectively incorporates relevant provisions of the WTO into the IIA, and hence breaches of those provisions also constitute breaches of the IIA. In contrast, Philip Morris' claim relating to expropriation[55] has no obvious analogy in the concomitant proceedings under the WTO. Philip Morris has, in any case, apparently withdrawn its umbrella clause claim.[56]

## 4.3 Good Faith and its Particularizations in Connection with Parallel Disputes

### 4.3.1 Good faith as a general principle of law affecting parallel disputes

As discussed in chapter 2 of this volume, the obligation on states to act in good faith finds expression in 'more or less all legal systems and legal cultures'[57] and has accordingly been recognized as a general principle of law[58] and a part of international law.[59] It is, however, an ambiguous and potentially elusive concept. Scholars have struggled to give it definition beyond general notions of 'honesty', 'fairness' and 'reasonableness'.[60] Indeed, even amongst these terms, the subjective notion of 'honesty' does not align precisely with the more objective qualities of 'reasonableness' and 'fairness'.[61] The difficulties in defining 'good faith' have led some to question its efficacy or utility as an obligation with autonomous content and applicability.[62]

[54] Notice of Arbitration by Philip Morris Asia Ltd to the Commonwealth of Australia (n 1) (21 November 2011) paras 7.15–7.17, para 8.2.

[55] ibid paras 7.3–7.14.

[56] *Philip Morris Asia Ltd v Australia (Procedural Order No 8)* (Ad Hoc Arbitral Tribunal, UNCITRAL, 14 April 2014) para 34.

[57] Markus Kotzur, 'Good Faith (Bona Fides)' in Wolfrum (n 22) para 1.

[58] *Statute of the International Court of Justice* art 38(1)(c).

[59] *Certain Norwegian Loans (France v Norway) (Judgment)* [1957] ICJ Rep 9, 53 (Lauterpacht J).

[60] John O'Connor, *Good Faith in International Law* (Dartmouth Publishing 1991) 118–19; Kotzur (n 57) para 21; Bin Cheng, *General Principles of Law as Applied by International Courts and Tribunals* (Grotius Publications 1987) 105 (citations omitted); Andrew Mitchell, 'Good Faith in WTO Dispute Settlement' (2006) 7 Melb J Intl L 339, 344–45.

[61] Mitchell, 'Good Faith' (n 60) 340.

[62] See, eg, Shabtai Rosenne, *Developments in the Law of Treaties 1945–1986* (CUP 1989) 135; Royston Goode, 'The Concept of Good Faith in English Law' (Paper presented at the Centro di Studi e Ricerche di Diritto Comparato e Straniero, Rome, March 1992); Disa Sim, 'The Scope and Application of Good Faith in the Vienna Convention on Contracts for the International Sale of Goods' in Pace Intl Law Rev (ed), *Review of the Convention on Contracts for the International Sale of Goods (CISG) 2002-2003* (Kluwer Law International 2004) 19, 61.

In practical terms, it usually finds expression in particularized contexts, such as in the interpretation of treaties or the doctrines of estoppel and abuse of rights.[63]

The existence of parallel litigation in different fora in relation to the same dispute or matter creates a range of problems. By increasing the costs of proceedings, parallel disputes drain the respondent's resources, which could potentially coerce the respondent into a premature settlement or jeopardize its ability to mount a strong defence.[64] By creating a situation in which two adjudicatory bodies make a determination regarding similar facts or laws, parallel disputes create the potential for conflicting outcomes in the same matter.[65] The successful party in the first-decided dispute may therefore be unable to enjoy the first judgment as a binding and final outcome.[66] From a more systemic viewpoint, the potential for conflicting outcomes could also undermine confidence in the legal regime by undermining its ability to function as originally designed—that is, to produce binding, objective, rules-based outcomes in relation to disputes.[67] Parallel litigation also gives rise to the potential for double remedies.[68] In particular, if parallel litigation could lead to two separate awards for compensation in relation to the same injury or damage (for example, claims brought against a single measure

[63] Mitchell, 'Good Faith' (n 60) 345–51. See also chapters 2 and 3 of this volume.

[64] See, eg, August Reinisch, 'The Issues Raised by Parallel Proceedings and Possible Solutions' in Michael Waibel et al (eds), *The Backlash against Investment Arbitration* (Kluwer Law International 2010) 113–14; Campbell McLachlan, *Lis Pendens in International Litigation* (Martinus Nijhoff 2009) 216; Jamie Shookman, 'Too Many Forums for Investment Disputes? ICSID Illustrations of Parallel Proceedings and Analysis' (2010) 27 J Intl Arb 361, 362.

[65] Joost Pauwelyn and Luiz Eduardo Salles, 'Forum Shopping before International Tribunals: (Real) Concerns (Im)Possible Solutions' (2009) 42 Cornell Intl LJ 77, 81–83; McLachlan (n 64) 217–18; Reinisch (n 64) 114–17; Frank Spoorenberg and Jorge Vinuales, 'Conflicting Decisions in International Arbitration' (2009) 8 LPICT 91, 91–92; August Reinisch, 'The Use and Limits of Res Judicata and Lis Pendens as Procedural Tools to Avoid Conflicting Dispute Settlement Outcomes' (2004) 3 LPICT 37, 38–42; Susan Franck, 'The Legitimacy Crisis in Investment Treaty Arbitration: Privatizing Public International Law through Inconsistent Decisions' (2005) 73 Fordham L Rev 1521, 1558; Ishaya Paul Amaza, 'Multiplicity of International Dispute Settlement Forums: Avoiding the Risk of Parallel Proceedings' (2012) 6 DRI 149, 151–52; Robin Hansen, 'Parallel Proceedings in Investor–State Treaty' (2010) 73 MLR 523, 538; Pedro Martinez-Fraga and Harout Jack Samra, 'The Role of Precedent in Defining Res Judicata in Investor–State Arbitration' (2012) 32 Northwest J Intl L & Bus 419, 435.

[66] McLachlan (n 64) 217–18.

[67] Reinisch, 'Parallel Proceedings' (n 64) 116; Amaza (n 65) 151–52; Pauwelyn and Salles (n 65) 81–83.

[68] See, eg, *Wena Hotels Ltd v Egypt (Decision on Annulment)* (ICSID Arbitral Tribunal, Case No ARB/98/4, 5 February 2002) para 63; Pauwelyn and Salles (n 65) 81; Zachary Douglas, 'The Hybrid Foundations of Investment Treaty Arbitration' (2003) 74 BYBIL 151, 236–37 (depending upon the nature of the alleged infringed rights, an investor may claim restitution or compensation in up to five different proceedings).

under two IIAs by the same investor), the claimant could receive compensation disproportionate to the harm suffered.

Consequences such as increased costs, conflicting outcomes, and double remedies are not necessarily evidence of a bad faith pursuit of parallel litigation. If, for instance, a claimant cannot pursue all of its claims in a given forum, the multiplication of costs through parallel litigation may simply be a by-product of the legitimate exercise of a right to pursue its other claims in a different forum.[69] Similarly, where conflicting outcomes arise from the application of different norms under international trade law and international investment law, the resulting systemic damage may reflect inadequacies in the delineation of a hierarchy of norms in public international law rather than evidence of bad faith on the part of a claimant. If, however, a claimant launches parallel litigation merely to increase its chances of winning, or if it takes a 'second bite of the cherry' by relitigating the same matter in a new forum after an initial adverse finding, the resulting systemic damage is likely to be germane to the principle of good faith.

Thus, the subjective motivation of claimants in launching parallel litigation is likely to be highly relevant in determining whether the principle of good faith constitutes a pertinent or applicable constraint on such action. McLachlan alludes to this in his discussion on *lis pendens*:

> *[w]hy* might litigants wish to pursue proceedings in more than one forum at the same time? The answer to that question may in turn assist in resolving how, in what circumstances, with what techniques and for what purpose should the law seek to control such a phenomenon.[70]

The principle of *lis pendens* examined by McLachlan is one tool available to constrain parallel proceedings, as we now explain.

## 4.3.2 Relevant particularizations of the principle of good faith

### *4.3.2.1* Lis pendens

In general terms, an adjudicatory body applying *lis pendens* will stay proceedings before it where the same matter is being litigated before another body.[71] While not always an expression or particularization of the principle of good faith, *lis pendens* can be deployed to remedy contraventions of good faith in certain contexts:

[69] McLachlan (n 64) 227–28. [70] ibid 224 (emphasis added).

[71] Various approaches and techniques exist for applying *lis pendens* and controlling competing jurisdictions: see ibid 243–54.

> The most common reason for granting a stay is that a foreign court is the natural or appropriate forum. However, there are some cases where a stay will be given even though the forum where the stay is sought is the natural forum, *because the court concluded that the case before it is an abuse of process, because it is abusive, or oppressive, or vexatious, or brought in bad faith.*[72]

Traditional conceptions of *lis pendens* apply the triple identity test, which requires an identity of parties, causes of action, and remedies available.[73] According to this traditional approach, *lis pendens* will be capable of correcting transgressions of good faith only if the triple identity test is fulfilled. To some extent, this seems fitting. If the parties to the claims are different (for example, an investor and a state), a fair presumption arises that they represent different sources of harm or different economic interests and are not coordinated or targeted in their parallel litigation over the same matter. As a result, bad faith is less likely, and double remedies become less of a concern. Similarly, if claims made by a single claimant in different fora arise out of substantively different rights and obligations, the claimant may be seen as availing itself of two legitimate avenues for redress, and the two fora will be making determinations on different norms and thus not in genuine conflict.

The principle of *lis pendens* is thus blind to most instances of parallel litigation in international economic law: where the claimant is formally or in fact different (for example, an investor claiming under an IIA as distinct from a WTO member claiming under WTO rules, or a corporate investor claiming under one IIA as distinct from its individual officers/owners claiming under another IIA); where the claims are different (for example, under different provisions in different IIAs, or under different obligations under an IIA and WTO law); or where the remedies are different (for example, financial compensation available under international investment law as opposed to ensuring compliance for the future and the potential for trade retaliation under WTO law). Moreover, considerable uncertainty exists as to the applicability of *lis pendens* as a general principle of law in the absence of express treaty text.[74] Although international adjudicatory bodies may be regarded as having inherent jurisdiction to safeguard their own proceedings against abuses and claims made in bad faith,[75] the denial of a claim pursuant to *lis*

[72] Filip De Ly and Aydley Sheppard, 'ILA Final Report on Lis Pendens and Arbitration' (2009) 24 Arb Intl 1, 9, 32 (recommendation 2) (emphasis added).

[73] Reinisch, 'Res Judicata and Lis Pendens' (n 65) 50–51; McLachlan (n 63) 226.

[74] McLachlan (n 64) 467; De Ly and Sheppard (n 72) 17.

[75] McLachlan (n 64) 465–66; Andrew Mitchell and David Heaton, 'The Inherent Jurisdiction of WTO Tribunals: The Select Application of Public International Law Required by the Judicial Function' (2010) 31 Mich J Intl L 561, 615; *Phoenix Action Ltd v Czech Republic (Award)* (ICSID Arbitral Tribunal Case No ARB/06/5, 15 April 2009) paras 92–93.

*pendens* in the absence of express authority could undermine a claimant's right to due process.[76] Accordingly, *lis pendens* appears to have little work to do in addressing the typical forms of parallel disputes that may arise in international trade law and international investment law, at least where the triple identity test is strictly applied.

#### *4.3.2.2 Estoppel*

The doctrine of estoppel—another particularization of the principle of good faith[77]—could also be potentially relevant to parallel litigation in international economic law. Estoppel would generally be considered a more established principle than *lis pendens* in international law.[78] In general terms, the essential features of estoppel under public international law are contained in the following passage of Judge Spender in the *Temple of Preah Vihear Case*:

> [T]he principle operates to prevent a State contesting before the Court a situation contrary to a clear and unequivocal representation previously made by it to another State, either expressly or impliedly, on which representation the other State was, in the circumstances, entitled to rely and in fact did rely, and as a result that other State has been prejudiced or the State making it has secured some benefit or advantage for itself.[79]

The International Court of Justice (ICJ) has taken a relatively strict approach to claims of estoppel, for example, holding in *Land and Maritime Boundary between Cameroon and Nigeria*:

> An estoppel would only arise if by its acts or declarations Cameroon had consistently made it fully clear that it had agreed to settle the boundary dispute submitted to the Court by *bilateral avenues alone*. It would further be necessary that, by relying on such an attitude, Nigeria had changed position to its own detriment or had suffered some prejudice.[80]

Thus, according to the ICJ, an agreement to settle a dispute by one means does not itself give rise to a representation that this is the exclusive and definitive means of dispute resolution.[81]

[76] McLachlan (n 64) 467. [77] Mitchell, 'Good Faith' (n 60) 348–49.

[78] ibid; Wehland (n 2) 129. See also *Petrobart Ltd v Kyrgyz Republic (Arbitral Award)* (Stockholm Chamber of Commerce, Arbitration No 126/2003, 29 March 2009) 67; *Pan American Energy LLC v Argentina (Decision on Preliminary Objections)* (ICSID Arbitral Tribunal, Case No ARB/03/13, 27 July 2006) para 159; *Pope & Talbot (Interim Award)* (n 17) para 111.

[79] *Temple of Preah Vihear (Cambodia v Thailand) (Merits)* [1962] ICJ Rep 101, 143–44 (Spender J); see also Thomas Cottier and Jörg Paul Müller, 'Estoppel' in Wolfrum (n 22).

[80] *Land and Maritime Boundary between Cameroon and Nigeria (Cameroon v Nigeria) (Preliminary Objections)* [1998] ICJ Rep 275 paras 57, 71 (emphasis added).

[81] See also *SGS v Pakistan (Decisions of the Tribunal on Objections to Jurisdiction)* (ICSID Arbitral Tribunal, Case No ARB/01/13, 6 August 2003) para 177.

Applying this principle in the context of parallel proceedings, a respondent might argue that initiating a claim in one forum constitutes an implied representation by the claimant to resolve the dispute in that forum, such that the claimant is estopped from bringing another claim in a different forum. However, further evidence would be required to establish that the complainant (or the parties) intended the first forum to be the *exclusive* forum for the dispute, such as the existence of an exclusive choice of forum provision in a relevant instrument, as discussed further below. Moreover, an estoppel is unlikely to be made out where the claimant is different (for example, an investor under an IIA and a WTO member under WTO law). Finally, the respondent might have difficulty demonstrating that it had relied on the alleged representation in such a way that it is unduly prejudiced by the second claim.

According to the more specific offshoot of estoppel known as 'collateral estoppel', claimants are barred from relitigating a matter before another forum where, in a prior proceeding: (i) the matter was distinctly put in issue; (ii) the prior forum decided the matter; and (iii) the resolution of the matter was necessary to resolve the claims before that forum.[82] Applying collateral estoppel in the context of parallel proceedings, a respondent could argue that the second forum seised of a given matter should decline to issue an award after the first forum has made final binding determinations regarding the same matter. However, collateral estoppel (as with the related concept of *res judicata*)[83] is usually applied in connection with claims launched *after* the conclusion of an earlier proceeding rather than claims brought in parallel (that is, launched around the same time).

#### *4.3.2.3 Abuse of rights*

The doctrine of abuse of rights (*abus de droit*) could present a more flexible legal tool than *lis pendens* or estoppel for curing contraventions of good faith through parallel litigation. Abuse of rights can be conceived as a particularization or application of the principle of good faith,[84] forbidding an actor from 'exercising a right either in a way which impedes the enjoyment by other States of their own rights or for an end different from that for which the right was created, to the injury of another State'.[85] An abuse of rights may

[82] See, eg, *RSM v Grenada (Award)* (ICSID Arbitral Tribunal, Case No ARB/10/06, 10 December 2010) para 7.1.2; *Petrobart* (n 78) 66–67.

[83] See Wehland (n 2) 123, 132.

[84] Bin Cheng (n 60) 121; Mitchell, 'Good Faith' (n 60) 349–50.

[85] Alexandre Kiss, 'Abuse of Rights' in Wolfrum (n 22).

include instances where a right is exercised solely for a malicious purpose and contrary to its intended operation.

The utility of the doctrine of abuse of rights in addressing parallel disputes in international trade law and international investment law is complicated by two factors. First, as discussed further below, both WTO tribunals and at least some investment tribunals[86] may be reluctant to apply a doctrine from outside the relevant treaty (that is, the relevant IIA or the WTO agreements) in the absence of specific treaty text. Second, even if a tribunal determines that the doctrine of abuse of rights is applicable in the relevant forum, the scope of the doctrine is restricted and its elements are likely to be made out only in rare circumstances.[87]

For example, in the context of parallel litigation, the relevant right that may be abused is the right to litigate a claim. As that right is generally intended to be used in order to facilitate an orderly rules-based resolution to a dispute and to remedy a wrong, the initiation of parallel litigation for other purposes—for example, to maximize the chances of success, to drain the resources of the respondent, or to obtain double remedies—could be considered contrary to the intended operation of the right, or even malicious. In such instances, the doctrine of abuse of rights could potentially be deployed to stymie bad faith initiations of parallel litigation. However, strong evidence would be required to demonstrate the illegitimate purposes, keeping in mind that a complainant is likely to have multiple purposes for commencing litigation.

## 4.4 Existing Approaches to Parallel Disputes in International Economic Law

### 4.4.1 Relevant treaty provisions

#### *4.4.1.1 Provisions in WTO law*

Article 23 of the WTO's *Understanding on Rules and Procedures Governing the Settlement of Disputes* (*Dispute Settlement Understanding* or *DSU*)[88] requires WTO members seeking the redress of violations of WTO law to 'have recourse to, and abide by, the rules and procedures' of the *DSU*.[89]

[86] See, eg, *Waste Management v Mexico (Award)* (ICSID Arbitral Tribunal Case No ARB(AF)/00/3, 30 April 2004) para 85.

[87] See, eg, *Chevron Corp and Texaco Petroleum Corp v Ecuador (Interim Award)* (Ad Hoc Arbitral Tribunal, UNCITRAL, 1 December 2008) paras 143, 146.

[88] *DSU* (n 21).

[89] ibid art 23.1.

Although this provision appears to endow the WTO dispute settlement system with 'compulsory and exclusive' jurisdiction over WTO violations, it 'cannot prohibit tribunals established by other treaties from exercising jurisdiction over the claims arising from their treaty provisions that run parallel to, or overlap with, the WTO provisions'.[90] Moreover, other *DSU* provisions make clear that WTO members are free to resolve their disputes amicably rather than through formal dispute settlement. Article 3.7 requires WTO members, before bringing a case, to exercise 'judgement as to whether action under these procedures would be fruitful'. The *DSU* also promotes 'mutually agreed solutions' to disputes, provided that such solutions are consistent with WTO law.[91]

In fact, then, the WTO dispute settlement system is neither compulsory nor exclusive, giving rise to the potential for issues of good faith to be used in determining whether a WTO panel should exercise jurisdiction in a given case, such as where another dispute over the same subject matter is pending under a PTA or IIA. Article 3.10 of the *DSU* provides that, in the event of a dispute, 'all Members will engage in these procedures in good faith in an effort to resolve the dispute'. Article 4.3 similarly requires members responding to a request for consultations to enter such consultations 'in good faith'.

On one view, textual references to good faith in the *DSU* indicate that an estoppel argument could be brought to prevent a WTO panel from proceeding in the face of an exclusive choice of forum provision in another forum.[92] For example, article 2005(4) of the *North American Free Trade Agreement* (*NAFTA*)[93] provides:

> In any dispute referred to in paragraph 1 that arises under Section B of Chapter Seven (Sanitary and Phytosanitary Measures) or Chapter Nine (Standards-Related Measures):
> (a) concerning a measure adopted or maintained by a Party to protect its human, animal or plant life or health, or to protect its environment, and
> (b) that raises factual issues concerning the environment, health, safety or conservation, including directly related scientific matters,
>
> where the responding Party requests in writing that the matter be considered under this Agreement, the complaining Party may, in respect of that matter, thereafter have recourse to dispute settlement procedures *solely under this Agreement*.[94]

[90] Kyung Kwak and Gabrielle Marceau, 'Overlaps and Conflicts of Jurisdiction between the World Trade Organization and Regional Trade Agreements' in Lorand Bartels and Federico Ortino (eds), *Regional Trade Agreements and the WTO Legal System* (OUP 2006) 465, 466, 476.

[91] *DSU* (n 21) arts 3.6–3.7.

[92] Mitchell and Heaton (n 75) 614–16.

[93] *North American Free Trade Agreement*, signed 17 December 1992 [1994] CTS 2 (entered into force 1 January 1994) (*NAFTA*).

[94] Emphasis added.

In *US—Tuna II (Mexico)*, the United States initially invoked NAFTA article 2005(4) to counter Mexico's request to establish a panel in the WTO.[95] However, presumably for systemic reasons (which may have included the United States' traditional aversion to general public international law being brought into the WTO context),[96] the United States did not proceed with these jurisdictional arguments before the WTO panel or the Appellate Body.[97]

### *4.4.1.2 Provisions in international investment agreements*

Unlike the WTO dispute settlement system, international investment law is decentralized. Arbitral tribunals convened to adjudicate investment claims are neither hierarchical nor vertically integrated,[98] sometimes leading to inconsistent and divergent strands of jurisprudence.[99] Furthermore, rather than each applying the same norms in the same instrument, arbitral tribunals are convened under one of the thousands of IIAs currently in existence and must base their awards on the specific text of the given treaty.[100]

Some IIAs expressly provide a mechanism for dealing with parallel proceedings in different fora. For instance, the updated IIA between Switzerland and China provides that 'disputes with respect to investments between a Contracting Party and an investor of the other Contracting Party' may be submitted to adjudication under domestic law or pursuant to international arbitration, but not both.[101] Under that treaty, an investor may submit a dispute to international arbitration only after it has withdrawn any corresponding domestic proceedings.[102] Once a dispute is submitted to international arbitration the other contracting party is prohibited from exercising diplomatic protection vis-à-vis its investor, unless the respondent party fails to comply with the arbitral award.[103]

[95] United States Trade Representative, 'United States Initiates NAFTA Dispute with Mexico over Mexico's Failure to Move Its Tuna-Dolphin Dispute from the WTO to the NAFTA' (Press Release, 9 November 2009) <www.ustr.gov/about-us/press-office/press-releases/2009/november/united-states-initiates-nafta-dispute-mexico-over> accessed 20 May 2014.

[96] United States Trade Representative, 'US Proposal for Additional Guidance on the Use of Public International Law' (undated) <www.ustr.gov/sites/default/files/asset_upload_file737_10409.pdf> accessed 20 May 2014, 7–9.

[97] Appellate Body Report, *United States—Measures Concerning the Importation, Marketing and Sale of Tuna and Tuna Products*, WTO Doc WT/DS381/AB/R (adopted 13 June 2012) paras 72–80; Panel Report, *United States—Measures Concerning the Importation, Marketing and Sale of Tuna and Tuna Products*, WTO Doc WT/DS381/R (adopted 13 June 2012) pt VIII.B.1.

[98] See, eg, Spoorenberg and Vinuales (n 65) 95–96; Newcombe and Paradell (n 35) 102–07.

[99] Newcombe and Paradell (n 35) 104–07; Spoorenberg and Vinuales (n 65) 95–96.

[100] For a listing of all IIAs, see the UNCTAD website, available at <http://www.unctadxi.org/templates/DocSearch____779.aspx>

[101] Swiss-China BIT (n 12) art 11.2. [102] ibid art 11.4. [103] ibid art 11.6.

The 2012 United States Model Bilateral Investment Treaty (US Model BIT) also includes a fork-in-the-road provision, requiring upon submission to arbitration a written waiver 'of any right to initiate or continue before any administrative tribunal or court under the law of either Party, or other dispute settlement proceedings, any proceeding with respect to *any measure alleged to constitute a breach*' of certain investment obligations.[104] Such a waiver might ground an estoppel or abuse of rights argument should the claimant initiate or continue a parallel claim in another forum.[105] Focusing on the impugned 'measure' rather than the relevant 'dispute' avoids difficulties in identifying the relevant 'dispute' and whether two or more matters form part of the same 'dispute'.[106] The US Model BIT also includes a provision to facilitate the consolidation of separate investment claims that have 'a question of law or fact in common and arise out of the same events or circumstances', if this would be 'in the interest of fair and efficient resolution of the claims'.[107]

Another treaty-based innovation to address parallel proceedings appears in the *Australia–Hong Kong BIT*:

> This Agreement shall not apply to a company organised under the law of a non-Contracting Party … where the provisions of an investment promotion and protection agreement with that non-Contracting Party have already been invoked in respect of the same matter.[108]

Through this provision, entities in the same corporate chain with different nationalities are barred from initiating parallel disputes under separate IIAs over the same matter, thus avoiding the *CME/Lauder* scenario discussed below.

The inclusion in IIAs of these kinds of dispute settlement provisions may obviate the need to apply good faith or its particularizations—as matters of international law independent of the treaty text—in resolving some parallel disputes. Although these various treaty-based mechanisms do not expressly use the term 'good faith', they are clearly grounded in normative considerations of what is acceptable or unacceptable in relation to parallel disputes. For instance, whereas parallel claims over *different* 'measures' or 'disputes' may be normatively permissible, those in relation to the *same* measures and disputes are barred.

[104] 2012 United States Model BIT (n 40) art 26.2 (emphasis added).

[105] See, eg, Mitchell and Heaton (n 75) 615.

[106] See Tania Voon, Andrew Mitchell and James Munro, 'Legal Responses to Corporate Manoeuvring in International Investment Arbitration' (2014) JIDS 41, 49–51.

[107] 2012 United States Model BIT (n 40) art 33.

[108] Australia–Hong Kong BIT art 13.2.

### *4.4.1.3 Provisions in preferential trade agreements*

Several PTAs contain dispute settlement provisions that seek to minimize the potential for multiple proceedings in respect of the same factual scenario. The relevant treaty provisions sometimes align with the particularizations of good faith discussed above. For example, the PTA between the EU and a group of Central American countries might be seen as reflecting the traditional conception of *lis pendens*: '[t]he disputing Parties shall avoid bringing identical disputes in different fora when based on the same legal claims and measures'.[109]

As another example of how treaty provisions may be used to resolve the problem of parallel proceedings in trade and investment law, the PTA between Australia and Malaysia provides:

> Where a dispute concerning any matter arises under this Agreement and under another international agreement to which the Parties are party, the Complaining Party may select the forum in which to address that matter and that forum shall be used to the exclusion of other possible fora in respect of that matter.[110]

Under this approach, the complainant may select the forum for resolving the dispute but is then precluded from raising the dispute in another forum.

Similarly, the PTA between Australia and Chile states:[111]

> 1. Where a dispute regarding any matter arises under this Agreement and under another free trade agreement to which both Parties are party or the WTO Agreement, the complaining Party may select the dispute settlement procedure in which to settle the dispute.
> 2. Once the complaining Party has requested a panel under an agreement referred to in paragraph 1, the forum selected shall be used to the exclusion of the others.

By limiting the application of the exclusive choice of forum provision to 'other free trade agreements or the WTO Agreement', this provision would not appear to prevent a party from pursuing a claim regarding the same matter under a non-trade treaty, including potentially a BIT.

[109] *Agreement Establishing an Association between Central America, on the one hand, and the European Union and its Member States, on the other*, signed 29 June 2012 (not yet in force) art 326.

[110] *Malaysia–Australia Free Trade Agreement*, signed 22 May 2012, [2013] ATS 4 (entered into force 1 January 2013) art 20.5.

[111] *Australia–Chile Free Trade Agreement*, signed 30 July 2008, [2009] ATS 6 (entered into force 6 March 2009) art 21.2.1.

### 4.4.2 Approaches of trade/investment tribunals

Dispute settlement tribunals within the WTO and international investment law have endorsed and rejected a variety approaches to dealing with parallel disputes, both treaty-based and non-textual.

#### *4.4.2.1 WTO panels and the WTO Appellate Body*

While no panel or Appellate Body report has yet authoritatively applied estoppel or good faith-based arguments to manage parallel proceedings, WTO case law contains a number of references to their potential applicability. The panels in both *EC—Aircraft* and *Argentina—Poultry* engaged with arguments to decline jurisdiction that were grounded in estoppel, albeit finding that the requirements for estoppel were not made out in those cases.[112] Similarly, the Appellate Body in *EC—Bananas III (Article 21.5—Ecuador II)* seemed to sketch a legal standard for estoppel-based defences when stating that 'if a WTO Member has not clearly stated that it would not take legal action with respect to a certain measure, it cannot be regarded as failing to act in good faith if it challenges that measure'.[113]

In *EC—Sugar Subsidies*, the Appellate Body found it 'reasonable for a panel to examine estoppel in the context of determining whether a Member has engaged "in these procedures in good faith," as required under Article 3.10 of the DSU'.[114] However, the Appellate Body has cautioned that 'even assuming *arguendo* that the principle of estoppel could apply in the WTO, its application would fall within these narrow parameters set out in the DSU'.[115] As such, a successful application of good faith-based principles or doctrines in general international law before a WTO panel would need to have firm textual foundations in the *DSU*.

Based on its reading of the *DSU*, the WTO Appellate Body has stated that a panel has 'no discretion to decline to exercise its jurisdiction in the case that

[112] See Panel Report, *Argentina—Definitive Anti-Dumping Duties on Poultry from Brazil* (n 3) paras 7.37–7.39; Panel Report, *European Communities and Certain Member States—Measures Affecting Trade in Large Civil Aircraft*, WTO Doc WT/DS316/R (adopted 1 June 2011) paras 7.101–7.104.

[113] Appellate Body Report, *European Communities—Regime for the Importation, Sale and Distribution of Bananas—Second Recourse to Article 21.5 of the DSU by Ecuador*, WTO Doc WT/DS27/AB/RW2/ECU (adopted 11 December 2008), and Corr 1, para 228.

[114] Appellate Body Report, *European Communities—Export Subsidies on Sugar*, WTO Doc WT/DS265/AB/R, WTO Doc WT/DS266/AB/R, WTO Doc WT/DS283/AB/R (adopted 19 May 2005) para 307.

[115] ibid para 312.

has been brought before it' and that any such decision by a panel would 'seem to "diminish" the right of a complaining Member to "seek the redress of a violation of obligations"'.[116] This statement was made in the Appellate Body's report in the *Mexico—Taxes on Soft Drinks* case,[117] in which Mexico had argued that the panel should decline to exercise jurisdiction in favour of a NAFTA panel.[118] Mexico had sought to frame its impugned taxation measures as part of a broader trade dispute with the United States relating to the parties' rights and obligations under NAFTA.[119] Mexico argued that only a NAFTA panel could resolve the whole underlying dispute and was therefore the 'appropriate forum',[120] while hinting at the unreasonableness of the United States' recalcitrance to engage under NAFTA.[121]

The Appellate Body rejected these jurisdictional arguments, finding no textual foundation in the *DSU* to decline jurisdiction over an otherwise valid claim under the WTO Agreement due to other more 'appropriate' fora.[122] Importantly, however, the Appellate Body explicitly declined to comment on the merits of an estoppel or abuse of rights-based defence, such as that entertained by the panel in *Argentina—Poultry* where one disputing party makes a representation to resolve a dispute exclusively in another forum.[123] Thus, the Appellate Body left open the possibility for using a properly-exercised exclusive choice of forum provision in another instrument as a basis for declining jurisdiction. As mentioned above, although the United States initially pursued this line of argument in *US—Tuna II (Mexico)*, it did not ultimately pursue it formally before the panel or Appellate Body.[124]

These cases leave WTO panels and the Appellate Body with a possible margin of discretion to suspend proceedings or defer to another tribunal in the event of parallel litigation under another agreement, particularly where one disputing party has represented that it would use the other forum to the exclusion of the *DSU*.

#### *4.4.2.2 Investment treaty arbitral tribunals*

Some investment tribunals have been willing to apply general principles of international law not founded in the text of a given IIA to manage proceedings running parallel to an investment claim, which have most often involved commercial arbitration or domestic proceedings involving the same (or related)

[116] Appellate Body Report, *Mexico—Taxes on Soft Drinks* (n 1) paras 53, 57.

[117] ibid para 3, paras 10–11, para 31.

[118] Panel Report, *Mexico—Tax Measures on Soft Drinks and Other Beverages*, WT/DS308/R (adopted 24 March 2006) paras 7.11–7.16.

[119] Appellate Body Report, *Mexico—Taxes on Soft Drinks* (n 1) para 10.

[120] ibid.

[121] ibid n 33.

[122] ibid para 53.

[123] ibid para 54.

[124] See part 4.4.1.1.

parties and the same impugned measures or conduct.[125] For instance, a number of tribunals have asserted the applicability of *lis pendens*.[126] In the words of one tribunal, 'in the interest of international judicial order, either of the tribunals [seised in parallel proceedings] may, in its discretion and as a matter of comity, decide to stay the exercise of its jurisdiction pending a decision by the other tribunal'.[127] However, tribunals have diverged on the degree of stringency with which to apply the 'triple identity' test for *lis pendens*. Some have taken an especially strict approach, finding that claims brought under separate instruments are inherently and necessarily different, even if those instruments contain the same substantive norms and disciplines.[128] Others have adopted a more flexible approach,[129] for example, viewing proceedings launched by related yet formally distinct corporate entities as having a single 'identity',[130] or viewing proceedings brought under a contract and an IIA as involving the same broader claim or matter, despite involving different instruments.[131]

An unduly strict conception of what amounts to an identity of parties could ignore the economic reality that the ultimate beneficiary of an interest or enterprise is capable of assuming multiple legal personalities. This was most clearly illustrated in the parallel *Lauder/CME/Czech Republic* investment treaty cases, in which Mr Ronald Lauder launched an investment treaty claim against the Czech Republic under the US–Czech IIA, followed by a claim based on the same facts and allegations by his Dutch holding company CME under the Netherlands–Czech IIA.[132] Despite Mr Lauder

[125] See, eg, *SGS Société Générale de Surveillance SA v Pakistan (Procedural Order No 2)* (ICSID Arbitral Tribunal, Case No ARB/01/13, 16 October 2002) paras 46–49; *SGS Société Générale de Surveillance SA v Philippines (Decision on Jurisdiction)* (ICSID Arbitral Tribunal, Case No ARB/02/6, 29 January 2004) paras 173–76; *Bureau Veritas, Inspection, Valuation, Assessment and Control, BIVAC BV v Paraguay (Further Decision on Objections to Jurisdiction)* (ICSID Arbitral Tribunal, Case No ARB/07/9, 9 October 2012) paras 284–90; *CMS v Argentina (Jurisdiction)* (ICSID Arbitral Tribunal, Case No ARB/01/8, 17 July 2003) paras 70–76; *CME v Czech Republic (Final Award)* (Ad Hoc Tribunal, UNCITRAL, 14 March 2003) para 410; *Petrobart* (n 78) 64 (discussing the twin concept of *res judicata*).

[126] See, eg, *Tokios Tokelés v Ukraine (Order No 1 Provisional Measures)* (ICSID Arbitral Tribunal, Case No ARB/02/18, 1 July 2003) para 7; *Ceskoslovenska Obchodni Banka v Slovak Republic (Decision of the Tribunal on Objections to Jurisdiction)* (ICSID Arbitral Tribunal, Case No ARB/97/4, 24 May 1999) para 9; *Milicom v Senegal (Decision on Provisional Measures)* (ICSID Arbitral Tribunal, Case No ARB/03/20, 9 December 2009) paras 47–51;

[127] *Southern Pacific Properties (Middle East) Ltd [SPP] v Egypt (Decision on Jurisdiction)* (ICSID Arbitral Tribunal, Case No Arb 84/3, 27 November 1985) para 84.

[128] See, eg, *SGS (Objections to Jurisdiction)* (n 81) para 182; *CME (Final Award)* (n 125) para 433.

[129] See, eg, *Milicom* (n 126) para 45(b), paras 47–51; See, eg, *Tokios Tokeles* (n 126) para 7; *Ceskoslovenska* (n 126) para 9.

[130] *Milicom* (n 126) para 45(b), paras 47–51.

[131] See, eg, *Tokios Tokeles* (n126) para 7; *Ceskoslovenska* (n 126) para 9.

[132] *Lauder v Czech Republic (Award)* (Ad Hoc Tribunal, UNCITRAL, 3 September 2001); *CME (Partial Award)* (n 2).

being the beneficiary of CME, both tribunals rejected arguments based on *lis pendens* due to, inter alia, the formal legal distinction between Mr Lauder and CME.[133] Since no formal legal identity arose between the two parties, the tribunal considered 'the Respondent's recourse to the principle of *lis alibi pendens* to be of no use'.[134]

The possibility for the same beneficiary to launch multiple proceedings and circumvent *lis pendens* through multiple legal personalities has led some commentators to call for a less strict application of the triple identity test. Reinisch argues that it 'may be appropriate to consider the economic realities of foreign investments' when applying the rule.[135] McLachlan argues that, where the relevant interests are indissociable or indivisible, 'parallel treaty arbitrations by company and shareholder relating to the same underlying facts should be held to meet' the identical parties test.[136] The International Law Association Final Report on *Lis Pendens* and Arbitration also cautioned against 'the application of… rigid criteria' through the triple identity test.[137] Despite these calls for a more flexible test, the dominant approach to *lis pendens* remains focused on formal distinctions of legal personality.

Some tribunals have also expressed a willingness to decline to exercise jurisdiction (or render a claim inadmissible) on the basis of the doctrine of abuse of right under general international law. As the tribunal in *Metal-Tech v Uzbekistan* explained:

> [T]he Contracting Parties to an investment treaty may limit the protections of the treaty to investments made in accordance with the laws and regulations of the host State. Depending on the wording of the investment treaty, this limitation may be a bar to jurisdiction… or a defense on the merits… Similarly, a breach of the general prohibition of abuse of right, which is a manifestation of the principle of good faith, may give rise to an objection to jurisdiction or to a defense on the merits.[138]

Thus, if parallel litigation is initiated in bad faith, a tribunal could find that it constitutes an abuse of the right to bring a claim and therefore decline to exercise jurisdiction. Such a finding would need to be grounded in positive evidence of a vexatious litigation strategy—for instance to obtain double remedies, to drain the respondent's resources, or to unduly maximize chances of success—and would likely be subject to a high threshold of proof.[139]

[133] *Lauder (Award)* (n 2) para 171; *CME (Partial Award)* (n 2) para 412.

[134] *Lauder (Award)* (n 2) para 171.

[135] Reinisch (n 64) 121.

[136] McLachlan (n 63) 415.

[137] De Ly and Sheppard (n 72) 32–33 (recommendations 1 and 6). See also Robin Hansen (n 65) 523, 543; Martinez-Fraga and Samra (n 65) 438.

[138] *Metal-Tech v Uzbekistan (Award)* (ICSID Arbitral Tribunal, Case No ARB/10/3, 4 October 2013) para 127.

[139] *Chevron* (n 87) paras 143–46.

Other tribunals have expressed a view diametrically opposite to that of *Metal-Tech v Uzbekistan*, asserting that no grounds exist for denying a claim on the basis of general international law in the absence of express textual authority in an IIA. This strict formalism was captured by the Annulment Committee in *RSM v Grenada*, which dismissed the respondent's plea to mitigate parallel proceedings on the basis of good faith by indicating that it was:

> not necessary… to find that the Applicant has committed an abuse of process in commencing separate proceedings against the Respondent. If the Applicant considers that it has legal rights, it is entitled to seek the vindication of those rights.[140]

The tribunal in *SGS v Pakistan* made a similar finding in relation to the applicability of estoppel:

> In the absence of such treaty language, we are not free to read into the Swiss–Pakistan BIT a requirement that would preclude a would-be claimant from resorting to other remedies in respect of contract claims prior to the exercise of its BIT rights. Moreover, given the general purpose of the ICSID Convention and the object and purpose of the BIT, we would be hesitant to imply estoppel (or waiver for that matter) with respect to BIT claims that have not in fact been alleged in another forum.[141]

Thus, the jurisprudence on good faith-based arguments for suspending proceedings or declining jurisdiction in instances of parallel proceedings is mixed and divergent.

Whereas the foregoing discussion relates to the same or related parties initiating parallel proceedings, precedent also exists for tribunals managing proceedings that involve *unrelated* parties litigating the same measures or conduct under the same IIA. The preferred tool in such cases is to consolidate the proceedings rather than shut down one of the claims. As mentioned above, some IIAs contain mechanisms that permit a tribunal to order the consolidation of claims that have 'a question of law or fact in common' where such consolidation would be 'in the interests of fair and efficient resolution of the claims'.[142] In other instances, separate claims by unrelated parties over the same matters have been de facto consolidated through the appointment of the same arbitrators in the separate tribunals or through the voluntary consolidation of claims into one tribunal.[143]

[140] *RSM v Grenada (Order of the Annulment Committee)* (ICSID Arbitral Tribunal, Case No ARB/05/14, 28 April 2011) para 65.

[141] *SGS (Objections to Jurisdiction)* (n 81) para 177.

[142] 2012 United States Model BIT (n 40) art 33.

[143] Catherine Yannaca-Small, 'Consolidation of Claims: A Promising Avenue for Investment Arbitration?' in OECD, *International Investment Perspectives 2006* (OECD 2006) 225, 232–33.

## 4.5 Conclusion

The foregoing analysis reveals only limited scope for managing parallel litigation under WTO law and investment law on the basis of principles of good faith, at least under current jurisprudential approaches. The nature of the two legal regimes is such that different sets of parties to parallel WTO and investment proceedings are the norm, with investment treaty claims frequently brought by a private actor and WTO proceedings limited to WTO members. The remedies available will also usually diverge, with WTO proceedings primarily aimed at the prospective withdrawal of an offending measures and investment claims directed at retrospective compensation for harm suffered. Further, despite a degree of normative overlap in the substantive disciplines of the two regimes, a given claim will often address other obligations that are particular to the specific regime, such as expropriation in investment claims.

Even on more liberal approaches to *lis pendens*, parallel proceedings taking place in the WTO and pursuant to an ISDS mechanism in an IIA are extremely unlikely to meet the 'triple identity' test. Differences between the international trade law regime and the international investment law regime would also make it difficult to establish a firm defence of abuse of rights, since an investor or state could argue that it is simply availing itself of separate and distinct legal rights and remedies as opposed to vexatiously pursuing the same claim in multiple fora.

The nature of jurisdiction in the WTO dispute settlement system also makes it unlikely that a panel or the Appellate Body would decline to exercise jurisdiction simply on the basis of a parallel claim brought under an IIA by a private actor. A good faith-based defence (for example, estoppel) might nevertheless be plausible in the face of a relevant provision in the IIA. For example, the requirement in some IIAs that an investor's home state cease affording it diplomatic protection after the investor brings a claim could be viewed as a representation that the home state will not initiate disputes on its investor's behalf, including at the WTO. However, as WTO disputes regularly relate to measures of general application that affect a range of actors rather than a single investor, representations relating to individual claims or investors may diminish in significance.

The WTO and IIA claims over Australia's plain packaging laws highlight some of these issues. Whereas Philip Morris is contesting the laws under the Australia–Hong Kong BIT, it has solicited the support of the Dominican Republic to contest the laws at the WTO, including by reportedly covering the Dominican Republic's legal costs.[144] Thus, it could be inferred that the same broad economic entity—Philip Morris—is a key figure and beneficiary behind the parallel WTO and investment proceedings. Further, as discussed above, Philip Morris at least originally claimed that certain breaches of WTO law also constitute violations of the IIA, which means that substantial overlap exists in relation to the normative standards being contested in the respective claims. Additionally, since Philip Morris is seeking a rescission of the laws through its investment claim, and since a withdrawal of the offending measures is the preferred and standard remedy sought in WTO proceedings, a degree of overlap is expected in the remedies sought. Based on these considerations, the pursuit by Philip Morris of parallel proceedings in relation to the same matter could be viewed as vexatious and contrary to principles of good faith. It creates the potential for conflicting outcomes, it maximizes the chance of success through multiple determinations, and it could be viewed as draining the respondent's resources.

Equally, however, Philip Morris is alleging breaches of the IIA that are not available in the WTO, such as those relating to expropriation and the impairment of investments. It is also seeking compensation for retrospective harm under its investment claim, which is unavailable under the Dominican Republic's WTO claim. Furthermore, the Dominican Republic is not the only WTO member to contest Australia's laws. Cuba, Honduras, Ukraine and Indonesia have initiated additional, concomitant WTO proceedings. While some of these WTO proceedings are reportedly being funded by other tobacco companies,[145] none has been directly connected to Philip Morris in the same way as the Dominican Republic. These considerations appear to mitigate inferences of bad faith in the initiation of the parallel proceedings in relation to the same matter. They make it difficult for either adjudicatory body to decline to exercise jurisdiction on the basis of parallel litigation in the other legal regime.

Nevertheless, within the bounds of their own domains, international trade law and international investment law do contain tools to manage

[144] Andrew Martin, 'Philip Morris Leads Plain Packs Battle in Global Trade Arena' *Bloomberg News* (22 August 2013) <www.bloomberg.com/news/2013-08-22/philip-morris-leads-plain-packs-battle-in-global-trade-arena.html> accessed 30 January 2014.

[145] See, eg, Mike Seccombe, 'Big Tobacco's Plan to Stub out Plain Packaging' *The Saturday Paper* (8 March 2014) <http://www.thesaturdaypaper.com.au/opinion/topic/2014/03/08/big-tobaccos-plan-stub-out-plain-packaging/1394197200> accessed 16 June 2014; Stephanie Nebehay, 'Australia Says Big Tobacco Aiding WTO Challengers' *Reuters* (23 May 2012) <www.reuters.com/article/2012/05/23/us-trade-tobacco-idUSBRE84M0IO20120523> accessed 16 January 2014.

the initiation of parallel proceedings in bad faith. If the entities bringing the claims and the questions of law and fact being litigated are aligned, a respondent has scope to plead a bad faith defence. In international trade law, the potential for this defence lies in the operation of exclusive choice of forum provisions in PTAs, which can operate on their own terms before a PTA panel or as a representation giving rise to an estoppel before a WTO panel. In international investment law, much depends on how strictly a tribunal construes the 'same' claim and the 'same' entity in applying *lis pendens*. When faced with parallel proceedings, tribunals in both regimes have grappled with an apparent tension between the text of the relevant treaty and general international law. While some decision-makers have been willing to draw on general principles of good faith and apply estoppel or abuse of rights independent of any textual foundation, others have been loathe to apply anything other than the precise words of the instrument under dispute. This tension, apparent in both regimes, points to a broader uncertainty concerning the relationship and primacy between different sources of international law. With the continued proliferation of both trade and investment dispute settlement mechanisms, questions of how to best manage parallel proceedings will likely garner increasing salience.

# 5

# Good Faith Limitations on Protected Investments and Corporate Structuring

*Stephan W Schill and Heather L Bray**

## 5.1 Good Faith Unbound—Good Faith Restrained

Good faith is omnipresent. It is a broad, general concept embedded in the architecture of all legal systems in the world, both national and international, as a fundamental element of every legal obligation.[1] As such, good faith may help to ease the strictness inherent in an overly formalistic application of legal rules and provide flexibility and openness towards unforeseen circumstances or future development. At the same time, it is inherently ambiguous, difficult to define and challenging to contextualize, and therefore carries with it the risk of being unpredictable in both its application and consequences. The mere mention of the term 'good faith' can befuddle even the most seasoned adjudicator, as it conjures abstract and elusive ideals of morality, ethical imperatives, and ideas of fairness, justice, honesty and trustworthiness. What is more, these notions are often tied to an adjudicator's individual experiences and values and therefore risk being filled with subjective biases rather than objective standards of normativity. In order to make the principle of good faith operative in a legal order that is faithful to

* This chapter was written with the support of a European Research Council Starting Grant on 'Transnational Private-Public Arbitration as Global Regulatory Governance: Charting and Codifying the Lex Mercatoria Publica' (LexMercPub, Grant agreement no 313355). The discussion of some of the cases in part 5.2 draws on Stephan W Schill, 'Illegal Investments in Investment Treaty Arbitration' (2012) 11 LPICT 281.

[1] In investment treaty arbitration, good faith has also been designated as a 'Janus concept': see *Phoenix Action Ltd v Czech Republic (Award)* (ICSID Arbitral Tribunal, Case No ARB/06/5, 15 April 2009) para 109. See also Markus Kotzur, 'Good Faith (Bona fide)' in Rüdiger Wolfrum (ed), *Max Planck Encyclopedia of Public International Law*, vol IV (OUP 2012) 508; Woo Pei Yee, '"Protecting Parties" Reasonable Expectations: A General Principle of Good Faith' (2001) 1 OUCLJ 195.

the rule of law and that balances between competing interests in a predictable manner, it is therefore important to avoid abuse of the principle and to concretize its operation and scope of application. Rather than good faith unbound, a legal order based on the rule of law should strive for good faith restrained.

International law is well aware of this task. As explained in chapter 2, the good faith principle constitutes a fundamental and ubiquitous principle of international law[2] that is embraced in both international instruments[3] and international jurisprudence.[4] It operates as both a general principle of law and as a principle of customary international law[5] and, as the International Court of Justice (ICJ) in the *Nuclear Tests Case* underscored, is 'one of the basic principles governing the creation and performance of legal obligations, whatever their source'.[6] In international law, the principle of good faith has multiple roles. In horizontal inter-state relations, as demonstrated in chapter 3, good faith guides the interpretation of treaties (pursuant to the *Vienna Convention on the Law of Treaties* (*VCLT*))[7] and facilitates their performance.[8] In the context of international dispute settlement, as indicated in chapter 4, good faith has manifestations linked to other legal terms of art, such as equity, estoppel, and abuse of rights.[9] But good faith also limits the exercise of international public authority and restricts the exercise of unilateral powers by states or international organizations.[10] Yet, while the ICJ has recognized that good

[2] See, eg, Robert Kolb, 'Principles as Sources of International Law (with Special Reference to Good Faith)' (2006) 53 Nether Intl L Rev 1; Andrew D Mitchell, 'Good Faith in WTO Dispute Settlement' (2006) 7 Melb J Intl L 339; Bernardo Cremades, 'Good Faith in International Arbitration' (2012) 27(4) Am U Intl L Rev 761.

[3] See, eg, *Charter of the United Nations* art 2(2): 'All Members, in order to ensure to all of them rights and benefits resulting from membership, shall fulfill in good faith the obligations assumed by them in accordance with the present Charter'.

[4] See, eg, *Nuclear Tests Case (New Zealand v France) (Judgment)* [1974] ICJ Rep 457, para 49.

[5] See, eg, *Certain Norwegian Loans (France v Norway) (Jurisdiction)* [1957] ICJ Rep 9, 53.

[6] *Nuclear Tests Case* (n 4) para 49.

[7] Opened for signature 23 May 1969, 1155 UNTS 331 (entered into force 27 January 1980) art 31(1) (referring to good faith treaty interpretation).

[8] ibid art 26 (referring to the *pacta sunt servanda* principle).

[9] See Yee (n 1) 200–08.

[10] This is the essence of the finding of the WTO Appellate Body in *Certain Shrimp and Shrimp Products* when it stated that good faith 'controls the exercise of rights by States' when invoking exceptions in GATT 1994 art XX: Appellate Body Report, *United States—Import Prohibition of Certain Shrimp and Shrimp Products*, WTO Doc WT/DS58/AB/R (adopted 6 November 1998) para 158. See also *Certain Questions of Mutual Assistance in Criminal Matters (Djibouti v France) (Judgment)* [2008] ICJ Rep 177, para 145. On the need for international organizations to act in good faith cf *Interpretation of the Agreement of 25 March 1951 between the WHO and Egypt (Advisory Opinion)* [1980] ICJ Rep 3, 93, 96; see also *Vienna Convention on the Law of Treaties between States and International Organizations or between International Organizations*, opened for signature 21 March 1986, UN doc A/CONF.129/15, preamble, arts 26, 31 (treaty not yet in force) (regarding contractual relations of international organizations).

faith governs all legal obligations, it added the caveat that good faith 'is not in itself a source of obligation where none would otherwise exist'.[11] Good faith cannot therefore be used as a source of an international legal obligation per se, but rather constitutes an ancillary principle governing the implementation of legal obligations. On the whole, international law therefore follows a notion of good faith restrained, rather than good faith unbound.

Originating in the ancient Roman law notion of *bona fides,* good faith also exists in all domestic legal systems worldwide and has application in both private and public law.[12] It is most pervasive in the area of contract law. In civil legal traditions,[13] good faith governs all aspects of contracts, beginning at formation and ending with performance and enforcement of contractual obligations.[14] Common law traditions,[15] in contrast, have a much narrower formulation of the principle, namely one that is applicable only to contract performance and enforcement.[16] Regardless of its scope, good faith in both legal traditions 'requires parties to perform their obligations under the contract fairly, honestly, and in a manner acceptable in their trade or business'.[17] Although less well-known, good faith also exists in areas of public law, including administrative law, tax law and criminal law.[18] In the public law context, good faith is chiefly used as a means to control the exercise of discretion by public authorities.[19]

In light of the different functions in domestic private law, domestic public law and public international law—acting as a corrective tool in the former and as a check on state authority in the latter two areas of law—good faith has a multidimensional nature. Investment treaty arbitration, as a discipline that brings together public international law, commercial arbitration and

[11] *Land and Maritime Boundary between Cameroon and Nigeria (Cameroon v Nigeria) (Preliminary Objections)* [1988] ICJ Rep 275, para 39, citing *Border and Transborder Armed Actions (Nicaragua v Honduras) (Jurisdiction and Admissibility)* [1988] ICJ Rep 69, para 94.

[12] Kotzur (n 1) paras 1, 3, 5–6.

[13] See, eg, *Bürgerliches Gesetzbuch* [Civil Code] § 242 (Germany); *Code Civil* [Civil Code] art 1134(3) (France).

[14] Arthur Hartkamp et al (eds), *Towards a European Civil Code* (4th rev edn, Kluwer Law International 2010) 628–34.

[15] Lord Mansfield in *Carter v Boehm,* 97 Eng Rep 1162, 1164 referred to good faith as '[t]he governing principle . . . applicable to all contracts and dealings'. But see Allan Farnsworth, 'Duties of Good Faith and Fair Dealings under the UNDROIT Principles, Relevant International Conventions, and National Laws' (1995) 3 Tul J Intl & Comp L 47.

[16] Paul Powers, 'Defining the Undefinable: Good Faith and the United Nations Convention on the Contracts for the International Sale of Goods' (1999) 18(2) J L & Commerce 336. See, eg, Section 1-2013 of the United States Uniform Commercial Code.

[17] Powers (n 16) 341.

[18] Saul Litvinoff, 'Good Faith' (1996–1997) 71(6) Tul L Rev 1671.

[19] ibid 1671.

domestic public law,[20] is not immune to the good faith concept.[21] In fact, investment treaty tribunals are regularly tasked with determining the applicability of the principle of good faith, as it exists in international investment law in a variety of contexts, as the various contributions to the present volume show. This chapter focuses on one area in which the good faith principle has played a role, namely as a discipline on whether certain foreign investments or their corporate structure benefit from investment treaty protection. In fact, on numerous occasions, tribunals make reference to the principle of good faith and suggest that only *bona fide* investments and *bona fide* investors can benefit from investment treaty protection, while excluding unwelcome investments or setting limits on initial and subsequent nationality planning.[22]

The benefits of relying on the principle of good faith when analysing whether a particular investment or investor is *bona fide* in investment arbitration are clear. Good faith inserts flexibility into the decision-making process, allowing arbitrators to escape the tight constraints of positivistic treaty language. The good faith principle can also be used as a mechanism for arbitral tribunals to react, or adapt, to the ever-changing arbitral climate and, importantly, act as a gateway for outside norms to enter arbitral decision-making.[23] Overall, good faith encourages investment arbitration to be receptive to competing concerns and global regulatory standards and, in this way, ensures that decisions are made not within a legal vacuum but with reference to the larger framework in which international investment law operates. But, problems also arise in using the principle of good faith. Reliance on a vague principle may lead to legal uncertainty, create a risk of unpredictability for foreign investors, and provide decision-makers with an abundance of discretion that is subject to personal valuation and biases, which may lead to arbitrary results or a development of investment law by arbitral tribunals that is not in line with what states as contracting parties intended.[24]

[20] See Stephan W Schill, 'International Investment Law and Comparative Public Law: An Introduction' in Stephan W Schill (ed), *International Investment Law and Comparative Public Law* (OUP 2010) 3, 10–17. See also Stephan W Schill, 'W(h)ither Fragmentation? On the Literature and Sociology of International Investment Law' (2011) 22 EJIL 875, 878, 883–902.

[21] For articles that look at the intersection between the good faith principle and investor–state arbitration, see Sanja Dajic, 'Mapping the Good Faith Principle in International Investment Arbitration: Assessment of Its Substantive and Procedural Value' (2012) 46 Zbornik Radova 207; Eric De Brabandere, '"Good Faith", "Abuse of Process" and the Initiation of Investment Treaty Claims' (2012) 3 JIDS 609.

[22] The relevant case law is discussed below in parts 5.2 and 5.3.

[23] On the function of open-ended norms, such as the principle of good faith, as a gateway for non-social norms and an instrument of adapting the law to a changed social environment, see Gunther Teubner, *Standards und Direktiven in Generalklauseln: Möglichkeiten und Grenzen der empirischen Sozialforschung bei der Präzisierung der Gute-Sitte-Klauseln im Privatrecht* (Athenäum 1971) 65–106.

[24] On the function of open-ended norms to delegate law-making activities to dispute settlement institutions, see ibid 106–15.

In order to keep these problems in check, and to arrive at an understanding of good faith restrained, rather than good faith unbound, we show in this chapter that in cases of limiting the scope of protection of foreign investments—both *ratione materiae* and *ratione personae*—good faith has only a marginal role to play in practice. Keeping the role of good faith in this context to a minimum is also convincing from a normative perspective. In almost all cases, (mis-)using corporate structures or engaging in unwelcome, but not illegal, investment activities can be dealt with through recourse to domestic law. Reliance on domestic law both strengthens predictability in this area and appeals to the powers and self-determination of host states in deciding which investments they want to attract and what corporate form these investments should take. By contrast, applying the principle of good faith in a broad manner would risk granting arbitrators overly broad discretion to override the choices made by host states under domestic law. Applying good faith—or another notion that forms part of this concept, such as abuse of right or abuse of process—to exclude certain investments from treaty protection should therefore be limited to exceptional circumstances.

Against this background, this chapter first addresses the role the principle of good faith has played when arbitral tribunals assess whether investments are protected under investment treaties even though they were contrary to domestic law and policies or international legal standards (part 5.2). In this context, we review how good faith interacts with domestic illegality both in cases involving an explicit 'in accordance with host state law' clause and in the absence of such clauses. In both instances, we show that good faith should primarily function as a limit on the host state's conduct and not as a limit on the investor's protection under the investment treaty in question. Instead, recourse to the domestic law of the host state to determine the scope of protection *ratione materiae* is the preferred approach. Only in cases where domestic law falls short of implementing international standards may recourse to good faith be had in order to ensure the investment's compliance with international standards, notably in the context of combatting corruption. However, as reflected in arbitral jurisprudence, in such circumstances it is preferable to use the notion of transnational public policy, rather than a freestanding concept of good faith, as the former is less prone to being filled with subjective notions and biases and instead suggests a more structured and objective analysis.

Part 5.3 then discusses how arbitral tribunals use good faith to impose limits on corporate structuring, both before an investment is made as well as during post-investment restructuring. Here, again, we consider that arbitral tribunals have made use of the concept of good faith in an unnecessarily broad manner, as many problematic cases of corporate structuring can be resolved more appropriately by focusing on the timing of the restructuring and taking into account the applicability of investment treaties *ratione temporis*. This approach considerably limits the need to have recourse to the concept of good faith. In fact, as part 5.4 concludes, a restrained use of good faith is mandated by the concept of the rule of law as an overarching principle governing international investment relations.

## 5.2 Good Faith and Compliance of Investments with Domestic and International Law

Identifying an investment protected under international investment law depends on the definition of 'investment' in the relevant international investment agreement and the *Convention on the Settlement of Investment Disputes between States and Nationals of Other States* (*ICSID Convention*).[25] However, the protection of an investment also depends on compliance with the domestic law in force in the host state as well as international standards, and, in the view of some tribunals, on the investment being made in good faith. In this context, arbitral tribunals have, in our view unnecessarily, understood good faith as an obligation incumbent upon the foreign investor even in cases where the investment in question was contrary to domestic law. In addition, good faith has been usefully found to discipline the host state's reliance on domestic illegality in limited circumstances. Finally, good faith can have an independent role to play in determining the scope of protection of an investment *ratione materiae* if the investment is contrary to international standards without at the same time contravening domestic law.

### 5.2.1 Good faith and the investor's duty to comply with domestic law

Arbitral tribunals, when dealing with the impact of domestic illegality, often make reference to the principle of good faith as a limitation on the scope of protection of foreign investment. In this context, good faith can interact with domestic illegality in two possible ways, depending on whether or not the treaty contains an explicit 'in accordance with host state law' clause.[26]

[25] Opened for signature 18 March 1965 (entered into force 14 October 1966).

[26] For a detailed analysis of how breaches of domestic law are dealt with in investment treaty arbitrations, see Stephan W Schill, 'Illegal Investments in Investment Treaty Arbitration' (2012) 11 LPICT 281. Cf Zachary Douglas, 'The Plea of Illegality in Investment Treaty Arbitration' (2014) 29 ICSID Rev 155; Jarrod Hepburn, 'In Accordance with Which Host State Laws? Restoring the "Defence" of Investor Illegality in Investment Arbitration' (2014) 5 JIDS 531.

Thus, in *Inceysa v El Salvador*, a case involving the interpretation of an explicit 'in accordance with host state law' clause, the tribunal found that the claimant obtained a government contract for mechanical inspection services only because of a fraudulent misrepresentation of the claimant's industry experience and financial capacities. The tribunal held that this was contrary not only to host state law but also to principles recognized under international law, including good faith, the principle *nemo auditor propriam turpitudinem allegans* (nobody can benefit from his or her own wrong), international public policy, and unlawful enrichment.[27]

While the tribunal reasoned that the bilateral investment treaty (BIT) in question did not protect investments made in contravention of good faith, the need to have recourse to this concept in addition to domestic law is questionable. Although the tribunal itself stated that it needed to assess compliance of the investment with the laws of El Salvador because of the 'in accordance with host state law' clause in the BIT,[28] it nonetheless continued with the circular argument that because the Constitution of El Salvador determined international law to be part of national law 'the BIT, as valid law in El Salvador, [was] the primary and special legislation this Tribunal must analyze to determine whether Inceysa's investment was made in accordance with the legal system of that Nation'.[29] Since the applicable law clause in the BIT made reference to generally recognized rules and principles of international and national law,[30] the tribunal considered that it had to apply general principles of law before having recourse to domestic law.[31] Thus, instead of assessing primarily whether the investor's fraudulent misrepresentations breached the law of El Salvador, the tribunal laboured over whether the conduct in question was contrary to generally recognized principles of international law, including the principle of good faith.

Arbitral tribunals have also made reference to the principle of good faith when faced with breaches of domestic law in the absence of an 'in accordance with host state law' clause. As the tribunal in *Yaung Chi Oo Trading v Myanmar* has suggested, there exists a 'general rule that for a foreign investment to enjoy treaty protection it must be lawful under the law of the host State'.[32] The main difficulty, however, relates to how to ground such a general

[27] *Inceysa Vallisoletana v El Salvador (Award)* (ICSID Arbitral Tribunal, Case No ARB/03/26, 2 August 2006) paras 230–57. Cf *Rumeli Telekom AS and Telsim Mobil Telekomunikasyon Hizmetleri AS v Kazakhstan (Award)* (ICSID Arbitral Tribunal, Case No ARB/05/16, 29 July 2008) paras 236–40, 323, 334–35.

[28] *Inceysa* (n 27) para 218.

[29] ibid para 220.

[30] See ibid para 222.

[31] ibid para 224.

[32] *Yaung Chi Oo Trading Pte Ltd v Myanmar (Award)* (Asean Arbitral Tribunal, Case No ARB/01/1, 31 March 2003) para 58. See also *Ioannis Kardassopoulos v Georgia (Decision on Jurisdiction)* (ICSID Arbitral Tribunal, Case No ARB/05/18, 6 July 2007) paras 185–94.

rule. One way in which arbitral tribunals have done this is by recourse to general principles of law, including the principle of good faith. Most explicit in this context was the tribunal in *Hamester v Ghana*. Even though the applicable Germany–Ghana BIT[33] contained an 'in accordance with host state law' clause, the tribunal stated in obiter dicta:

> An investment will not be protected if it has been created in violation of national or international principles of good faith; by way of corruption, fraud, or deceitful conduct; or if its creation itself constitutes a misuse of the system of international investment protection under the ICSID Convention. It will also not be protected if it is made in violation of the host State's law ... These are general principles that exist independently of specific language to this effect in the Treaty.[34]

Similarly, in *Phoenix v Czech Republic*, although the applicable BIT contained an explicit 'in accordance with host state law' clause,[35] the tribunal noted that:

> States cannot be deemed to offer access to the ICSID dispute settlement mechanism to investments not made in good faith. The protection of international investment arbitration cannot be granted if such protection would run contrary to the general principles of international law, among which the principle of good faith is of utmost importance.[36]

In the view of both the *Hamester* and *Phoenix* tribunals, the principle of good faith can therefore be seen as serving the function of substituting for a non-existent 'in accordance with host state law' clause. At the same time, the tribunals suggest that the obligation to comply with good faith exists independently of the investor's duty to comply with domestic law.

The question arises, however, whether reliance on a good faith obligation is needed when the activity in question is already found contrary to domestic law, or whether an analysis of domestic illegality is sufficient to exclude illegal investments from treaty protection. It seems that the latter is the case. After all, in the presence of an 'in accordance with host state law' clause, arbitral tribunals generally recognize that illegal investments are excluded from treaty protection and decline jurisdiction without the need to resort to good faith. Similarly, in the absence of such a clause, arbitral tribunals, while accepting

33 *Agreement between the Federal Republic of Germany and the Republic of Ghana for the Encouragement and Reciprocal Protection of Investments*, signed 24 February 1995 (entered into force 23 November 1998).

34 *Gustav FW Hamester GmbH & Co KG v Ghana (Award)* (ICSID Arbitral Tribunal, Case No ARB/07/24, 18 June 2010) paras 123–24.

35 See *Phoenix* (n 1) paras 56 and 134.

36 ibid para 106.

jurisdiction over any ensuing dispute, deal with the breach of domestic law as a matter of the merits and equally limit the investment's protection.[37] In both cases, good faith has no additional value and only grants unnecessary discretion to arbitral tribunals to alter domestic law.

The insignificance of a good faith obligation also becomes apparent when analysing the above mentioned cases that have conflated compliance with domestic law and the principle of good faith. Thus, the *Inceysa* tribunal could have restricted itself to determining whether the investment was made 'in accordance with host state law' by reference to the relevant national law of El Salvador. Such an approach would have been more consistent with the terms of the treaty and the clear reference in the 'in accordance with host state law' clause to the national law of the host state.

Limiting the analysis to domestic law was, for example, the approach preferred in *Fraport v Philippines*,[38] which involved the prohibition for foreign investors under the Philippine Constitution to hold more than 40% of the shares of locally incorporated companies holding concessions in the public utilities sector—a prohibition that was backed by a so-called Anti-Dummy Law that criminally sanctioned Philippine nationals acting as straw men for foreigners in circumvention of the constitutional prohibition in question.[39] The tribunal majority found that the German claimant had violated the domestic law in question, because the claimant had concluded secret shareholder agreements ensuring that it had a controlling influence over the local company holding a concession to build and operate a new terminal at Manila's international airport, in full knowledge that this was contrary to Philippine law.[40] With direct reference to the applicable national law, the majority of the tribunal found that the investor had not made an investment 'accepted in accordance with the respective laws and regulations' of the Philippines, as required by the Germany–Philippines BIT,[41] and declined jurisdiction.[42]

[37] For a detailed analysis of jurisprudence see the references at n 26.

[38] *Fraport AG v Philippines (Award)* (ICSID Arbitral Tribunal, Case No ARB/03/25, 16 August 2007). Although the decision was later annulled, the grounds for annulment did not turn on the interpretation of the 'in accordance with host state law' clause at hand: see *Fraport AG v Philippines (Annulment)* (ICSID Arbitral Tribunal, Case No ARB/03/25, 23 December 2010). The award can therefore still be considered as relevant for the general understanding and interpretation of 'in accordance with host state law' clauses.

[39] *Fraport (Award)* (n 38) paras 287, 349.

[40] ibid paras 349–56.

[41] *Agreement between the Federal Republic of Germany and the Republic of the Philippines on the Promotion and Reciprocal Protection of Investments,* signed 18 April 1997 (entered into force 2 February 2000) art 1(1).

[42] See *Fraport (Award)* (n 38) paras 281–83. Cf Dissenting Opinion paras 14, 15–27.

Other arbitral tribunals dealing with a variety of explicit 'in accordance with host state law' clauses have subsequently followed this approach.[43]

In cases not involving express 'in accordance with host state law' clauses, the duty to comply with domestic law can still be established without recourse to the principle of good faith. This was suggested by the *Fraport* tribunal in an obiter dictum when stating that foreign investors are under a general 'obligation to make the investment in accordance with the host state's law'.[44]

More directly on point is the decision in *Plama v Bulgaria* that dealt with domestic illegality in the absence of a specific treaty clause.[45] In this case, the tribunal found that the claimant had misled the host state as to the identity of the members of a consortium participating in a bid for the privatization of a state-owned oil refinery. Although the Energy Charter Treaty (ECT)[46] did not have an 'in accordance with host state law' clause, the tribunal found that illegal investments were not protected under the treaty:

> Unlike a number of Bilateral Investment Treaties, the ECT does not contain a provision requiring the conformity of the Investment with a particular law. This does not mean, however, that the protections provided for by the ECT cover all kinds of investments, including those contrary to domestic or international law ... In accordance with the introductory note to the ECT '*[t]he fundamental aim of the Energy Charter Treaty is to strengthen the rule of law on energy issues ...*'. Consequently, the ECT should be interpreted in a manner consistent with the aim of encouraging respect for the rule of law. The Arbitral Tribunal concludes that the substantive protections of the ECT cannot apply to investments that are made contrary to law. The Tribunal finds that the investment in this case violates not only *Bulgarian law* ... but also '*applicable rules and principles of international law*'.[47]

[43] See, eg, *Desert Line Projects LLC v Yemen (Award)* (ICSID Arbitral Tribunal, Case No ARB/05/17, 6 February 2008) para 104; *Alasdair Ross Anderson v Costa Rica (Award)* (ICSID Arbitral Tribunal, Case No ARB(AF)/07/3, 10 May 2010) paras 51–53, 58; *Metal-Tech Ltd v Uzbekistan (Award)* (ICSID Arbitral Tribunal, Case No ARB/10/3, 4 October 2013) para 165; *Ambiente Ufficio SPA (Case formerly known as Giordana Alpi) v Argentina (Decision on Jurisdiction and Admissibility)* (ICSID Arbitral Tribunal, Case No ARB/08/9, 8 February 2013) para 517; *Nordzucker AG v Poland (Partial Award (Jurisdiction))* (UNCITRAL, 10 December 2008) para 167.

[44] *Fraport (Award)* (n 38) para 402.

[45] *Plama Consortium Ltd v Bulgaria (Award)* (ICSID Arbitral Tribunal, Case No ARB/03/24, 27 August 2008) para 133. For a recent case accepting the *Plama v Bulgaria* approach see *Yukos Universal Ltd (Isle of Man) v Russian Federation (Final Award)* (Permanent Court of Arbitration, Case No AA 227, 18 July 2014). See also *SAUR v International SA v Argentina (Jurisdiction and Liability)* (ICSID Arbitral Tribunal, Case No ARB/04/4, 6 June 2012) para 308, where the tribunal held that compliance with domestic law is an implicit requirement for the protection of an investment even in the absence of an 'in accordance with host state law' clause.

[46] *Energy Charter Treaty*, signed 17 December 1994, 2080 UNTS 95 (entered into force 16 April 1998).

[47] *Plama* (n 45) paras 138–40 (emphasis in original) (citations omitted).

Referring to the applicable law clause in article 26(6) of the ECT, which provides that '[a] tribunal established under [the ECT] shall decide the issues in dispute in accordance with this treaty and applicable rules and principles of international law', the tribunal reasoned that international law prohibited an investment obtained by deceitful conduct from receiving treaty protection. Specifically, the tribunal relied on the decisions in *Inceysa v El Salvador* and *World Duty Free v Kenya* as authority for the proposition that fraud constitutes a violation of the principles of good faith and *nemo auditor propriam turpitudinem allegans* and is contrary to 'international public policy'.[48] The tribunal concluded that the misrepresentation by the claimant was contrary to these principles of international law, with the result that the substantive protections under the ECT should not be afforded to the investment.[49]

That the tribunal stressed not only illegality under Bulgarian law, but also breaches of principles of international law, was probably due to the absence of an explicit reference to domestic legality in the ECT. Moreover, the tribunal may have understood article 26(2) of the ECT as precluding the tribunal from considering domestic law, therefore using principles of international law, including good faith, as a functional equivalent to the *renvoi* to domestic law effectuated by an 'in accordance with host state law' clause. Yet, reliance on good faith seems by no means necessary as an independent obligation incumbent on foreign investors to ground the binding nature of domestic law in the absence of explicit 'in accordance with host state law' clauses.

Instead, compliance with domestic law should more simply be understood as a general duty incumbent on foreign investors as a general principle of law that requires no specific recognition in an international investment agreement. This understanding stresses the host state's responsibility for determining which investments it wants to admit and reduces the risk of tribunals excluding from investment treaty protection investments that are perfectly legal under domestic law. In other words, a breach of good faith, without more, should not be used to exclude an investment from protection under an investment treaty and to deprive a treaty-based tribunal of jurisdiction under an 'in accordance with host state law' clause.

### 5.2.2 Good faith limitations on the host state's invocation of domestic illegality

Rejecting an independent role for good faith as a source of investor obligation in the case of domestic illegality does not mean, however, that the concept of good faith has no application at all in this context. On the contrary, good

[48] ibid paras 141–42. [49] ibid paras 143–46.

faith can play a role in moderating how the host state invokes domestic illegality. More specifically, the concept of estoppel, as an element of good faith, can be relied upon to prevent the host state from invoking domestic illegality in situations where the host state breached its own laws or where the host state knew about the investor's illegality and accepted it—either by (incorrectly) suggesting that the investment in question complied with domestic laws, or by continuing to cooperate with the investor on the basis of an illegal investment.

Thus, the tribunal in *Kardassopoulos v Georgia* held that the respondent could not maintain that state-owned enterprises with whom the claimant had entered into contractual agreements had acted ultra vires, contrary to domestic law. The tribunal clarified that the host state's control over access and conduct of foreign investors under an 'in accordance with host state law' clause:

> relates to the investor's actions in making the investment. It does not allow a State to preclude an investor from seeking protection under the BIT on the ground that its own actions are illegal under its own laws. In other words, a host State cannot avoid jurisdiction under the BIT by invoking its own failure to comply with its domestic law.[50]

In order to arrive at this result, the tribunal invoked the concept of estoppel, which prevented the respondent from invoking domestic illegality when the state's conduct had been 'cloaked with the mantle of Governmental authority',[51] given that two presidents and two prime ministers had endorsed the relevant agreements and implemented them.[52] The tribunal therefore found 'that Respondent created a legitimate expectation for Claimant that his investment was, indeed, made in accordance with Georgian law and, in the event of breach, would be entitled to treaty protection'.[53] Furthermore, the tribunal pointed to article 7 of the International Law Commission's 'Articles on State Responsibility',[54] which attribute to the state conduct of

[50] *Kardassopoulos* (n 32) para 182 (emphasis in original). See also *Inmaris Perestroika Sailing Maritime Services Gmbh v Ukraine (Decision on Jurisdiction)* (ICSID Arbitral Tribunal, Case No ARB/08/8, 8 March 2010) para 139; cf *Alpha Projektholding Gmbh v Ukraine (Award)* (ICSID Arbitral Tribunal, Case No ARB/07/16, 8 November 2010) para 299. See also Rahim Moloo and Alex Khachaturian, 'The Compliance with the Law Requirement in International Investment Law' (2011) 34 Fordham Intl LJ 1473, 1497–99; Hepburn (n 26) 549–58.

[51] *Kardassopoulos* (n 32) paras 193 and 194, quoting *Southern Pacific Properties (Middle East) Ltd v Egypt (Award)* (ICSID Arbitral Tribunal, Case No ARB/84/3, 20 May 1992) paras 81–83, 85.

[52] See *Kardassopoulos* (n 32) para 191. [53] ibid para 192.

[54] *Responsibility of States for Internationally Wrongful Acts*, GA Res 56/83, UN GAOR, 56th sess, 85th plen mtg, Supp No 49, UN Doc A/RES/56/83, A/45/49(Vol I)/Corr.4 (28 January 2002, adopted 12 December 2001) annex.

an entity exercising governmental authority even if the acts in question were ultra vires.[55] In any event, estoppel requires that the host state knew about the illegality and deliberately accepted it.[56]

While *Kardassopoulos* relates to the application of estoppel in the presence of an 'in accordance with host state law' clause in the underlying treaty, the same reasoning should apply when no such clause is at issue. The only difference, again, will be the context in which estoppel is to be addressed, namely as a question of the merits, rather than jurisdiction as is the case with an 'in accordance with host state law' clause. In both situations, arbitral tribunals should therefore apply the concept of estoppel in order to reject the state's claim that breaches of domestic law entailed a loss of treaty protection of the investment in question. In estoppel cases, good faith therefore functions as a discipline on the invocation by the host state of its own laws, in line with the role of good faith in public law to limit a state's exercise of authority.

### 5.2.3 Good faith and compliance with international law

Situations in which an investment breaches domestic law should be distinguished from the scenario where there is no breach of domestic law, but the investment is contrary to international standards, such as transnational public policy.[57] In such a scenario, good faith may legitimately have an independent role to play in determining the scope of protection of an investment *ratione materiae* and has been invoked accordingly by arbitral tribunals. For example, in *Phoenix v Czech Republic*, the tribunal held that 'investments made in violation of the most fundamental rules of protection of human rights, like

[55] *Kardassopoulos* (n 32) para 90; *Railroad Development Corp v Guatemala (Second Decision on Objections to Jurisdiction)* (ICSID Arbitral Tribunal, Case No. ARB/07/23, 18 May 2010) para 146.

[56] *Fraport (Award)* (n 38) paras 347 and 387.

[57] We purposefully use the term 'transnational public policy' in order to refer to a universal conception of public policy that transcends state boundaries and not a notion, such as 'international public policy', which is often tied to policy considerations of a particular national legal system in a transborder context. The International Law Association, in its *Interim Report on Public Policy as a Bar to Enforcement of International Arbitral Awards* (London Conference, 2000) succinctly defined transnational public policy or 'truly international public policy' as 'comprising fundamental rules of natural law, principles of universal justice, jus cogens in public international law, and the general principles of morality accepted by what are referred to as civilized nations'. For other similar definitions of transnational public policy see: Pierre Lalive, 'Transnational (or Truly International) Public Policy in International Arbitration' in Pieter Sanders (ed), *Comparative Arbitration Practice and Public Policy in Arbitration* (ICCA Congress Series No 3, 1987) 295–96; Martin Hunter and Gui Conde E Silva, 'Transnational Public Policy and Its Application in Investment Arbitrations' (2003) 4(3) JWIT 367; Michael Pryles, 'Reflections on Transnational Public Policy' (2007) 24(1) J Intl Arb 1; David Cairns, 'Transnational Public Policy and the Internal Law of State Parties' (2009) 6(1) TDM 27.

investments made in pursuance of torture or genocide or in support of slavery or trafficking of human organs' should not be granted investment protection, regardless of whether such acts are contrary to domestic law.[58] Foreign investments, in other words, must comply not only with domestic law but also with international law.

Such an analysis makes sense, as it is difficult to argue that one part of international law protects certain investment activities that other parts of international law plainly prohibit. Yet, since international law usually does not impose obligations directly on foreign investors, international legal prohibitions must be transformed into obligations that bind foreign investors. Domestic law is the usual vehicle for this transformation. In the absence of relevant domestic law, however, the obligation of foreign investors to comply with the principle of good faith may bring compliance with international law into the investment protection context.

At the same time, in order to counter the dangers inherent in the use of a broad notion of good faith, which risks importing subjective biases of the arbitrator into the decision-making process, it seems preferable to conduct the analysis in question with compliance of foreign investment with transnational public policy as the focal point. Although reliance on transnational public policy is similar to reliance on good faith, transnational public policy is arguably a more concrete concept that requires arbitrators to make a reasoned decision based on international legal instruments that prohibit the investment activities at stake. In other words, the thought process used and reasoning laid out by a tribunal will be different when relying on good faith as compared to transnational public policy. As cautioned by the tribunal in *World Duty Free v Kenya*, arbitrators are required to 'carefully check the objective existence of a particular transnational public policy rule in identifying it through international conventions, comparative law and arbitral awards'.[59]

Practically, the most relevant example for the invocation of transnational public policy is where corruption is not contrary to the national law of the host state, even though it is contrary to international law and international (or transnational) public policy.[60] Particularly noteworthy for the development of the notion of transnational public policy is the decision in *World Duty Free v Kenya*, which involved a foreign investor bribing the Kenyan

[58] *Phoenix* (n 1) para 78.

[59] *World Duty Free Co Ltd v Kenya (Award)* (ICSID Arbitral Tribunal, Case No ARB/00/7, 4 October 2006) para 141.

[60] Other situations, which are not further discussed here, would be investments in industries that are contrary to internationally outlawed activities, such as investments in the production of illegal drugs.

president in order to be awarded a contract for the construction, maintenance, and operation of duty-free complexes at the Nairobi and Mombassa international airports.[61] This act of corruption, the tribunal decided, not only breached Kenyan law, with the effect that the contract was voidable,[62] but was also contrary to 'international public policy' or 'transnational public policy', understood as 'signifying an international consensus as to universal standards and accepted norms of conduct that must be applied in all fora'.[63] The tribunal noted that the concept of transnational public policy must be applied cautiously,[64] and it relied not only on Kenyan law at the time of the incident but also on various international agreements sanctioning corruption, universally as well as specifically in Europe and Africa, and on decisions of arbitral tribunals sitting in commercial arbitrations.[65] The tribunal concluded:

> In light of domestic laws and international conventions relating to corruption, and in light of the decisions taken in this matter by courts and arbitral tribunals, this Tribunal is convinced that bribery is contrary to the international public policy of most, if not all, States or, to use another formula, to transnational public policy. Thus, claims based on contracts of corruption or on contracts obtained by corruption cannot be upheld by this Arbitral Tribunal.[66]

In this case, strictly speaking, illegality could have been based on domestic law. Nevertheless, in light of Kenya's compliance with international norms on corruption, the case is important for its careful analysis of international legal instruments in determining the content of transnational public policy. This methodology is exemplary, and could be employed similarly, in cases where the domestic law in question falls short of accepted international standards in other respects, such as investments in the production of illegal drugs or enterprises that facilitate the recruitment of children or human trafficking.

Another more recent contract-based ICSID arbitration, *Niko Resources v Bangladesh,* is equally noteworthy in its treatment of corruption and its analysis of the content of transnational public policy. The tribunal

[61] *World Duty Free* (n 59) para 136. [62] See ibid para 164.

[63] ibid para 139, citing Pierre Lalive, *Transnational (or Truly International) Public Policy and International Arbitration* (1986) 3 ICCA Congress Series 257 and International Law Association, 'International Commercial Arbitration on Public Policy as a Bar to Enforcement of International Arbitral Awards' (Report of the 70th Conference, New Delhi, 2002).

[64] *World Duty Free* (n 59) para 141.

[65] See ibid paras 142–57. On how corruption has been addressed by tribunals in commercial arbitration, see Abdulhay Sayed, *Corruption in International Trade and Commercial Arbitration* (Kluwer 2004).

[66] *World Duty Free* (n 59) 157.

ultimately found that the payment of bribes in 2005 to Bangladesh's then State Minister of Energy and Mineral Resources in connection with the development of gas fields, which resulted in a criminal conviction of the investor in Canada, had no influence on the investor–state contract in question.[67] The tribunal accepted the statement in the *World Duty Free v Kenya* case that corruption is 'contrary to international public policy of most, if not all, States or, to use another formula, to transnational public policy',[68] but it distinguished the case before it based on the absence of a causal link between the act of corruption and the earlier conclusion of the investor–state contract.[69]

Even though the contracts were not obtained by corruption, the respondent argued that the 'act of bribery linked to the investment' should deny the foreign investor protection. The respondent invoked three arguments: (i) that the offer of ICSID arbitration applied only to investments made in good faith; (ii) that accepting jurisdiction would jeopardize the integrity of the ICSID dispute settlement mechanism; and (iii) that the unclean hands doctrine would exclude the tribunal's jurisdiction.[70]

With regard to the first argument, the tribunal distinguished between cases in which jurisdiction is based on an investment treaty and those brought pursuant to a contractual dispute. In the former situation, states make an offer to 'an unknown number of unidentified foreign investors', and in such circumstances the host state may be justified in 'offer[ing] access to the dispute settlement regime provided by the treaty only subject to certain conditions'.[71] In the latter situation, however, involving 'a firm agreement binding both parties to submit their disputes to ICSID arbitration … the alleged or established lack of good faith in the investment does not justify the denial of jurisdiction but must be considered as part of the merits of the dispute'.[72]

The tribunal also rejected the second argument, based on the need to safeguard the integrity of the ICSID system, because according to the tribunal 'such integrity is promoted, and not violated, by the adjudication of disputes submitted to the Centre under a valid consent to arbitrate'.[73]

Finally, the tribunal addressed the clean hands argument. Although it recognized that the clean hands doctrine 'in international law remains controversial and its precise content is ill defined',[74] the tribunal referred to a three part test developed by an arbitral tribunal established pursuant to the *UN*

[67] *Niko Resources (Bangladesh) Ltd v Bangladesh (Decision on Jurisdiction)* (ICSID Arbitral Tribunal, Case No ARB/10/11, ARB/10/18, 19 August 2013) paras 423–29.

[68] ibid para 431. [69] ibid para 455. [70] ibid para 466. [71] ibid para 469.

[72] ibid paras 470–71. [73] ibid para 474. [74] ibid para 477.

*Convention on the Law of the Sea*:[75] '(i) the breach must concern a continuing violation, (ii) the remedy sought must be "*protection against continuance of that violation in the future*", not damages for past violations and (iii) there must be a relationship of reciprocity between the obligations considered'.[76] In applying this test, the tribunal in *Niko Resources* found that the criteria had not been met:

> Here the violation on which the Respondents rely is not continuing, but consisted in two acts that have been completed long ago; the remedy which the Claimant seeks does not concern protection against this past violation; and there is no relation of reciprocity between the relief which the Claimant now seeks in this arbitration and the acts in the past which the Respondents characterise as involving unclean hands.[77]

In both *World Duty Free* and *Niko Resources,* the tribunals resorted to transnational public policy. Especially noteworthy is the rigorous analysis conducted by the *World Duty Free* tribunal, which was later accepted by *Niko Resources*, in order to determine that the prohibition of bribery forms part of transnational public policy. The detailed review of both international and domestic legal sources as well as secondary sources of learned writers provides an important check on arbitrator discretion. Compared to the principle of good faith, which often imports subjective prejudices and biases of the arbitrator, transnational public policy is less open to such abuse. This is as true for contract-based investment arbitration cases as it is for treaty-based disputes.

In sum, as regards the impact of good faith as a limitation on the scope of protection of foreign investments *ratione materiae*, in our view only two situations arise in which good faith should legitimately enter the discussion. First, good faith can be used as a mechanism of estoppel, whereby a host state may be barred from raising an illegality claim because it either accepted or encouraged the illegality committed by the foreign investor. Second, good faith can be used to limit investment protection where the foreign investor contravened transnational public policy but, because the domestic laws of the host state have not implemented such policy, the domestic laws of the host state were not breached. Beyond these two limited cases, good faith should have no scope in restricting the scope of protected investments.

[75] The tribunal referred to the test set out by Hudson J in *Guyana v Suriname (Award)* (Permanent Court of Arbitration, 17 September 2007) paras 420–21.

[76] *Niko Resources* (n 67) para 481 (emphasis in original).

[77] ibid para 483. But see the decision in *Yukos v Russia* (n 45) paras 1338–63, where the tribunal held that a general principle of law does not exist that would bar an investor from making a claim under an investment treaty because of unclean hands.

## 5.3 Corporate Structuring and Good Faith

In addition to the legality of an investment, good faith may also enter the decision-making process in regard to the legality of the investor. This can occur at two entry points. The first is in regard to nationality planning at the pre-investment stage. While there is nothing per se illegal or improper with an investor strategically organizing its investment in ways that maximize protection under an applicable investment treaty, good faith may be used as a tool to place limits on nationality planning where there has been an abuse of corporate form. The second way that good faith can enter a discussion regarding the legality of the investor concerns corporate restructuring after the investment was made. In this context, several tribunals have relied on good faith, under the guise of an abuse of process, to dismiss jurisdiction. However, as these cases focus on the timing of the restructuring, most of them could have been easily resolved using a *ratione temporis* analysis rather than an abuse of process analysis. This considerably limits the need to have recourse to the concept of good faith and hence decreases the risk of an overly broad discretion in the hands of arbitrators when good faith is used.[78]

### 5.3.1 Nationality planning at the pre-investment stage

Good faith has a very small, if any, role to play in controlling nationality planning at the pre-investment stage. In principle, there is nothing either illegal or improper per se with an investor that engages in nationality planning in order to avail itself of protection under an applicable investment treaty.[79] As Christoph Schreuer notes:

> The establishment of companies so as to obtain benefits from domestic law and treaties is neither unethical nor illegal and is standard practice in international economic relations. Nationality planning has become as much a standard feature of diligent management as tax planning.[80]

Similarly, arbitral tribunals have continuously rejected arguments made by respondents to pierce the corporate veil to determine the true nationality

[78] For a different view see Tania Voon, Andrew Mitchell and James Munro, 'Legal Responses to Corporate Maneuvering in International Investment Arbitration' (2014) 5 JIDS 41, 60–66, arguing that greater acceptance of principles such as good faith and the doctrine of abuse of rights 'could increase coherence in international investment law and provide for more principled decision-making' (ibid 65).

[79] See Christoph Schreuer, 'Nationality Planning' in Arthur Rovine (ed), *Contemporary Issues in International Arbitration and Mediation* (Martinus Nijhoff 2013) 17; Mark Feldman, 'Setting Limits on Corporate Nationality Planning in Investment Treaty Arbitration' (2012) 27(2) ICSID Rev 281.

[80] Schreuer (n 79) 19.

of a locally incorporated company, instead preferring to rely on the text of the applicable investment treaty. This was the approach taken by the majority of the tribunal in *Tokios Tokelés v Ukraine.* In this case, a company that was incorporated in Lithuania but fully owned and controlled by Ukrainian nationals brought a claim against Ukraine.[81] The respondent urged the tribunal 'to "pierce the corporate veil" ... and determine the nationality of the company according to the nationality of its predominant shareholders and managers' because 'find[ing] jurisdiction in the case would be tantamount to allowing Ukrainian nationals to pursue international arbitration against their own government, which ... would be inconsistent with the object and purpose of the ICSID Convention'.[82]

While resounding in the forceful dissent of the tribunal's president,[83] the fact that the company was controlled by nationals of the host state did not matter in the view of the majority. The majority relied on the object and purpose of the investment treaty (protecting and promoting investments in order to justify a broad interpretation of the notion of investor)[84] and also, making an *e contrario* argument, pointed to the non-existence of a 'denial of benefits' clause that other investment treaties used in order to exclude the protection of such investments.[85] As a result, the tribunal allowed the claim by the corporate investor to proceed, despite its being owned and controlled by nationals of the host state.

However, referring to the *Barcelona Traction* case, the tribunal accepted exceptions granting treaty protection to corporate structures if this was necessary 'to prevent the misuse of the privileges of legal personality, as in certain cases of fraud or malfeasance, to protect third persons such as a creditor or purchaser, or to prevent the evasion of legal requirements or of obligations'.[86] This statement can be understood as a reference to the principle of good faith.

The dissent of the tribunal's president notwithstanding, subsequent jurisprudence has largely continued the trend of the majority decision in *Tokios Tokelés* to allow the protection of host state reinvestments under investment

[81] *Tokios Tokelés v Ukraine (Decision on Jurisdiction)* (ICSID Arbitral Tribunal, Case No ARB/02/18, 29 April 2004) paras 21–71.

[82] ibid para 22.

[83] ibid Dissenting Opinion by Prosper Weil.

[84] *Tokios Tokelés* (n 81) para 31, quoting *SGS v Philippines (Decision on Jurisdiction)* (ICSID Arbitral Tribunal, Case No ARB/02/6, 29 January 2004) para 116.

[85] *Tokios Tokelés* (n 81) paras 35–36, citing *Compañia de Aguas del Aconquija v Argentina (Decision on Annulment)* (ICSID Arbitral Tribunal, Case No ARB/97/3, 3 July 2002) para 112. In addition, the tribunal argued that its view was consistent with a number of other ICSID awards and the opinions of ICSID scholars: paras 40–52.

[86] *Tokios Tokelés* (n 81) para 53, citing *Barcelona Traction, Light and Power Co Ltd (Belgium v Spain) (Judgment)* [1970] ICJ Rep 3, 58.

treaties and to decline looking behind the corporate veil.[87] In the absence of limiting language, arbitral jurisprudence therefore allows even mere shell or mailbox companies to be protected as investors under an investment treaty that determines corporate nationality according to the place of incorporation.

This jurisprudence is consistent with the ordinary meaning approach to treaty interpretation under the *VCLT* and also with the determination of corporate nationality under customary international law, which, as the ICJ in *Barcelona Traction* observed, 'traditional[ly] attribute[d] the right of diplomatic protection of a corporate entity to the State under the laws of which it is incorporated and in whose territory it has its registered office'.[88] Moreover, from a policy perspective, there is no reason to interpret corporate nationality restrictively by requiring substantial links beyond incorporation, and thus to deny the protection of an investment treaty to shell or mailbox companies. What is decisive is not how investment activity is channelled into a foreign country but rather that such investment activity takes place. In view of the object and purpose of investment treaties to promote foreign investments, it should matter little for the host state where the capital for such investments comes from and what relations a corporate investor has with the state of its incorporation.

At the same time, arbitral tribunals have also acknowledged that the only time the corporate veil should be pierced is when there has been an abuse of corporate form and such piercing will 'prevent the misuse of the privileges of legal personality',[89] or where the 'real beneficiary of the business misused corporate formalities in order to disguise its true identity and to avoid liability'.[90] Unfortunately, the jurisprudence has not identified circumstances where abusive corporate form would meet the exceptions identified in the *Barcelona Traction* case and successfully deprive the tribunal of jurisdiction. The *Tokios Tokelés* tribunal confessed that '[t]he ICJ did not attempt to define in *Barcelona Traction* the precise scope of conduct that might prompt a tribunal to pierce the corporate veil' but nonetheless was

[87] See, eg, *Aguas del Tunari SA v Bolivia (Decision on Repondent's Objections to Jurisdiction)* (ICSID Arbitral Tribunal, Case No ARB/02/3, 21 October 2005) para 237; *ADC v Hungary (Award)* (ICSID Arbitral Tribunal, Case No ARB/03/16, 2 October 2006) paras 335–62; *Saluka v Czech Republic (Partial Award)* (UNCITRAL, 17 March 2006) paras 222–42; *Rompetrol Group NV v Romania (Decision on Respondent's Preliminary Objections on Jurisdiction and Admissibility)* (ICSID Arbitral Tribunal, Case No ARB/06/3, 18 April 2008) para 83; *KT Asia Investment Group BV v Kazakhstan (Award)* (ICSID Arbitral Tribunal, Case No ARB/09/8, 17 October 2013) para 134.

[88] See *Barcelona Traction* (n 86) 70.

[89] *Tokios Tokelés* (n 81) 53.

[90] *ADC* (n 87) para 358. See also *Aguas del Tunari* (n 87) para 245; *Saluka* (n 87) para 230; *KT Asia v Kazakhstan* (n 87) para 134.

satisfied 'that none of the Claimant's conduct ... constitute[d] an abuse of legal personality'.[91] Similarly, the tribunal in *Autopista v Venezuela* failed to identify any circumstances in which an abuse of right exception to nationality planning may warrant a dismissal of the case. The tribunal simply stated that '[n]o such circumstances are present' in this case.[92] Such reasoning fails to provide any content to the abuse of right exception.[93] While there may be cases in which an abuse of form argument is compelling, no such case has yet arisen. As future tribunals explore the abuse of right exception first articulated in the *Barcelona Traction* and more fully articulate the role of good faith in this context, the scope of application of this exception should be limited.

### 5.3.2 Corporate restructuring

The principle of good faith has also entered arbitral decisions concerning post-investment corporate restructuring. In these cases, tribunals have relied on good faith to dismiss claims based on an abuse of process.[94] With corporate restructuring cases, the main issue for the tribunals has been the timing of the restructuring—ie whether it occurs before or after the dispute has arisen. The cases in *Phoenix v Czech Republic* and *Mobil v Venezuela* are prime examples of such an approach.

In *Phoenix v Czech Republic*, Phoenix, an Israeli incorporated company that was controlled by a Czech citizen, Mr Beno, acquired two Czech companies in 2002 while the two companies were involved in ongoing litigation in the Czech courts. Two months after the purchase of the Czech companies, Phoenix gave notice to the Czech Republic of the existence of an investment dispute. The respondent argued that the tribunal lacked jurisdiction *ratione temporis* because the acts alleged by the claimant occurred before Phoenix had acquired the two Czech companies.[95] Additionally, the respondent argued that the tribunal lacked jurisdiction *ratione materiae* because there was no 'investment' within the meaning of article 25 of the *ICSID Convention*

[91] *Tokios Tokelés* (n 81) para 56.

[92] *Autopista Concesionada de Venezuela v Venezuela (Decision on Jurisdiction)* (ICSID Arbitral Tribunal, Case No ARB/00/5, 27 September 2001) para 67.

[93] For other cases that follow a similar approach see: *Saluka* (n 87) para 238; *ADC* (n 87) para 358.

[94] By contrast, in *Banro American Resources v Democratic Republic of the Congo (Award of the Tribunal)* (ICSID Arbitral Tribunal, Case No ARB/98/7, 1 September 2000) para 24, the tribunal relied on transnational public policy rather than good faith to analyse corporate restructuring that had taken place in order to have access to ICSID arbitration only after the dispute had arisen and shortly before initiating an ICSID claim.

[95] *Phoenix* (n 1) para 36. For acts that may have occurred after the acquisition, the respondent argued that they should be 'analyzed as a logical extension of the prior acts'.

and the relevant BIT.[96] Finally, the respondent maintained that the claims should be dismissed based on an abuse of process as the claimant company was 'nothing more than an *ex post facto* creation of a sham Israeli entity created by a Czech fugitive from justice, Vladimir Beno, to create diversity of nationality'.[97] According to the respondent, 'such abusive treaty-shopping is directly at odds with the fundamental object and purpose of the ICSID Convention and the BIT, which are meant to encourage *international* investment'.[98]

The tribunal's analysis focused on whether the tribunal had jurisdiction *ratione materiae* (ie whether there was a legal dispute arising directly out of an investment).[99] The tribunal modified the well-known *Salini* criteria used to determine whether an investment exists under the *ICSID Convention*. In addition to the four *Salini* criteria ((i) a contribution in money or other assets; (ii) a certain duration; (iii) an element of risk; and (iv) an operation made in order to develop an economic activity in the host state) the tribunal appended two additional criteria—(v) assets invested in accordance with the laws of the host state and (vi) assets invested *bona fide*.[100] The tribunal's assessment focused on the last criterion (ie whether the underlying investment was made in good faith). The tribunal stated:

> States cannot be deemed to offer access to the ICSID dispute settlement mechanism to investments not made in good faith. The protection of international investment arbitration cannot be granted if such protection would run contrary to the general principles of international law, among which the principle of good faith is of utmost importance.[101]

The tribunal recalled that the principle of good faith exists in both the national and international legal orders.[102] The tribunal held that the principle of good faith governs not only 'the relations between States' in public international law 'but also the legal rights and duties of those seeking to assert an international claim under a treaty', as in the case of investment treaty arbitration.[103] In regard to the case at hand, the 'tribunal [was] concerned … with the *international principle of good faith as applied to the international arbitration mechanism of ICSID*'.[104]

[96] ibid para 38. [97] ibid para 34 (emphasis in original).

[98] ibid para 34 (emphasis in original). [99] ibid paras 72–73.

[100] ibid paras 114–44. This approach was expressly refuted in both *Metal-Tech* (n 43) para 127 and *Quiborax SA v Bolivia (Decision on Jurisdiction)* (ICSID Arbitral Tribunal, Case No ARB/06/2, 27 September 2012) para 226, where the tribunals rejected the argument that a legality requirement forms part of the objective definition of an investment under *ICSID Convention* art 25. See also *Vannessa Ventures Ltd v Venezuela (Award)* (ICSID Arbitral Tribunal, Case No ARB(AF)/04/6, 16 January 2013) para 113.

[101] *Phoenix* (n 1) para 106. [102] ibid para 109. [103] ibid para 107.

[104] ibid para 113 (emphasis in original).

The tribunal provided four factors to consider when determining whether an investment is made 'in compliance with the international principle of good faith':[105] (i) the timing of the investment; (ii) the timing of the claim; (iii) the substance of the transaction; and (iv) the true nature of the operation.[106] Applying these facts, the tribunal found that the claimant's initiation and pursuit of ICSID arbitration constituted an abuse of process.[107] Specifically, the tribunal found that: (i) 'all damages claimed by Phoenix had already occurred and were inflicted on the two Czech companies, when the alleged investment was made;'[108] (ii) 'Phoenix notified the host state of the existence of an investment dispute even before'[109] it registered ownership of the two Czech companies; (iii) the 'investment was a mere redistribution of assets within the Beno family';[110] and (iv) there were 'strong indicia that no economic activity in the market place was either performed or even intended by Phoenix'.[111] Overall, the tribunal found that the purchase of the two Czech companies 'was an attempt to render their purely domestic disputes subject to the protections of the BIT rather than to conduct business'.[112] Consequently, the tribunal found no protected investment under the *ICSID Convention* and BIT because of an abuse of right.[113]

Similarly, in *Mobil v Venezuela*, an arbitral tribunal had to consider whether corporate restructuring for the sole purpose of gaining access to ICSID arbitration constituted an abuse of process. Mobil Corporation invested in the exploration and production of petroleum in Venezuela in the 1990s. In 2004, Venezuela took a number of measures to regulate the petroleum industry including royalty and tax increases and in 2007, by decree, Venezuela nationalized Mobil's investments. In 2005, Mobil, a US company, inserted a Netherlands entity, Venezuela Holdings, into its ownership structure for the purpose of obtaining protection under the Netherlands–Venezuela BIT.[114] The respondent submitted that Venezuela Holdings was a mere 'corporation of convenience' created for the sole purpose of gaining access to ICSID arbitration. The respondent characterized this restructuring as an 'abuse of the corporate form and blatant treaty-shopping'.[115]

[105] ibid para 113. [106] ibid paras 136–40. [107] ibid para 144.
[108] ibid para 136. [109] ibid para 138. [110] ibid para 139.
[111] ibid para 140. [112] ibid para 141. [113] ibid para 144.

[114] *Agreement on Encouragement and Reciprocal Protection of Investments between the Kingdom of the Netherlands and the Republic of Venezuela*, signed 22 October 1991, 1788 UNTS 45 (entered into force 1 November 1993).

[115] *Mobil Corp, Venezuela Holdings BV v Venezuela (Decision on Jurisdiction)* (ICSID Arbitral Tribunal, Case No ARB/07/27, 10 June 2010) para 27.

Like the *Phoenix* tribunal, the *Mobil* tribunal referred to the general principle of good faith to determine whether Mobil's restructuring to create a Dutch holding company constituted an abuse of right. The tribunal mentioned that, 'in all systems of law, whether domestic or international, there are concepts framed in order to avoid misuse of the law' and that one of these concepts includes the principle of good faith.[116] The tribunal maintained that a contextual approach, which takes into account the circumstances of each case, must be used to determine whether a restructuring constitutes an abuse of right.[117] The tribunal found that 'the main, if not the sole purpose of the restructuring was to protect Mobil investments from adverse Venezuelan measures in getting access to ICSID arbitration through the Dutch-Venezuela BIT'.[118] Interestingly, the tribunal recognized that such restructuring purpose would not always constitute an abuse of process. Depending on the circumstances, restructuring could be either 'legitimate corporate planning' or an 'abuse of right'.[119]

In this case, the deciding factor for the tribunal was the timing of the restructuring. The tribunal distinguished between claims that arose prior to Mobil's corporate restructuring and those that arose afterwards. With regard to prospective disputes, the tribunal found that the restructuring for the purpose of gaining access to ICSID arbitration through the BIT 'was a perfectly legitimate goal'.[120] However:

> [w]ith respect to pre-existing disputes, the situation is different and the Tribunal considers that to restructure investments only in order to gain jurisdiction under a BIT for such disputes would constitute, to take the words of the Phoenix Tribunal, 'an abusive manipulation of the system of international investment protection under the ICSID Convention and the BITs'.[121]

Thus, the tribunal held that it had jurisdiction over the claims that came into existence after the restructuring (ie those concerning nationalization of the investment) but declined jurisdiction over the claims that had already existed prior to the restructuring (ie those concerning the tax and royalty increases).[122]

In both *Phoenix* and *Mobil*, the tribunals focused on whether the timing of the restructuring occurred before or after the dispute arose, and in both cases the dispute was analysed from an abuse of process perspective.[123]

[116] ibid para 169. [117] ibid para 177. [118] ibid para 190. [119] ibid para 191.
[120] ibid para 204. [121] ibid para 205 (quoting *Phoenix* (n 1) para 144).
[122] ibid para 206.
[123] The same approach was subsequently adopted in *Tidewater v Venezuela (Decision on Jurisdiction)* (ICSID Arbitral Tribunal, Case No ARB/10/5, 8 February 2013) paras 146–48 and

Yet, instead of relying on the vague concepts of good faith and abuse of process not found within the text of the treaty, the tribunals could have simply followed a more predictable approach based on the temporal scope of application of investment protection treaties (ie jurisdiction *ratione temporis*). Indeed, the general principle of non-retroactivity in the application of international treaties is well-established in international law[124] and is articulated in article 28 of the *VCLT*, according to which 'provisions do not bind a party in relation to any act or fact which took place or any situation which ceased to exist before the date of the entry into force of the treaty with respect to that party'. Analogously, the investment treaties at stake would not have applied *ratione personae* to conduct that had occurred prior to the restructuring of the investment.

In fact, in the *Phoenix* decision, the tribunal briefly analysed the temporal argument and found that it had no jurisdiction over claims arising prior to the purchase by Phoenix of the two Czech companies in 2002 or for acts occurring after the sale of the Czech companies in 2008.[125] Its introduction of an additional good faith requirement to limit investors' access to investment treaty arbitration in cases of corporate restructuring was therefore wholly superfluous. Likewise, the *Mobil* tribunal could have simply asked whether the alleged violation by the host state occurred before or after the claimant became an investor.[126] The tribunal would lack jurisdiction over acts that took place before the restructuring (ie before there was a qualified investor) but would maintain jurisdiction over acts taking place after the restructuring. In either *Phoenix* or *Mobil*, there would was no need to rely on good faith to determine jurisdiction.

Finally, the dispute in *Pac Rim v El Salvador* also concerned the legitimacy of a corporate restructuring for the purpose of gaining access to investment arbitration. The tribunal, in adopting the approach in *Mobil*, focused on the issue of timing to determine when a restructuring constituted legitimate corporate planning or an abuse of right.[127] However, the *Pac Rim* tribunal went a step further in clarifying exactly when a change of nationality will

*ConocoPhilips v Venzuela (Decision on Jurisdiction and the Merits)* (ICSID Arbitral Tribunal, Case No ARB/07/30, 3 September 2013) paras 279–80.

[124] See Nick Gallus, *The Temporal Scope of Investment Protection Treaties* (British Institute of International and Comparative Law 2008).

[125] *Phoenix* (n 1) paras 67–71.

[126] This was the approach taken by *ST-AD GmbH (Germany) v Bulgaria (Award on Jurisdiction)* (UNCITRAL, 18 July 2013) para 304.

[127] *Pac Rim Cayman LLC v El Salvador (Decision on the Respondent's Jurisdictional Objections)* (ICSID Arbitral Tribunal, Case No ARB/09/12, 1 June 2012) para 2.45. See also *ST-AD GmbH* (n 126) paras 412, 416–17.

become an abuse of process. In attempting to set out a standard for distinguishing between an actual dispute and an emerging dispute, the tribunal explained that:

> the dividing-line occurs when the relevant party can see an actual dispute or can foresee a specific future dispute as a very high probability and not merely as a possible controversy. In the Tribunal's view, before that dividing-line is reached, there will be ordinarily no abuse of process; but after that dividing-line is passed, there ordinarily will be. The answer in each case will, however, depend upon its particular facts and circumstances, as in this case.[128]

In the case at hand, the tribunal concluded that the restructuring occurred before the dispute was known or foreseen by the claimant and thus the abuse of right defence failed.[129] At the same time, the tribunal also recognized that this dividing-line will 'include a significant grey area'.[130]

Interestingly, unlike *Phoenix* and *Mobil*, the *Pac Rim* tribunal examined the timing issue both from a temporal and abuse of process perspective. It found that the time frame for determining an abuse of process is not the same as the time frame for determining an objection *ratione temporis*. With regard to jurisdiction *ratione temporis*, the relevant time frame 'is the date on which the measure, act, or fact that constitutes the alleged breach took place'[131] and, unlike cases of abuse of process, '[t]here is no reference to a claimant's knowledge or awareness of an alleged breach or present or future dispute'.[132] In situations involving an abuse of process, the time frame 'must necessarily be earlier in time than the date for deciding the Ratione Temporis issue',[133] and the claimant's knowledge is particularly important. The tribunal explained that it:

> is clearly an abuse for an investor to manipulate the nationality of a company subsidiary to gain jurisdiction under an international treaty at a time when the investor is aware that events have occurred that negatively affect its investment and may lead to arbitration. In particular, abuse of process must preclude unacceptable manipulations by a claimant acting in bad faith who is fully aware prior to the change in nationality of the 'legal dispute', as submitted by the Respondent.[134]

When dealing with a continuous act—an act or measure occurring before the claimant's change of nationality and continuing after the change—the tribunal would have jurisdiction *ratione temporis* but would lack jurisdiction on

[128] *Pac Rim* (n 127) para 2.99.

[129] ibid para 2.109. The tribunal found it lacked jurisdiction as a result of the 'denial of benefits' clause.

[130] ibid para 2.99.

[131] ibid para 2.102.

[132] ibid para 2.102.

[133] ibid para 2.107.

[134] ibid para 70.

the basis of an abuse of process because 'the Claimant had changed its nationality during that continuous practice knowing of an actual or specific future dispute'.[135]

The tribunal's emphasis on the intention of the claimant as the main distinction between *ratione temporis* and abuse of process unfortunately was not grounded in any legal authority or justification. Why intention matters for an abuse of process analysis, therefore, is not clear. Recently, in the *Lao Holdings v Lao People's Democratic Republic* case, the tribunal adopted the distinction made by the *Pac Rim* case. The tribunal imputed an element of bad faith intention into an abuse of process analysis and found that an abuse of process, unlike *ratione temporis*, mandates that the investor has knowledge or awareness 'that events have occurred that negatively affect its investment and may lead to arbitration'.[136]

The great problem with such reasoning is that it may be wholly unpredictable for investors and host states when exactly corporate restructuring becomes abusive and when it still complies with the good faith principle. Therefore, it is preferable that host states clearly set the conditions for which corporate restructuring is acceptable in their domestic laws or in investor–state contracts, as a question relating to the admission of foreign investments. As a result, the principle of good faith has little room to enter the interpretative process either at the nationality planning stage, where tribunals should rely on the explicit wording of the BIT, or at the corporate restructuring phase, where tribunals should approach the timing issue primarily from a *ratione temporis* angle rather than from the perspective of abuse of process.

## 5.4 Conclusion: Good Faith and the Rule of Law in International Investment Relations

Good faith is a concept that saturates all legal systems in the world, including investment treaty arbitration. However, given that investment treaty arbitration resembles neither a purely public nor a purely private law system, a dilemma arises when trying to inform the scope and content of the principle of good faith through reasoning by analogy. In public law, both national and international, the good faith principle operates, as part of the concept of the rule of law, so as to limit the authority or discretion of states. In private law, in contrast, good faith is used as a means of corrective justice to maintain or restore equality between two

[135] ibid para 2.107.

[136] *Lao Holdings v Lao People's Democratic Republic (Decision on Jurisdiction)* (ICSID Arbitral Tribunal, Case No ARB(AF)/12/6, 21 February 2014) para 70. The issues of *ratione temporis* analysis and abuse of process are also clearly and properly distinguished in *Renée Rose Levy and Gremcitel SA v Republic of Peru (Award)* (ICSID Arbitral Tribunal, Case No ARB/11/17, 9 January 2015) paras 182–6.

private parties.[137] In most cases, international investment arbitration follows the public law approach, imposing an obligation on the state rather than the foreign investor.[138] Nonetheless, arbitral tribunals have also assessed good faith through a private law lens and imposed an obligation not only on the state but also on the foreign investor. This has occurred when the investor is in a horizontal relationship with the state (ie contract-based arbitration) or where the investor engaged in internationally illegal activity in complicity with the host state, in particular corruption. Investment treaty arbitration therefore has used good faith as both a public and private law tool.

In this chapter, we have looked at the dual function of good faith in assessing the protection of *non-bona fide* investment activities and corporate structures under the relevant investment treaty. Yet, in both situations, good faith plays only a marginal role in existing arbitral jurisprudence. With regard to the compliance of investments with applicable rules, good faith enters the discussion through two avenues. The first is when arbitral tribunals review the relationship between good faith and domestic illegality, both with and without an explicit 'in accordance with host state law' clause. In both of these situations, in our view, there is no role for good faith in limiting the protection of investments—instead, the preferred yardstick is solely the domestic laws of the host state. Good faith, however, could be legitimately used as a public law tool to limit host state reliance on its own laws, in particular in estoppel cases. The second avenue for good faith to play a role occurs when the acquisition of the investment or the investment activity is contrary to transnational public policy, albeit compliant with domestic law. In these cases, good faith is properly used as a mechanism to limit the protection of foreign investments or access to investment arbitration.

In cases involving the protection *ratione personae* of investor-claimants, the role of good faith in assessing the legitimacy of nationality planning and corporate restructuring is equally negligible. Thus, arbitral jurisprudence has consistently accepted nationality planning as a legitimate instrument at the pre-investment stage, subject only to the reservation that an abuse of corporate form, as a sub-category of the principle of good faith, could lead to an exclusion of investment treaty protection in exceptional cases. However, no tribunal so far has relied on this exception, which, in any event, should be handled extremely restrictively. In cases of corporate restructuring, although

[137] Steven Reinhold, 'Good Faith in International Law' (2013) 2 UCL JL & Jur 6–7.

[138] For instance, good faith often arises in the context of a host state's obligation to perform its international agreements. See, eg, *Saar Papier Vertriebes GmbH v Poland (Final Award)* (UNCITRAL, 16 October 1995) para 92; *Waste Management Inc v Mexico II (Final Award)* (ICSID Arbitral Tribunal, Case No ARB(AF)/00/3, 30 April 2004, para 138; *Canfor Corp v United States (Decision of Preliminary Question)* (UNCITRAL, 6 June 2006) para 182.

tribunals have relied on good faith where an abuse of process has been alleged, most cases could have just as effectively been analysed using a more stringent analysis of the temporal restrictions in the scope of application of investment treaties. Only the *Pac Rim* decision went further, by linking an abuse of corporate restructuring to the investor's intention to have access to investment treaty protection. Why such an intention is abusive was, however, not further explained. Reliance on good faith also seems unnecessary, because host states can make use of domestic law to regulate corporate structures of foreign investment projects.

Overall, arbitral tribunals that use good faith in analysing whether certain foreign investments or their corporate structure benefit from investment treaty protection should tread lightly. Although there are benefits in maintaining the principle, such as flexibility in interpreting and applying investment treaties and in keeping investment law open to outside norms, extensive reliance on good faith creates an unpredictable and uncertain legal environment that is subject to broad arbitrator discretion. This can endanger the rule of law in international investment relations. As a consequence, in order to keep an appropriate balance between arbitral flexibility and stability and predictability of investor–state relations, good faith should remain at the sidelines. The only times good faith should enter the discourse is in situations where the domestic law of the host state fails to regulate internationally objectionable activity and as a mechanism of estoppel. Otherwise, the emphasis should be on the responsibility of host state to regulate foreign investments and foreign investors through domestic law. Restricted in this way, the principle of good faith would allow both the national and the international rule of law to thrive in international investment relations.

# 6

# Good Faith, Corporate Nationality, and Denial of Benefits

*M Sornarajah*

## 6.1 Introduction

Good faith is an amorphous concept without specific content. Its application can be scoffed at for its uncertainty, lack of definite content, use as a vehicle for subjective preferences, and as a last ditch attempt at substantiating a difficult argument. But its inner core as a doctrine that deters obvious fraud and ensures that only those with clean hands are afforded a remedy can hardly be contested. In this core sense, it has an overarching presence that deters decisions in disputes that feature even a hint of fraud or malevolence on the part of the claimant. It is in that narrow and well-accepted sense that it needs to be used in considering the issue of corporate nationality in investment arbitration. Bad faith is indicated by fraud or malpractice on the part of the claimant. Law abjures fraud or anything tainted by fraud. Good faith is present in the absence of fraud and malpractice, when the claimant's hands are clean. There is no uncertainty involved in the use of this core principle of good faith. No instability occurs as a consequence of its use. It is in the interests of the international community as a whole that principles that oppose fraud and corruption are favoured over those that seek to justify chicanery by using formalistic interpretation of the written law.

In treaty law, it follows that when a treaty is fraudulently performed or there is malpractice even where the letter of the law is satisfied, there is bad faith. As the leading writer on treaties puts it, 'even if the words of the treaty are clear, if applying them would lead to a result that would be manifestly absurd or unreasonable, the parties must seek another interpretation'.[1] He justifies this view on the basis of the good faith principle. This view must

[1] Anthony Aust, *Modern Treaty Law and Practice* (CUP 2000) 185.

apply to the use of the device of corporate nationality in investment arbitration. Unfortunately, the picture that emerges is bleak: malpractices of investors have been permitted to triumph on the strained basis that the words of the treaty permit such a course. It is precisely such arguments that the good faith doctrine is designed to counter.

The series of awards on corporate nationality as the basis for invoking jurisdiction demonstrate that good faith has not deterred tribunals to any significant extent in expanding the jurisdictional scope of investment treaties by relying on a purely textual interpretation of the use of incorporation in the treaties as the test of corporate nationality.[2] The tribunals have not considered the extent to which the good faith principle should guide the outcome of the consideration of the issues of corporate nationality. They have often used the test of incorporation, the traditional test of corporate nationality in international law, [3] which is stated in the investment treaties concluded by common law states,[4] in a manner that defeats the object and purpose of both the investment treaties and the *Convention on the Settlement of Investment Disputes between States and Nationals of Other States* (*ICSID Convention*).[5] Such use raises the possibility that the tribunals may not have arrived at the conclusions they did had they considered the good faith principle.

The treaties in question had the object of promoting flows of foreign investment so that such investment could promote economic development in the poorer countries of the world. The result that the arbitrators have arrived at ensures that jurisdictional protection is given to corporations even though

[2] *ADC Affiliate Ltd v Hungary (Award)* (ICSID Arbitral Tribunal, Case No ARB/03/16, 2 October 2006) paras 357–58; *Tokios Tokelés v Ukraine (Decision on Jurisdiction)* (ICSID Arbitral Tribunal, Case No ARB/02/18, 29 April 2004) para 82; *Saluka Investments BV v Czech Republic (Partial Award)* (Permanent Court of Arbitration, 17 March 2006) paras 227–30; *Rompetrol Group NV v Romania (Decision on Respondent's Preliminary Objections on Jurisdiction and Admissibility)* (ICSID Arbitral Tribunal, Case No ARB/06/3, 18 April 2008) paras 83, 88, 92.

[3] *Barcelona Traction, Light and Power Co Ltd (Belgium v Spain) (Judgment)* [1970] ICJ Rep 3, paras 38, 39, 41; *Ahmadou Sadio Diallo (Republic of Guinea v Democratic Republic of the Congo) (Preliminary Objections)* [2007] ICJ Rep 552, paras 61, 62, 64. This was not always the test. Effectiveness and genuine connection played a role in determining nationality of physical persons: *Nottebohm Case (second phase) (Judgment)* [1955] ICJ Rep 4, 23–24.

[4] *Energy Charter Treaty*, signed 17 December 1994, 2080 UNTS 95 (entered into force 16 April 1998) art 1(7)(a); *North American Free Trade Agreement*, signed 17 December 1992 [1994] CTS 2 (entered into force 1 January 1994) art 201(1); *Agreement between the Government of the United Kingdom of Great Britain and Northern Ireland and the Government of the United Mexican States for the Promotion and Reciprocal Protection of Investments*, signed 12 May 2006 (entered into force 25 July 2007) art 1.

[5] *Convention on the Settlement of Investment Disputes between States and Nationals of Other States*, opened for signature 18 March 1965 (entered into force 14 October 1966) (*ICSID Convention*).

the assets of the corporation belong to nationals of the host country, or the corporation is inserted into a corporate structure of a multinational corporation only to enable the investor to acquire standing under an investment treaty with the respondent state. Neither situation promotes the object of states' economic development. The continuation of these trends led to the inclusion of denial of benefits clauses in investment treaties[6] (see the example in the annex) so that the respondent state could determine whether or not protection should be given to a foreign corporation. Through a denial of benefits clause, the state reserved to itself the power to decide whether the claimant entity has sufficient nexus with its contracting state partner to be considered a foreign investor of that state. But arbitrators have construed denial of benefits provisions narrowly,[7] so that the textual interpretations they had favoured continue to be accepted. Good faith has not played a role in the making of these decisions.

There is a problem to be examined here as to whether, in the light of the good faith doctrine, corporate standing has been properly found in the different jurisdictional awards relating to it.[8] They are the subject of discussion in the literature. Some regard these awards as illustrating one of the many instances in which the arbitrators have gone against the intent of states making the treaties.[9] Others regard them as instances of strict and proper construction of the relevant treaties. But the latter are not able to demonstrate why arbitrators—quite often the same arbitrators—adopt a teleological interpretation when it comes to other provisions in the treaties so as to favour the expansion of the law in investment treaties. This may demonstrate the absence of good faith in the arbitrators themselves, exposing them to the allegation of institutional bias.[10]

[6] *Treaty between the United States of America and the Argentine Republic concerning the Reciprocal Encouragement and Protection of Investment*, signed 14 November 1991 (entered into force 20 October 1994) art 1(2); *Agreement between the Republic of Austria and the Republic of Uzbekistan for the Promotion and Protection of Investments*, signed 2 June 2000 (entered into force 18 August 2001) art 10; *Agreement between Japan and the Socialist Republic of Viet Nam for the Liberalization, Promotion and Protection of Investment*, signed 14 November 2003 (entered into force 22 August 2006) art 22(2).

[7] *Generation Ukraine Inc v Ukraine (Final Award)* (ICSID Arbitral Tribunal, Case No ARB/00/9, 16 September 2003) para 15.7; *Plama Consortium Ltd v Bulgaria (Decision on Jurisdiction)* (ICSID Arbitral Tribunal, Case No ARB/03/24, 8 February 2005) paras 149–51.

[8] The situation of direct and indirect control of corporations with a hierarchy in the corporate structure is not considered here. See further chapter 5 of this volume.

[9] M Sornarajah, 'A Coming Crisis: Expansionary Trends in Investment Treaty Arbitration' in Karl Sauvant (ed), *Appeals Mechanism in International Investment Disputes* (OUP 2008) 39, 41.

[10] Gus Van Harten, *Investment Treaty Arbitration and Public Law* (OUP 2007) 167–75.

## 6.2 Corporate Nationality and Standing

This section focuses on the denial of benefits provisions in the context of corporate nationality, building on the broader discussion of good faith's role in this context in chapter 5. States began including a denial of benefits provision in investment treaties to cure problems arising from the literal interpretation of incorporation as the basis of corporate nationality in two principal situations: 'round-tripping' and 'the Dutch sandwich'. These two situations, necessitating the denial of benefits provisions, are the foci of this chapter. The literal interpretation permitted companies through mere incorporation of a company in the contracting state to acquire corporate nationality and thereby standing to sue under the treaty without having channelled any foreign investment into the other contracting party or without having any significant nexus with the state of incorporation.

The first situation in which corporate nationality is manipulated is where nationals of the respondent state take investment assets located in the respondent state to the territory of the other contracting party and incorporate a company in that state, vesting the assets in that company and then through the corporate vehicle bringing the investments back into the respondent state, which is in fact their home state. This was the situation in *Tokios Tokelés v Ukraine*.[11] This 'round-tripping' of investments seeks to exploit the incorporation theory of corporate nationality to secure investment protection for local investors. The literal interpretation of the investment treaty would permit recourse to establishing standing on the basis of such incorporation, as the company would be a national of the other contracting state, despite the fact that the owners of the assets as well as the assets themselves originated in the respondent state. The persons controlling the company are nationals of the respondent state. The situation qualifies the claimant corporation for protection based on the literal meaning of the treaty, as it has become a corporate national of the other contracting state. But, on a teleological interpretation, as the source of the funds is in the respondent state, no foreign investment flows into it and consequently no economic development (the objective of the treaty) arises. On that interpretation, the corporation will not qualify for protection. Likewise, since the *ICSID Convention* applies, as its title indicates, to disputes between states and nationals of other states, the dispute does not qualify for settlement by ICSID, as nationals of the respondent state control the investment.

The second situation of corporate nationality manipulation addressed in this chapter is referred to as the 'Dutch sandwich', because of the frequent

[11] *Tokios Tokelés* (n 2). The president of the tribunal, Professor Prosper Weil, dissented.

employment of Dutch treaties in using the technique. It involves the introduction of a subsidiary in the corporate structure through its incorporation in a state with favourable terms of investment protection purely for the sake of qualifying for investment protection, often in contemplation of arbitration or while a dispute is pending.[12] The subsidiary is often a 'postbox' company rather than a significant conduit for the transfer of funds. Its role is merely to provide standing to sue under the more advantageous investment treaty. Again, on a literal meaning, the treaty requirements for standing are satisfied, no foreign investment flows into the respondent state. The postbox company often does not have any funds to invest. Prima facie, any reasonable onlooker could see that both these situations involve techniques that subvert the aim of the investment treaty in promoting the flow of foreign investment for purposes of economic development. But that is not how arbitral tribunals have looked at the techniques. They have been permissive of both techniques.

In the context of these arbitral awards and corporate manipulation, states began to attempt in later treaties to prevent the abuse of incorporation through a provision on the denial of benefits. This provision enables the respondent state to deny the benefits of the treaty to a claimant company incorporated in the partner state where the incorporation was purely for the purpose of obtaining jurisdiction under the treaty and not for the purpose of making an investment through the company of funds belonging to the partner state. The intended cure has not always worked, as arbitrators have given a narrow interpretation to the denial of benefits clause. The manner in which tribunals have interpreted the denial of benefits provision raises the question whether the good faith principle has had any impact in this area of investment arbitration. The restoration of the good faith principle may help in dealing with the problems that have arisen in this field.

## 6.3 The Relevance of Good Faith to Corporate Nationality

Good faith is relevant as the basis for assessing the two situations relating to the interpretation of the provision on corporate nationality in the relevant treaties. The relevant treaties are the investment treaty on which the claim is based and the *ICSID Convention*, which provides for standing before ICSID tribunals. Both treaty instruments are premised on the fact

[12] As in the case in *Phillip Morris Asia Ltd v Australia* (Permanent Court of Arbitration, Case No 2012-12 (pending)). See Tania Voon, Andrew Mitchell and James Munro, 'Legal Responses to Corporate Manceuvring in International Investment Arbitration' (2014) 5 JIDS 41.

that the guarantee of investment protection will enhance flows of foreign investment and, consequently, the economic development of poorer states. The premise is stated in the preambular provisions of both treaty instruments. The *travaux préparatoires* of the *ICSID Convention* make clear that developing countries were given the understanding that secure means of settlement of investment disputes would promote flows of foreign investment. It is this understanding that led to a large number of developing states becoming party to the *ICSID Convention*.[13] Securing the stability of the investments is no doubt an objective, but the ultimate end of such security is the flow of investments to promote the economic development of the host state. A good faith interpretation requires adherence to the purposes of these treaty instruments so that investments that do not promote foreign investments and investors who do not make such beneficial investments are not protected under the instruments.

Analysis of the two situations where incorporation is used as the technique to enable standing for access to arbitration and thereby protection of the treaties, prima facie, indicates that good faith standards are not met. At one stage, leading law firms advertised that they would advise on how to obtain ICSID jurisdiction under favourable treaties. The simple secret, requiring no great expertise, was to incorporate postbox companies in the relevant states with effective treaties that relied on incorporation in the hope that the creation of a new subsidiary company within the corporate structure would be sufficient to enable the use of the treaty of the state of incorporation. Some tribunals announced that such 'corporate restructuring' or 'migration of companies' was permissible, the euphemisms hiding a naked abuse of the incorporation test of nationality.[14] Such restructuring was permitted even after the dispute had arisen, enabling the claimant to seek out a better treaty under which the claim could be brought.[15]

[13] The discussions leading to the signing of the *ICSID Convention* are found in Antonio Parra, *The History of ICSID* (OUP 2012); Anthony Sinclair, 'The Substance of Nationality Requirements in Investment Treaty Arbitration' (2005) 20 ICSID Rev 368.

[14] In *HICEE BV v Slovak Republic (Partial Award)* (Permanent Court of Arbitration, Case No 2009-11, 23 May 2011), the tribunal said: 'structured investments are not unusual, nor is there anything in the least reprehensible about it; structured investments are commonplace': para 103. In *Soufraki v United Arab Emirates (Award)* (ICSID Arbitral Tribunal, Case No ARB/02/7, 7 July 2004), the tribunal gratuitously suggested that the private claimant could have avoided the discomfiture of a successful jurisdictional contest by merely incorporating a company and contracting through it (para 83), thereby encouraging a possibly fraudulent practice. Arbitrators concede that something is wrong and profess 'some sympathy' for the view that shell companies that do no benefit the host state invoke the provisions of the treaty (*Saluka* (n 2) paras 240–41), but they seldom move towards finding irregularity. A possible explanation is subjective bias on the part of arbitrators.

[15] See part 6.6.2 below for detailed discussion.

The same argument arises in interpreting the *ICSID Convention*, which deals with a corporate national's standing to bring a claim before an ICSID tribunal. As indicated earlier, the title of the treaty states that it applies to disputes between states and nationals of other states. In the situation of round-tripping, the corporation is controlled by nationals of the same state. The preamble of the *ICSID Convention* mentions, as the object of the treaty, economic development through the flow of foreign investment resulting from a secure form of dispute settlement. For example, the preamble refers to the 'need for international cooperation for economic development and the role of private international investment therein'. The *ICSID Convention* itself was sold to developing countries by the World Bank on the basis that becoming party to the *ICSID Convention* would lead to greater flows of foreign investment. Thus, when the *ICSID Convention* was adopted the Bank stated that 'adherence to the Convention by a country would provide additional inducement and stimulate a larger flow of private international investment into its territories, which is the primary purpose of the Convention'.[16]

Neither of the two situations addressed here (round-tripping and the Dutch sandwich) involve any possibility of furthering the primary purpose of the *ICSID Convention*, as they give rise to no fresh investment flows. In both situations, the relevance of good faith may lead the tribunal to adopt an interpretation that takes account of the intention of the parties, which can be drawn from identifying the object and purpose of the treaty. Such intention is more relevant in arbitration, as the jurisdiction of the tribunal is dependent on the consent of the parties, which is evidenced in their intention in creating the tribunal and submitting to its jurisdiction. The role of good faith in treaty interpretation is therefore of crucial importance in determining the scope of incorporation as the test of nationality in foreign investment arbitration.

## 6.4 The Role of Good Faith in the Law of Treaties

### 6.4.1 Good faith in the *Vienna Convention on the Law of Treaties*

The issue as to whether corporate nationality could be used in establishing the standing of a corporation to sue under an investment treaty is a matter of interpretation of the relevant treaty. As discussed in chapter 3 of this volume,

[16] International Bank for Reconstruction and Development, *Report of the Executive Directors on the Convention on the Settlement of Investment Disputes Between States and Nationals of Other States* (International Bank for Reconstruction and Development 1965) para 12.

the *Vienna Convention on the Law of Treaties* (*VCLT*) recognizes that good faith is relevant in making such an interpretation. Article 31(1) of the *VCLT* states: 'A treaty shall be interpreted *in good faith* in accordance with the ordinary meaning to be given to the terms of the treaty *in their context and in the light of its object and purpose*'.[17] The next sub-paragraph states that the context shall include the preamble to the treaty and annexes.[18] I return to good faith in treaty interpretation below.

Good faith is mentioned in two other contexts in the *VCLT*. Article 18 requires a state to adhere in good faith to obligations in a treaty prior to ratification, which has no significance to the present discussion. But Article 26 of the *VCLT*, which requires good faith performance of the obligations of the treaty, is of great significance. Such an obligation can be meaningful only if the intention of the parties as evidenced in the object and purpose of the treaty is understood.[19] In the investment treaty, a claimant exercises a right to arbitration, which is usually obtained as a result of the corporate nationality of a contracting party to an investment treaty. The right forms part of the performance obligations under the treaty. The right to arbitration of the contracting party that originally arose from the rules on state responsibility under customary international law is exercised under the treaty by the investor itself, so that the contracting party is removed from the scene. This aspect of investment treaties was explained as achieving the depoliticization of investment dispute settlement by entrusting dispute settlement to ICSID. ICSID and the World Bank are performers in the treaty structure. The corporate citizen exercises the right of the contracting state to provide diplomatic protection.[20]

A home state is unlikely to want to protect a postbox company[21] or a company that is incorporated for the fraudulent purpose of obtaining standing under an investment treaty through round-tripping. Equally, the host state will

[17] *Vienna Convention on the Law of Treaties*, opened for signature 23 May 1969, 1155 UNTS 331 (entered into force 27 January 1980) (*VCLT*) (emphasis added). The next provision, art 31(2), states that the context shall include, among other things, the preamble of the treaty.

[18] *VCLT* (n 17) art 31(2). See Steven Reinhold, 'Good Faith in International Law' (2013) 2 UCL JL & Jur 40.

[19] Olivier Corten and Pierre Klein, *The Vienna Convention on the Law of Treaties: A Commentary* (OUP 2011).

[20] Different views exist, some regarding the right as derivative and others as an independent right. See, eg, the discussion in Tania Voon, Andrew Mitchell and James Munro, 'Parting Ways: The Impact of Mutual Termination of Investment Treaties on Investor Rights' (2014) 29(2) ICSID Rev 451, 454–56.

[21] Some states—such as Mauritius, the Netherlands, and Singapore—are small states, which perform the function of platform states from which large companies launch their investments into the region. But these states will also not be interested in mere postbox companies.

not want to recognize companies whose intentions are fraudulent and in no way benefit the host state. When a foreign investor exercises a right to arbitration transferred by the state, it does so in good faith. The right is not exercised in good faith when the device of corporate nationality is employed to obtain jurisdiction through a sandwich corporation or through a corporation that is set up to round-trip assets originating in the respondent state. An abuse of rights takes place in these circumstances (as discussed further below), and good faith is violated in a multitude of ways. The foreign investor violates good faith in seeking protection on grounds that diverge from the purpose of the treaty. The home state, in knowingly supporting such a claim, does not act in good faith if it permits the treaty to be abused for a purpose contrary to its objectives. The arbitrator who finds jurisdiction may not be acting in good faith in permitting a possibly fraudulent scheme to found jurisdiction. ICSID, as an institution performing a function under the treaty, does not act in good faith if it allows a fraudulent transgression to found jurisdiction of its tribunal. The complicity of all these performers of the treaty obligation must be seriously considered.

### 6.4.2 Good faith in treaty interpretation

The notion of good faith in the interpretation of treaties is also inherent in the principle of effectiveness. The principle of effectiveness is contained within article 31 of the *VCLT*. The principle was not explicitly included due to the fear that it could be used in order to create law through excessively teleological interpretations.[22] Yet, the principle does have relevance. As the International Law Commission has stated, the maxim *ut res magis valeat quam pereat* (that the thing may rather have effect than be destroyed) is embodied in Article 31.[23] It further explained: 'When a treaty is open to two interpretations, one of which does and the other does not enable the treaty to have appropriate effects, *good faith and objects and purposes* of the treaty demand that the former interpretation should be adopted'.[24] A purely textual interpretation going against the object and purpose of the treaty has been disapproved.[25] The interpretation of the provision of the investment treaty on which standing rests has been a crucial factor in foreign investment arbitration. The extent to which good faith plays a role in such interpretation has not been adequately considered. This chapter seeks to remedy that deficiency. It takes the stance that good faith requires the rejection of a purely textual

[22] 'Treaties' in Robert Jennings and Arthur Watts (eds), *Oppenheim's International Law*, vol 1 (9th edn, Longman Group 1992) 1266, 1280–81.

[23] [1966] II Yearbook ILC 219.

[24] ibid (emphasis added).

[25] *Territorial Dispute (Libya Arab Jamahiriya v Chad) (Merits)* [1994] ICJ Rep 6, para 47.

interpretation in order to achieve the object and purpose of the treaty and thus reflect the intention of the parties in the two situations of the use of corporate nationality identified here.

A further relevance of good faith in interpretation is that the *VCLT* requires that treaties be interpreted in the context of public international law, that is, 'any relevant rules of international law applicable in the relations between the parties'.[26] Good faith, as the tribunal in *Phoenix Ltd v Czech Republic* pointed out (and as elaborated in chapter 2 of this volume), is a general principle of international law.[27] As a general principle, good faith always has relevance to outcomes in international law, including as regards corporate nationality in investment treaties. Put in this sense, good faith becomes part of an effort to create an international law applicable to the foreign investment process. Good faith, very much a principle of interpretation of treaties, would then become an overriding factor, as the foreign investor should have regard to the obligations a host state has under these different laws affecting foreign investment.

### 6.4.3 Good faith and abuse of rights

As foreshadowed above, another relevant aspect of good faith in the context of the law of treaties is abuse of rights.[28] Good faith cannot exist in circumstances where a right is exercised in an unreasonable manner so as to defeat the purpose for which the right was created. The exercise of the right should not be unreasonable, and pursued in an arbitrary manner, without due consideration of the legitimate expectations of the other state. The treaty creates a right in the foreign investor to unilateral recourse to arbitration. This right flows from the right to accord diplomatic protection, which the home state of the investor has against the host state.[29] The investor should not abuse its derivative right; nor should a contracting state permit the abusive exercise of that right. When the foreign investor acts so as to defeat the purpose of the investment treaty, an abuse of rights may arise. A state permitting a right derived from it to be so abused becomes complicit in that abuse of right. The state may have an active duty to prevent the abusive exercise of a right derived from it or created by it. In a cosmopolitan world, when international law moves towards the recognition of wider obligations, a rule requiring

[26] *VCLT* (n 17) art 31(3)(c).

[27] *Phoenix Action Ltd v Czech Republic* (ICSID Arbitral Tribunal, Case No ARB/06/5, 15 April 2009) paras 106–13.

[28] Bin Cheng, *General Principles of Law* (Stevens & Sons Ltd 1953) 123; see also Michael Byers, 'Abuse of Rights: An Old Principle, A New Age' (2002) 47 McGill LJ 389.

[29] This is notwithstanding the view that the foreign investor enforces his own right that has been transferred to him by treaty. In terms of international law, this does not make sense. See Zachary Douglas, *The International Law of Investment Claims* (CUP 2009) 151–60.

prevention of an abusive exercise of a right by a multinational corporation could be advanced as a matter of policy.

The notion of abuse of rights was considered in the context of corporate nationality in *Phoenix v Czech Republic*.[30] The respondent state had argued that the claimant was a sham company incorporated in Israel, after the dispute had arisen, only to create standing. The respondent state pointed out that limitless jurisdiction could be created if unrestricted use could be made of corporate nationality.[31] The tribunal however was content in dismissing jurisdiction on the ground that the claimant had made no *bona fide* investment.[32] The award gives rise to the interesting issue as to whether an investment made by an investor through a sandwich corporation or a corporation intent on round-tripping can be described as a good faith investment. This issue is discussed further below.

Generally, good faith is arguably significant in the construction of a principle of arbitrability in investment arbitration. As the examples given in *Phoenix* relating to genocide and torture indicate,[33] a foreign investment having the objective of breaking a *jus cogens* principle is not arbitrable,[34] because the dispute involves community interests that transcend the interests of the parties. It is not within the realm of good faith to have such disputes settled by tribunals resting on the consent of two states when the dispute implicates international community interests. Is it then possible to argue that where a fraudulent incorporation of companies takes place to seek the protection of investment treaties designed to promote the economic development of the poor, similar good faith considerations justify denying the jurisdiction of a tribunal devoted to considering disputes from the angle of foreign investment alone? These considerations must be kept in mind when dealing with the hitherto wholly rule-based treatment of corporate nationality and standing.

## 6.5 Analysis of Corporate Nationality as a Basis for Jurisdiction

Unlike a physical person whose loyalties and ties to the state demonstrate citizenship of the state, mere incorporation in the state is sufficient for a corporation to acquire nationality of that state. A paradox exists in the treaty in that

[30] *Phoenix* (n 27). [31] ibid para 43. [32] ibid paras 142–44. [33] ibid para 78.

[34] ibid para 77. The tribunal relied on the observations of the WTO Appellate Body in *United States—Standards for Reformulated and Conventional Gasoline*, WTO Doc WT/DS2/AB/R (adopted 20 May 1996) 18.

its wording requires little to be satisfied in the case of a corporate national besides incorporation, whereas the citizen acquires nationality through satisfaction of legal criteria set out in the domestic law. As such, the rule that incorporation alone is sufficient to create nationality in the corporation lends itself to abuse. In civil law countries of Europe (except in the Netherlands, where the incorporation theory is retained for reasons of policy, ensuring that the Netherlands remains a platform state that serves as a host for export of investments),[35] corporate nationality is purposefully based on the *siège social* theory, which emphasizes the place of actual management of the company in determining corporate nationality, with the specific objective of avoiding fraudulent claims to nationality.[36] Problems of corporate nationality have therefore seldom arisen in treaties of the civil law states, which require substantial links with the state whose nationality is claimed, very much as in the case of physical persons.[37]

Adoption of the *siège social* theory effectively eliminates fraudulent claims of nationality. Its universal adoption should be kept in mind as an alternative to the denial of benefits provision, as it enables a state to argue against the entitlement of a claimant who uses incorporation as the sole basis for jurisdiction. Such prevention of fraudulent invocation of corporate nationality does not take place where incorporation is the basis of corporate nationality. This surely must not be taken to mean that these states condone its fraudulent use. Except where the corporate veil is lifted, it would not be possible to determine the true nationality of the corporation when incorporation determines corporate nationality. There has been a marked reluctance to lift the corporate veil in the common law jurisdictions,[38] which is reflected in the awards in foreign investment arbitration.[39] The inclusion of a denial of benefits provision enables the respondent state to lift the veil so as to determine whether

[35] Other small states—eg Hong Kong, Mauritius and Singapore—also work on this premise but are largely common law systems, whereas the Netherlands has a civil law system.

[36] 2008 German Model BIT, art 1(3)(a) <http://www.italaw.com/sites/default/files/archive/ita1025.pdf> accessed 8 October 2014; *Agreement between the Republic of Columbia and the Swiss Confederation on the Promotion and Reciprocal Protection of Investments*, signed 17 May 2006 (entered into force 6 October 2009) art 1(2)(b).

[37] But see *Yaung Chi Oo Trading Pte Ltd v Myanmar*, 42 ILM 540 (ASEAN Arbitral Tribunal, 31 March 2003). The *ASEAN Comprehensive Investment Agreement* (signed 26 February 2009, entered into force 29 March 2012) art 1(f) uses a combined formula of incorporation and effective management. This may be due to the inclusion of states with civilian legal systems. But in *Yaung Chi Oo*, the requirement of effective management was underplayed, the tribunal holding that complying with the legal requirement of the state of incorporation such as the presentation of annual reports satisfied the requirement of effective management: para 52.

[38] Paul Davies, *Gower and Davies: The Principles of Modern Company Law* (8th edn, Sweet & Maxwell 2008) 193–209.

[39] *Saluka* (n 2) para 214.

the incorporation is used merely as a technique to found jurisdiction. The view that corporate planning to take advantage of the treaty is permissible should be rejected outright.

The tussle in the area has been between two competing considerations. The first is to ensure that the intention of the states parties to the treaty is given effect by confining jurisdiction to companies that effectively operate within those states parties. The true intention of the parties is to be found in the preamble of the relevant treaty, which typically states that the aim of the treaty is the promotion of economic relations between the two states, 'particularly with respect to nationals of one Contracting Party in the territory of the other Contracting Party'.[40] As already noted, the rationale behind the treaty is the flow of foreign investment as a result of the protection given to it by the treaty. The rationale behind the *ICSID Convention*, which also talks about the personality of the corporation, is that foreign investment flows will help in the economic development of the state. Indeed, the World Bank has no competence to provide general arbitration services. ICSID is premised on the fact, as evidenced in its preamble, that flows of foreign investment promoted as a result of a definite dispute settlement mechanism will promote economic development. The round-tripping of the funds of nationals or the existence of postbox companies can hardly be consistent with the purposes of investment treaties or the *ICSID Convention*. Indeed, it would not be far-fetched to say that there is bad faith in any argument that protection should be permitted on the basis of round-tripping through companies established in the other contracting party or through postbox companies through which no investments actually flow.

The competing argument depends on the strict interpretation of the words of the treaty. Taken as a whole, investment arbitrators have not uniformly championed strict treaty interpretation. They have often read meaning into words and constructed new theories on the basis of the object and purpose of investment treaties.[41] The most glaring example of this is the revival of the fair and equitable standard as protecting the legitimate expectations of the foreign investor.[42] There is no basis in the text of the treaties for this

[40] *ICSID Convention* (n 5) preamble, art 25(1).

[41] *Metalclad Corp v Mexico* (Award) (ICSID Arbitral Tribunal, Case No ARB(AF)/97/1, 30 August 2000) para 76; *Waste Management Inc v Mexico ('Number 2') (Award)* (ICSID Arbitral Tribunal, Case No ARB(AF)/00/3, 30 April 2004) paras 78–85; *Compañía del Desarrollo de Santa Elena SA v Costa Rica (Award)* (ICSID Arbitral Tribunal, Case No ARB/96/1, 17 February 2000) paras 71–72; *Siemens AG v Argentina (Award)* (ICSID Arbitral Tribunal, Case No ARB/02/8, 17 January 2007) para 290.

[42] *Alex Genin, Eastern Credit Limited Inc and AS Baltoil v Estonia (Award)* (ICSID Arbitral Tribunal, Case No ARB/99/2, 25 June 2001) para 367; *Técnicas Medioambientales Tecmed SA v Mexico (Award)* (ICSID Arbitral Tribunal, Case No ARB (AF)/00/2) para 154.

innovation. It is based on the subjective preference of arbitrators to identify the purpose of the treaties as creating rules for stability of investment.[43] Strangely, the same group of arbitrators have shown fidelity to the strict construction of words when it comes to the interpretation of the provisions on corporate nationality.[44] This selectivity by this group of arbitrators detracts from consistency in arbitration and leads to questioning of the legitimacy of the techniques used in it to arrive at results that are more conducive to investment protection than to the application of the intention of the parties on which the jurisdiction of the arbitrators rests.

Good faith can possibly be used to support both views. It could be argued that good faith demands that a treaty devised to promote flows of foreign investment is not thwarted by a fraudulent investor who uses a postbox company either to channel funds originating in the home state back through the company incorporated in the host state or as a means of treaty shopping to ensure better treaty protection. Equally, it could be argued that good faith requires the strict interpretation of the terms of the treaty and that the strict interpretation of the relevant treaty words requires that such protection be given.

Curiously, the permissive view of corporate nationality is expansionist, as it works against the objective of the treaties themselves, which is the promotion of investment flows and not the strict construction of the terms of the treaties. It is expansionist as it enables a wider category of investors, including physical nationals of the home state, to secure jurisdiction despite the fact that the re-routing of their capital through a company in the home state cannot possibly achieve the purpose of promoting foreign investments.

Professor Schreuer has written that aspects of the law are 'unsavoury from an ethical standpoint'.[45] One could go further and identify the schism that has opened up in this area as a conflict between expansionary arbitrators who seek to extend the scope of investment arbitration well beyond the intention of the states which created it, and those who advocate caution lest states simply pull out of the system. It is also an observable factor that arbitrators have not been consistent in applying techniques of interpretation of treaties. As noted above, the arbitrators who insist on the strict meaning of words when considering standing based on corporate nationality are also the ones who adopt a teleological interpretation when considering the scope of the

[43] M Sornarajah, 'Mutations of Neo-Liberalism in International Investment Law' (2011) 3 Trade L & Dev 204, 213–15; Van Garten (n 10) 136–43.

[44] See Sergio Puig, 'Social Capital in the Arbitration Market' (2014) 25 EJIL 387.

[45] Christoph Schreuer, 'Nationality Planning' in Arthur Rovine (ed), *Contemporary Issues in International Arbitration and Mediation* (Martinus Nijhoff 2013) 17, 26.

fair and equitable standard. This attitude taints the whole field of investment arbitration. States have retaliated in various ways. The milder backlash has been the use of the denial of benefits clause to deal with problems posed by corporate nationality.

## 6.6 Revisiting the Awards

The two problems that had arisen in investment arbitration that the inclusion of a denial of benefits clause sought to cure were identified earlier as: (i) the round-tripping of investments; and (ii) postbox or sandwich companies inserted only so as to obtain the protection of a particular treaty. The awards involving these two situations are analysed more fully in the following section, before dealing with how denial of benefits provisions seek to overcome them.

### 6.6.1 Round-tripping of investments

*Tokios Tokelés v Ukraine*[46] is the award in which round-tripping of investments for the purpose of obtaining investment protection under the treaties was successful. The majority of the tribunal[47] held that the claimant—a company incorporated in Lithuania by Ukrainian nationals—was entitled to the protection[48] of the Lithuania-Ukraine bilateral investment treaty (BIT),[49] despite the fact that the purpose of the incorporation appeared to have been to channel money originating in Ukraine through the company back to Ukraine with the protection of the investment treaty.[50] There was no doubt that 99% of the shares in the Lithuanian company were controlled by nationals of Ukraine.[51] What was effected through ICSID arbitration was the protection of funds that originated in Ukraine under an investment treaty that was intended to promote investment flows between the two treaty partners and under the *ICSID Convention*, which was likewise intended to promote such flows through provision of a mechanism 'for the settlement of disputes between states and nationals of other states'.[52] There was no *international investment*; nor was the dispute *international*.

46 *Tokios Tokelés* (n 2). 47 That is, arbitrators Piero Bernadini and Daniel Price.

48 *Tokios Tokelés* (n 2) para 71.

49 *Agreement between the Government of Ukraine and the Government of the Republic of Lithuania for the Promotion and Reciprocal Protection of Investments*, signed 8 February 1994 (entered into force 27 February 1995).

50 *Tokios Tokelés* (n 2) paras 21–22. 51 ibid para 21.

52 The title of the *ICSID Convention* contains these words. Its full title is *Convention for the Settlement of Investment Disputes between States and Nationals of other States*.

Clearly, no benefit arose to Ukraine when its own money was recycled through a company incorporated in Lithuania. The claiming of the protection of the Lithuania–Ukraine investment treaty was clearly a fraud on the system of investment treaties. The fact that the claim was made several years after the incorporation did not change the nature of the assets as Ukrainian assets brought back into the country. Yet, the majority adopted a strict interpretation of the treaty,[53] which simply stated that any company incorporated in Lithuania was entitled to such protection, even one incorporated by Ukrainian nationals.[54] The underlying reasoning was probably that the test to be applied had no limitations. The tribunal also took the object and purpose of the treaty to be the protection of investment.[55] That purpose was said to be facilitated by the strict interpretation of the treaty to the effect that incorporation alone was sufficient to invoke the protection of the treaty.[56]

The president of the tribunal, Professor Prosper Weil, wrote an anguished dissent. His reasoning was unassailable. He pointed out that the *ICSID Convention* was based on arbitration of disputes between foreigners making investments and the host state. This basis is absent where funds are re-routed.[57] In addition, the object of the *ICSID Convention*, which is to promote flows of funds and thereby the economic development of the host state, is not satisfied when assets originating in the state are brought back into it. This is also the purpose of investment treaties.[58]

The *VCLT* demands a good faith interpretation of a treaty having regard to its object and purpose. But good reasoning has not deterred subsequent arbitrators from holding, as the majority did in *Tokios Tokelés*, that what matters is that a corporate national of the other state is sending assets into the respondent state. Twenty-one awards have accepted this view.[59] Strict construction has thus been used to defeat the purpose of the treaties. Prosper Weil declaimed in disgust that the ICSID system would lose credibility as a result of the decision.[60] Yet the error he declaimed has been consistently made in other awards. It is an indictment of the system of foreign investment arbitration that an interpretation that clearly defeats the intention of the parties and the object of the relevant treaties has had such acceptance within the system. It is necessary to search for reasons. The obvious one is the prevalence of an

[53] *Tokios Tokelés* (n 2) para 52. [54] Lithuania–Ukraine BIT (n 49) art 1(2).

[55] *Tokios Tokelés* (n 2) para 31. [56] ibid paras 42–45.

[57] ibid dissenting opinion paras 10–11. [58] ibid dissenting opinion para 3.

[59] *KT Asia Investment Group BV v Kazakhstan (Award)* (ICSID Arbitral Tribunal, Case No ARB/09/8, 17 October 2013) para 121. The tribunal cited and disagreed with Weil. The respondent argued that there were 21 awards that decided that mere incorporation was sufficient.

[60] *Tokios Tokelés* (n 2) dissenting opinion para 1.

in-built bias of arbitrators towards investment protection and the expansion of the system.[61]

Good faith has not triumphed. Rather, a system has been created that enables fraud to be perpetrated on the respondent state so that funds originating from it can be cycled back with the protection of an investment treaty when such funds are channelled through a company incorporated in the treaty partner. These cases did not even consider the good faith principle. In *KT Asia v Kazakhstan*, for example, the reasoning is simply that the large majority of cases have followed *Tokios Tokelés*.[62]

Also in *KT Asia v Kazakhstan*, the tribunal found that Kazakhstan was aware of the outcome of using the incorporation test, as it had used that test in 24 treaties and the alternative formula of *siège social* in 11 treaties.[63] This had to do less with awareness than with the fact that common law treaty partners used the incorporation test whereas civil law states (with the exception of the Netherlands) used the *siège social* theory. The formulation used in the relevant treaty was not deliberately selected by a state like Kazakhstan with any understanding of how arbitrators would come to employ the incorporation test. This selection has not been so explained in the literature on investment treaties, which simply states that common law countries used incorporation while civil law states used the alternative of the *siège social* theory.[64] Tribunals seek to give additional but unconvincing reasons to bolster the erroneous view of the majority in *Tokios Tokelés*, while conceding the substance of the dissent of Professor Weil.[65]

### 6.6.2 Postbox or sandwich companies

The technique of inserting a subsidiary in a favourable treaty jurisdiction (usually the Netherlands and hence the 'Dutch sandwich') simply to obtain the better protection standards of that jurisdiction has been accepted in many awards, even where the insertion took place after proceedings were

[61] See generally Van Garten (n 10). [62] *KT Asia* (n 59) para 137.

[63] ibid para 123.

[64] Rudolf Dolzer and Margrete Stevens, *Bilateral Investment Treaties* (Martinus Nijhoff 1995).

[65] *Tokios Tokelés* (n 2) paras 121, 135. In the unrelated area of control of the corporate vehicle through which investment is channeled in the host country, the test of control that is applied has involved the lifting of the veil to determine who has real control: *TSA Spectrum de Argentina SA v Argentina (Award)* (ICSID Arbitral Tribunal, Case No ARB/05/5, 19 December 2008) paras 160–62; *National Gas SAE v Egypt (Award)* (ICSID Arbitral Tribunal, Case No ARB/11/7, 3 April 2014) (unpublished). This view had been established quite early in *Vacuum Salts v Ghana (Award)* (ICSID Arbitral Tribunal, Case No ARB/92/1, 16 February 1994) paras 42–44, 54.

contemplated. In *Aguas del Tunari v Bolivia*, such 'migration' was held permissible,[66] though the insertion of the company was effected during the course of the dispute. The temporal factor was not considered an obstacle. In *Mobil v Venezuela*, the situation was rationalized on the basis that corporation reorganization is always possible,[67] even though the reorganization in that case was done to obtain jurisdiction that would otherwise not have existed, through the incorporation of a new subsidiary in the Netherlands. In such circumstances, no flows of funds take place from the Dutch postbox company.

The incorporation of shell companies within the corporate structure cannot satisfy the objects of investment treaties, in that such companies cannot promote economic development or economic cooperation between the states. As Professor Weil stated in his dissenting award in *Tokios Tokelés*, such schemes put the success of ICSID arbitration 'at risk by extending its scope and application beyond the limits so carefully assigned to it by the Convention'.[68]

Allowance of these corporate extensions frustrates the objectives of both the investment treaty and the *ICSID Convention*, which protect only investment flows and not the re-nomination of existing foreign investment through other states simply to achieve protection. The objects of the treaty from the point of view of the host country are not in any way furthered by corporate migration or reorganization. The fact that a company 'migrates' so as to benefit from a treaty by the simple act of incorporation in a state with the most favourable treaty can bring no economic development to the host country, which is the main purpose of any investment treaty as well as of the *ICSID Convention*. Such movement creates only economic hardship to the host state in creating an unanticipated method of arbitration. This idea leads to widespread treaty shopping and creates doubts about the treaty regime as a whole, as the uncertainties that are involved lead states to rethink the wisdom of entering into treaties that are capable of infinite extensions and that create liability to an unlimited number of corporations. As Bolivia argued in *Aguas del Tunari v Bolivia*, this interpretation would mean that the Netherlands–Bolivia treaty[69] would become 'a treaty between Bolivia and the world', as every foreign investor could 'migrate' or insert a postbox, subsidiary company

[66] *Aguas del Tunari SA v Bolivia (Decision on Respondent's Objections to Jurisdiction)* (ICSID Arbitral Tribunal, Case No ARB/02/3, 21 October 2005) paras 166, 174–75.

[67] *Mobil Corp, Venezuela Holdings BV v Venezuela (Decision on Jurisdiction)* (ICSID Arbitral Tribunal, Case No ARB/07/27, 10 June 2010) paras 190–91, 203–05.

[68] *Tokios Tokelés* (n 2) dissenting opinion para 30.

[69] *Agreement on encouragement and reciprocal protection of investments between the Kingdom of the Netherlands and the Republic of Bolivia*, signed 10 March 1992 (entered into force 1 November 1994).

into the Netherlands and secure the protection of the treaty—hardly a result that Bolivia could have intended when signing the BIT.[70]

It is as if, in the case of Bolivia, what was intended as a bilateral treaty was converted into a multilateral treaty, a result that would have greatly enhanced neo-liberal strategies of foreign investment protection. That indeed was the justification given by the tribunal, saying:

> This Decision reflects the growing web of treaty based referrals to arbitration of certain investment disputes. Although titled 'bilateral' investment treaties, this case makes clear that which has been clear to negotiating states for some time, namely, that through the definition of 'national' or 'investor', such treaties serve in many cases more broadly as portals through which investments are structured, organized, and, most importantly, encouraged through the availability of a neutral forum. The language of the definition of national in many [bilateral investment treaties] evidences that such national routing of investment is entirely in keeping with the purpose of the instruments and the motivations of the state parties.

The only object of such rationalizations is to ensure broad latitude for treaty shopping by multinational corporations. States did not agree to arbitration tribunals converting their bilateral treaties into multilateral treaties. If they had such desires, they would have made multilateral treaties. States, including the Netherlands, have no desire to do so, as the experience of the failed Multilateral Agreement on Investment[71] sponsored by the Organisation for Economic Co-operation and Development among developed countries shows. These rationales have nothing at all to do with the original purpose of the investment treaty or of the *ICSID Convention*. In these circumstances, one must query whether there is an institutional duty on the part of ICSID to take a stance as to the appropriateness of the interpretation, as ICSID is obviously condoning a situation that was not anticipated by the parties or by the institution.

In *Alps Finance v Slovakia*,[72] the tribunal was conscious of the harm that the emphasis on incorporation and expansion of jurisdiction could bring about. The tribunal held that more than mere incorporation is required to establish corporate nationality.[73] The provision must be interpreted in good faith.[74] Shell companies cannot satisfy the object of the treaty, which is to bring about greater economic cooperation between the states and economic benefits that the preamble of the treaty mentions.[75] The tribunal took a

[70] *Aguas del Tunari* (n 66). See also argument of the Czech Republic in *Phoenix* (n 29) para 43.

[71] See Jürgen Kurtz, 'A General Investment Agreement in the WTO? Lessons from Chapter 11 of NAFTA and the OECD Multilateral Agreement on Investment' (2002) 23 U Pa J Intl Econ L 713.

[72] *Alps Finance and Trade AG v Slovak Republic (Award)* (UNCITRAL, 5 March 2011).

[73] ibid para 224. [74] ibid paras 225–26. [75] ibid para 226.

contrary view to previous expansionist views. It found the claim to be seriously defective.[76] Departing from practice, the tribunal awarded full costs to the respondent state[77] in obvious recognition of the defective claim. One could then, in this area, as well, clearly distinguish between expansionist tribunals and tribunals that show fidelity to the limits of jurisdiction expressed in the consent of the parties.

The division of views is emblematic of two strands within investment arbitration. One desires expansion of the investment treaty system, seeking the multilateralization of the system through several means, including the use of the incorporation theory. The other seeks to resist such a process. The second strand is more consistent with the views of states, as states' efforts to introduce denial of benefits provisions into new investment treaties show.

### 6.6.3 Construing denial of benefits provisions

Denial of benefits provisions found in more recent investment treaties are reactions to the expansionary use of corporate nationality by arbitrators eager to increase the jurisdictional scope of investment arbitration. In the light of that prevailing mindset of expansionary interpretation of investment treaties, ad hoc solutions are not bound to work, as arbitrators will seek to interpret the provisions as narrowly as possible so that their expansionary venture is not affected. Arbitration tribunals have reacted to the 'bandaid' solution by construing denial of benefits provisions narrowly so as not to affect investment protection.

In *Liman Caspian Oil v Kazakhstan*, the tribunal held that the denial of benefits clause could not be used where Dutch companies brought the claim though the real controllers were Canadian.[78] The tribunal suggested that the respondent state should have been aware of the facts at the time of the request for arbitration and should have raised the issue of denial of benefits at that time and not one year later, during the jurisdictional phase.[79] This is difficult reasoning, deliberately calculated to ensure that the investor benefits despite the fact that the denial of benefits provision itself was not specified to be time limited. The claimants knew of the facts and had a duty to disclose them. They could not have been adversely affected by facts of which they had knowledge. Instead, the tribunal willingly put the onus

[76] ibid para 266. [77] ibid paras 268–70.

[78] *Liman Caspian Oil BV and NCL Dutch Investment BV v Kazakhstan (Award)* (ICSID Arbitral Tribunal, Case No ARB/07/14, 22 June 2010) 2 (summary of facts).

[79] ibid paras 226–27.

on the respondent to know the facts and plead them at the commencement of proceedings.

In *Plama v Bulgaria*, the tribunal held that the respondent must notify a denial of benefits to the claimant in advance of the claim,[80] placing the onus on the respondent state to anticipate possibilities of future claims. Similarly, in *Yukos v Russia*, round-tripping was alleged and the state relied on the denial of benefits provision.[81] The tribunal brushed aside this argument, holding that the origin of the capital used to acquire the relevant assets is not relevant to the question of jurisdiction under the *ICSID Convention*.[82]

The reasoning in these awards seems faulty. Denial of benefits provisions seek to cure what states see as wrongful behaviour. These provisions are designed to give notice to foreign investors that investments falling within their scope are not protected under the treaty. The foreign investor has the best knowledge of the source of its funds and the place of control. The claimant cannot be adversely affected by the respondent's identification of those facts at any stage of the proceedings. Restricting the stage of proceedings at which the respondent must invoke a denial of benefits provision undermines the purpose of the provision. In these awards tribunals have deliberately set out to find restrictions on states' attempts to overcome what they consider unsuitable claims. This willingness of tribunals to overcome impediments placed in the way of foreign investors may provoke states to renounce the investment treaty system, as these kinds of awards indicate that the ad hoc solutions advanced by states to keep the treaty system legitimate and effective are not taken seriously by arbitrators. The tribunals making such decisions are, once again, selective as to the rules of interpretation to be applied. They use a strict interpretation technique rather than examining the mischief sought to be remedied by the insertion of a denial of benefits provision.

Good faith is relevant to denial of benefits, as evidenced by the context of corporate nationality cases. Thus, the tribunal in *Rizvi v Indonesia* stated that if the investor does not adequately disclose its relevant circumstances at the time of making the investment, a tribunal could draw the inference that the investor is attempting to evade the laws of the state regarding the entry of investments. This rule could be extended to the entry of investments through

[80] *Plama Consortium Ltd v Bulgaria (Decision on Jurisdiction)* (ICSID Arbitral Tribunal, Case No ARB/03/24, 8 February 2005) paras 157–58.

[81] *Yukos Universal Limited (Isle of Man) v Russian Federation (Interim Award on Jurisdiction and Admissibility* (UNCITRAL, Permanent Court of Arbitration, Case No AA 227, 30 November 2009) para 447.

[82] ibid para 432.

round-tripping or interposition of postbox companies. The state would then have the option of excluding protection for such companies at the outset.[83]

### 6.6.4 Lifting the corporate veil

In comparative company law, the courts will look at abuse of the corporate form under certain circumstances, by 'lifting the corporate veil' to see whether it cloaks abuse or fraud.[84] The International Court of Justice in the *Barcelona Traction* case adverted to this possibility in situations where the true purpose of the use of the corporate form becomes relevant:

> [T]he wealth of practice already accumulated on the subject in municipal law indicates that the veil is lifted, for instance, to prevent the misuse of the privileges of legal personality, as in certain of fraud or malfeasance, to protect third persons such as a creditor or purchaser, or to prevent the evasion of legal requirements or of obligations.

Strictly construing relevant treaty provisions, investment treaty arbitrators have found it unnecessary to use the facility that the law provides for examining whether the corporate nationality was used only to secure protection of the treaty by nationals, in which case scope exists for a finding of fraud or that the investment proceeded from a sandwich company that could not have furthered the objective of economic development of the host state. The failure of investment treaty tribunals to consider lifting the veil in the disputes that have arisen concerning corporate nationality effectively condones deliberate efforts to commit fraud or to evade the objective of the treaty (in either case involving fraudulent intent).[85] In such circumstances, bad faith is attributable not only to the claimants, who used the technique of incorporation to obtain standing, but also to the arbitrators, who accepted the use of this technique. The domestic law reluctance to lift the veil results largely from the fact that the outcome would entail imposing liability on the shareholders.[86] In contrast, in the case of investment treaty arbitration, the only reason to lift the veil is to determine whether the shareholders are genuinely entitled to jurisdiction. Consequently, little reason exists to avoid lifting the veil in ICSID disputes.

[83] *Rafat Ali Rizvi v Indonesia (Award on Jurisdiction)* (ICSID Arbitral Tribunal, Case No ARB/11/13, 16 June 2013) para 68. The present author was an arbitrator in this case and issued a separate concurring opinion on some issues.

[84] Albert Badia, *Piercing the Veil of State Enterprises in International Arbitration* (Kluwer Law International 2014).

[85] As indicated earlier, tribunals have not refused to lift the veil to find out who really controls the company incorporated in the host state as the vehicle for the foreign investment.

[86] See generally Sornarajah, 'Neo-Liberalism' (n 43).

### 6.6.5 Use of the *siège social* theory

With the exception of *Yaung Chi Oo v Myanmar*,[87] no award involving round-tripping or sandwich companies has considered a treaty that embodies the *siège social* theory of corporate nationality. The *Yaung Chi Oo* dispute involved allegations of round-tripping under a treaty that required proof of effective management as well as incorporation to establish nationality for the purposes of a protected investment.[88] The tribunal was willing to accept the mere filing of annual reports with the Registrar of Companies of the state of incorporation as sufficient to show management of the company from the state of incorporation.[89] This was an aberration, albeit of limited effect, as the tribunal held that the investment was not protected as it had not been approved in writing as required by the treaty.[90]

The arbitrators in *Yaung Chi Oo* were clearly wrong in their decision on corporate nationality. The purpose of the limitation in the treaty was to give effect to the *siège social* theory of corporate nationality used in investment treaties of the Philippines.[91] The notion of effective management would have required more than mere filing of the statements required under the company law of the state of incorporation. It would have required the location of the centre of administration in the state. Insistence on actual management in the state of incorporation may be effective in overcoming the issues presented by round-tripping and sandwich companies. The requirement of management ensures that incorporation is not used for the fraudulent purpose of defeating the objectives of the treaty.

### 6.6.6 Use of good faith

Given the existence of an intransigent attitude towards investment protection, the application of a good faith criterion is likely to be ignored in investment arbitration as a means of dealing with corporate nationality. This is unfortunate, as arbitral tribunals have a definite duty to avoid circumvention of the objects of the treaty by reliance on its precise terms. The doctrine of

87 *Yaung Chi Oo* (n 37). 88 *ASEAN Comprehensive Investment Agreement* (n 37).

89 *Yaung Chi Oo* (n 37) para 52.

90 ibid para 60. The present writer was chief counsel for the claimant in *Yaung Chi Oo Trading Pte Ltd v Myanmar*. The object of the exercise was to convert the case into an exposure of the human rights abuses of the Myanmar government. This failed as jurisdiction was denied.

91 *Agreement between the Federal Republic of Germany and the Republic of the Philippines for the Promotion and Reciprocal Protection of Investments*, signed 18 April 1997 (entered into force 1 February 2000) art 3(a); *Agreement between the Republic of Turkey and the Republic of the Philippines concerning the Reciprocal Promotion and Protection of Investments*, signed 22 February 1999 (entered into force 17 February 2006) art 1(iii).

good faith mandates that such abusive use of the treaties be avoided. The doctrine is beginning to emerge to a greater extent in the awards. Its further use may result in avoiding abuses. But given the entrenched trends, this is an optimistic assessment. If the trends persist, states may see in these episodes relating to the use of the incorporation theory of nationality a further reason to resile from investor–state arbitration.

## 6.7 Conclusion

Good faith is of limited use, if one takes the view that both round-tripping and the insertion of sandwich companies into the corporate structure are fraudulent means of obtaining standing in a manner that defeats the purpose of the treaty. In that case, the tribunal must find fraud and deny jurisdiction. The only relevance of good faith is where the tribunal is unwilling to find fraud, in which case, finding an absence of good faith in the claimant may enable the refusal of jurisdiction without condemnation of the claimant. Good faith could also help to reverse the large number of awards, reputedly over 21 in the case of company migration, where these corporate techniques have been approved on the basis that they accord with a treaty provision indicating that incorporation is sufficient for standing, despite the fact that this defeats the purpose of the treaty. Good faith could well be used to effect a change in this line of cases. It could form the basis of an argument that where the incorporation is clearly for the abusive purpose of obtaining standing, a rebuttable presumption against standing arises. The claimant could rebut this presumption by showing another purpose for the incorporation, although in the majority of instances such a purpose is unlikely to exist. However, arbitrators seem unlikely to take up this approach to good faith as a means of limiting investment protection.

The law on corporate nationality devised in investment arbitration will stand as evidence of the many instances in which arbitrators have developed a law that promotes arbitration and the interests of foreign investors beyond the intention of the states that made the treaties. This development does not bode well for the investment treaty system. Efforts of states to overcome the situation through denial of benefits provisions have also been rebuffed. In that context, states that want to continue with the investment treaty system will have to devise alternatives. The wholesale adoption of the *siège social* theory for identifying corporate nationality is an obvious solution, given that round-tripping and sandwich companies are not used to obtain protection under the treaties that have adopted this theory. The eventual solution may not lie in the application of a principle of good faith by arbitrators, for they seem to have distanced themselves from such notions at least in relation to corporate nationality. The answer then lies in the hands of states. If they want to retain a system of investment treaties, denial of benefits provisions do not offer an answer. The answer lies in the adoption of the *siège social* theory in a secure way, indicating the nature of the management that accompanies incorporation for the identification of corporate nationality.

# ANNEX

## ASEAN COMPREHENSIVE INVESTMENT AGREEMENT

(signed 26 February 2009, entered into force 29 March 2012).

### Article 19 Denial Of Benefits

1. A Member State may deny the benefits of this Agreement to:
    1. (a) an investor of another Member State that is a juridical person of such other Member State and to investments of such investor if an investor of a non-Member State owns or controls the juridical person and the juridical person has no substantive business operations in the territory of such other Member State;
    2. (b) an investor of another Member State that is a juridical person of such other Member State and to investments of such investor if an investor of the denying Member State owns or controls the juridical person and the juridical person has no substantive business operations in the territory of such other Member State; and
    3. (c) an investor of another Member State that is a juridical person of such other Member State and to an investment of such investor if investors of a non-Member State own or control the juridical person, and the denying Member State does not maintain diplomatic relations with the non-Member State.
2. Following notification to the Member State of the investor, and without prejudice to paragraph 1, a Member State may deny the benefits of this Agreement to investors of another Member State and to investments of that investor, where it establishes that such investor has made an investment in breach of the domestic laws of the denying Member State by misrepresenting its ownership in those areas of investment

which are reserved for natural or juridical persons of the denying Member State.

3. A juridical person is:
   1. (a) 'owned' by an investor in accordance with the laws, regulations and national policies of each Member States;
   2. (b) 'controlled' by an investor if the investor has the power to name a majority of its directors or otherwise to legally direct its actions.

# 7

# Good Faith and Fair and Equitable Treatment in International Investment Law

*Martins Paparinskis**

## 7.1 Introduction

Good faith is a general principle of international law, which in different forms permeates the entirety of international legal order and process.[1] Fair and equitable treatment is, in a structural sense, a rule of much more modest ambition: merely a legal term of art well known in the field of overseas investment protection.[2] However, what the rule of fair and equitable treatment lacks in conceptual importance,[3] it makes up in the considerable practical effect in international dispute settlement on the basis of investment treaties. Judging from publicly available awards, this is the obligation that investment treaty tribunals are most likely to find to have been breached.[4] Of course, to

* This chapter borrows from arguments published elsewhere, particularly: Martins Paparinskis, 'Investment Treaty Arbitration and the (New) Law of State Responsibility' (2013) 24 EJIL 617; Martins Paparinskis, *The International Minimum Standard and Fair and Equitable Treatment* (OUP 2013).

[1] *Nuclear Tests (Australia v France) (Judgment)* [1974] ICJ Rep 253, para 49; Robert Kolb, *La bonne foi en droit international public* (Presses Universitaires de France 2000); Hugh Thirlway, *The Law and Procedure of the International Court of Justice* (OUP 2013) 9–66, 1111–42.

[2] *Oil Platforms (Iran v United States) (Preliminary Objections)* [1996] ICJ Rep 803, 847 para 39 (Higgins J). See generally Martins Paparinskis, *The International Minimum Standard and Fair and Equitable Treatment* (OUP 2013).

[3] The reading of fair and equitable treatment as a conceptually unremarkable primary obligation is not shared by everyone. For example, an argument for viewing fair and equitable treatment as a gateway for systemic integration of other sources of international law appears in Roland Kläger, *'Fair and Equitable Treatment' in International Investment Law* (CUP 2011) ch 4.

[4] From 1 August 2012 to 1 June 2014, 20 publicly available awards on merits in treaty cases have been rendered, of which nine found breaches of fair and equitable treatment, either on its own or together with one or more other obligations, and two awards recognized breach of expropriation rules only: Martins Paparinskis, 'Introduction to the Paperback Edition' in Martins Paparinskis, *The International Minimum Standard and Fair and Equitable Treatment* (OUP 2014) xliii. Cf the

suggest that a general principle and a particular primary obligation occupy different places in the architecture of the international legal order is not particularly original—one could make a similar point about many, if not all, principles and rules. But there may be something more that catches the eye in this particular instance, which makes it an important topic for analysis.

Whether international investment law is a hybrid regime in search of its identity, an accidental combination of different unrelated developments, a run-of-the-mill regime of international law, or something entirely different, is a question about which reasonable people may disagree.[5] The proper role and function of international arbitration and adjudication in investment treaty law, just as in international dispute settlement more broadly,[6] is a topic equally unlikely to lead to immediate consensus.[7] But whatever analytical perspective one adopts, the great importance of investment arbitration tribunals for articulating and elaborating key legal issues cannot be ignored.[8] When dealing with good faith and fair and equitable treatment, investment treaty tribunals appear to have suggested that good faith plays a particular role in the process of reasoning. A few examples will serve to illustrate the variety of ways in which good faith has been introduced into the argument.

In the early *Tecmed v Mexico* case, the tribunal elaborated exacting requirements of legitimate expectations and transparency, flowing from fair and equitable treatment, without any obvious legal source[9] other than the good faith principle in international law.[10] In *Merril & Ring v Canada*, the tribunal noted, in response to an argument by Canada that good faith does not impose any obligations of its own, that good faith must be applied as a general principle that has a close connection with a secure legal environment

relevant data regarding 2010–2011, suggesting similar relative importance for fair and equitable treatment: Paparinskis, *International Minimum Standard* (n 2) 4.

[5] Cf respectively Anthea Roberts, 'Clash of Paradigms: Actors and Analogies Shaping the Investment Treaty System' (2013) 107 AJIL 45; Joost Pauwelyn, 'At the Edge of Chaos?' (2014) 29 ICSID Rev 372; Martins Paparinskis, 'Analogies and Other Regimes of International Law' in Zachary Douglas, Joost Pauwelyn, and Jorge Viñuales (eds), *The Foundations of International Investment Law* (OUP 2014) 73.

[6] Chester Brown, *A Common Law of International Adjudication* (OUP 2007) 72–78; Gleider Hernández, *The International Court of Justice and the Judicial Function* (OUP 2014) ch 8.

[7] W Michael Reisman, '"Case-Specific Mandates" v "Systemic Implications": How Should Investment Tribunals Decide?' (2013) 29 Arb Intl 131.

[8] Great, but, of course, not exclusive: see Anthea Roberts, 'Power and Persuasion in Investment Treaty Arbitration: The Dual Role of States' (2010) 104 AJIL 179.

[9] Zachary Douglas, 'Nothing if Not Critical for Investment Arbitration: *Occidental, Eureko* and *Methanex*' (2006) 22 Arb Intl 27, 27.

[10] *Tecnicas Medioambientales TECMED SA v Mexico (Award)* (ICSID Arbitral Tribunal, Case No ARB(AF)/00/2, 29 May 2003) paras 154–55.

and perhaps also transparency.[11] In the recent *Micula v Romania* arbitration, the tribunal considered the investor's argument that conduct in good faith is an element of the primary obligation of fair and equitable treatment, and described its content as akin to estoppel.[12] And in another recent case, the tribunal in the *TECO v Guatemala* arbitration had no doubt that 'the minimum standard is part and parcel of the international principle of good faith ... and that a lack of good faith on the part of the state or of one of its organs should be taken into account in order to assess whether the minimum standard was breached'.[13] As these awards show, good faith might relate to different sources: a rule of interpretation of treaties in *Micula*, an obligation under customary law in *TECO*, or a general principle, through which treaties are interpreted or obligations imposed, in *TECMED*. And good faith also seems to occupy a number of roles in the argument about the content of the obligation: from being the obligation itself in *TECO*; to bad faith or absence of good faith being one of the elements of the obligation in *Micula* and *TECO*; to good faith being the basis for, being particularized as, or informing the content of more specific rules regarding respect for expectations in *TECMED* and lack of arbitrariness in *Micula*.

The diversity in the approaches outlined above does not show a necessarily impermissible conflation of different issues: after all, good faith operates in many guises in the international legal order.[14] A principle and its different particularizations may play different roles at different stages of legal reasoning. But it does suggest a potential for confusion, for the avoidance of which one should draw clear distinctions between different forms of legal arguments employing good faith. Keeping this caution in mind, the relationship between good faith and fair and equitable treatment will be addressed in this chapter in three parts. While good faith is '[o]ne of the basic principles governing the creation and performance of legal obligations, whatever their source',[15] the structural differences between different sources will lead to differences of mechanics in its operation. Some disagreement exists about the manner in which fair and equitable treatment fits within the structure of sources of international law, therefore the chapter will first explain the impact of this disagreement on the role of good faith (7.2). The second part of the chapter will address, in a relatively brief manner, selected issues of

[11] *Merril & Ring Forestry LP v Canada (Award)* (Ad Hoc Arbitral Tribunal, UNCITRAL, 31 March 2010) para 187.

[12] *Ioan Micula v Romania (Award)* (ICSID Arbitral Tribunal, Case No ARB/05/20, 11 December 2013) paras 831–34.

[13] *TECO Guatemala Holdings LLC v Guatemala (Award)* (ICSID Arbitral Tribunal Case No ARB/10/17, 19 December 2013) para 456 (citations omitted).

[14] See (n 1); chapters 2 and 3 of this volume.

[15] *Nuclear Tests* (n 1) para 46.

state responsibility for the breach of fair and equitable treatment, regarding which good faith could play a particular role (7.3). The third (and the main) part will address the extent to which the primary obligation of fair and equitable treatment particularizes good faith (7.4). The chapter does not purport to address exhaustively all the different ways in which good faith has been invoked and applied regarding fair and equitable treatment,[16] focusing instead on a limited number of representative and illustrative instances.

Overall, the chapter calls for nuance and light touch in assessing the role of good faith in articulating fair and equitable treatment. While the open-textured language of both concepts intuitively suggests a necessary or at least useful normative relationship, the translation of this intuition into the technical language of sources and interpretation may lead to less insightful and illuminating conclusions than one might have initially expected. To loosely paraphrase Robert Jennings from a related context, what is now required in a sphere such as fair and equitable treatment is the development not so much of very general principles and standards as of detailed rules of technical law. No doubt, these rules may then be said to represent the contemporary content or particularization of good faith in the particular area, but they will not be reduced a priori from the idea of good faith.[17] Of course, this perspective should not lead to a downplaying of the systemically important role of good faith in framing, underpinning, and informing particular primary obligations. But equally one should not rush to employ good faith as a ubiquitous shortcut to the conclusion of the legal argument, merely because the mundane exercise of competently identifying and applying the small print of international law turns out to be more vexing than expected.

## 7.2 Good Faith and Different Sources of Fair and Equitable Treatment

Obligations to provide fair and equitable treatment to foreign investment are included in the majority of existing treaties that address the protection of foreign investment. But the manner in which the rules are formulated may be significantly different, raising questions about the interplay between treaty

[16] See Rudolf Dolzer and Christoph Schreuer, *Principles of International Investment Law* (2nd edn, OUP 2012) 156–58; Patrick Dumberry, *The Fair and Equitable Treatment Standard: A Guide to NAFTA Case Law under Article 1105* (Kluwer Law International 2013) 222–24; Deyan Draguiev, 'Bad Faith Conduct of States in Violation of "Fair and Equitable Treatment" Standard in International Investment Law and Arbitration' (2014) 5 JIDS 273.

[17] Robert Jennings, 'State Contracts in International Law' (1961) 37 BYBIL 156, 180–81.

and customary law.[18] A number of recent developments may serve to illustrate this variety: the 2004 *Dominican Republic–Central America–United States Free Trade Agreement* defines fair and equitable treatment as prescribing and not going beyond what is required by the customary standard of treatment;[19] the 2009 ASEAN *Comprehensive Investment Agreement* expresses the obligation in treaty terms, but its explanation by reference to denial of justice and the principle of due process may have the effect of a reference to general international law;[20] and the negotiators of the *EU–Canada Free Trade Agreement* (*CETA*) have chosen to provide a detailed definition of fair and equitable treatment, yet without an obvious engagement with other rules of international law.[21] To considerably simplify the subtlety and nuance between and within different positions adopted in treaty practice, arbitral decisions, and legal writings, two dominant views have been taken regarding the relationship between the (treaty law concept of) fair and equitable treatment and (customary law concept of) international standard. Treaty rules on fair and equitable treatment may be taken to refer to customary minimum standard; or the interpretation of the autonomous treaty terms does not require taking into account the customary standard. This is not the place to untangle the normative web surrounding fair and equitable treatment,[22] merely to employ the distinctions drawn in practice between the role of treaty law and general international law to structure the discussion of good faith in three parts: in treaty law (7.2.1), general international law (7.2.2), and in equity, both within and outside the law (7.2.3).

### 7.2.1 Good faith and the law of treaties

Good faith underpins many aspects of the law of treaties,[23] but it may be convenient to focus here on its role in the interpretation of treaties. As elaborated in chapter 3, the general rule of interpretation in article 31(1) *Vienna Convention on the Law of Treaties* (*VCLT*) provides that '[a] treaty shall be interpreted *in good faith* in accordance with the ordinary meaning to be given

[18] Paparinskis, *International Minimum Standard* (n 2) 90–96.

[19] Adopted 5 August 2004 (entered into force 1 March 2006) art 10.5(1)–(2).

[20] *ASEAN Comprehensive Investment Agreement*, adopted 26 February 2009 (entered into force 29 March 2012) art 11(1)–(2).

[21] Consolidated *CETA* Text (26 September 2014) <http://trade.ec.europa.eu/doclib/docs/2014/september/tradoc_152806.pdf> accessed 1 October 2014, art X.9.

[22] For an attempt at that, suggesting that 'fair and equitable treatment' is a term of art that refers to customary international law, whether the process of reference is explicitly spelled out or not, see Paparinskis, *International Minimum Standard* (n 2) chs 5–6.

[23] Kolb (n 1) 179–314; 'Index' in Olivier Corten and Pierre Klein (eds), *The Vienna Conventions on the Law of Treaties* (OUP 2011) 1879, 1952–53.

to the terms of the treaty in their context and in the light of its object and purpose'.[24] Taking a bird's-eye-view,[25] good faith in interpretation operates through specific canons and the overall approach to interpretation,[26] but it may possibly provide for an additional overall preference for reasonableness of interpretation.[27] Moving more particularly to fair and equitable treatment, tribunals tasked with its interpretation have sometimes seemed troubled by the looseness of treaty language. Other investment obligations seem, by comparison, models of clarity: fair and equitable treatment does not require significance of interference (as explicit or necessarily implicit in concepts such as 'expropriation', 'taking', or 'deprivation'), comparison of treatment in different situations (as in national and most-favoured-nation treatment), protection of a particular legal relationship (as in umbrella clauses), or an indication regarding its structure (as in full protection and security). Could the principle of good faith be of assistance in this interpretative endeavour?

One could conceivably imagine how good faith might be relied upon to press the interpretative argument in a number of directions, three of which will be outlined here, in somewhat caricatured terms. The first argument would start from the ordinary meaning in the dictionaries: '"just", "even-handed", "unbiased", "legitimate"'.[28] An uncharitable description of this argument is: '[t]o say [that] is quite frankly to state a tautology. Such formulations are not judicially operational in the sense that they lend themselves to being readily applied to complex, concrete investment fact situations'.[29] From the perspective of good faith, this dismissal underplays the importance that good faith plays through the ordinary meaning—protecting reasonable reliance on the common and expected meaning and precluding the introduction of unusual and unexpected meanings.[30] The tribunal cited above therefore puts the cart before the normative horse. If the ordinary meaning of a treaty rule is not judicially operational, the prima facie implication is that the rule does not impose an obligation of such a character, rather than that the technique of ordinary meaning has failed. To resolve the quandary by reading the clause as imposing an expansive obligation would go against the principle

[24] *Vienna Convention on the Law of Treaties*, opened for signature 23 May 1969, 1155 UNTS 331 (entered into force 27 January 1980) art 31(1) (emphasis added).

[25] For a detailed analysis, see chapter 3 of this volume.

[26] Kolb (n 1) 272–78; Thirlway (n 1) 270, 1129–30.

[27] Kolb (n 1) 266–72; Richard Gardiner, *Treaty Interpretation* (OUP 2008) 155–57.

[28] *Saluka v Czech Republic (Partial Award)* (UNCITRAL, 17 March 2006) para 297.

[29] *Suez, Sociedad General de Aguas de Barcelona SA, and InterAgua Servicios Integrales del Agua v Argentina (Decision on Liability)* (ICSID Arbitral Tribunal, Case No ARB/03/19, 30 July 2010) para 202.

[30] Kolb (n 1) 272–73.

of reasonable interpretation as part of good faith, in requiring something from a party that could not have reasonably been envisaged.[31] The contextual interpretation, reflecting good faith in calibrating the ordinariness on which reliance could be placed, would support the narrow reading, in contrast with other obligations usually included in investment treaties, which have much easier identifiable technical meanings. The narrow interpretation would also be reasonable in the broader context of international law. For example, in a number of cases dealing with 'friendship, commerce, and navigation' treaties the International Court of Justice (ICJ) has found that certain rules are 'formulated in a broad and general manner, having an aspirational character' or are only 'such as to throw light on the interpretation of the other Treaty provisions'.[32] Overall, a good faith interpretation of fair and equitable treatment would narrow the obligation down to either an aspirational or a very limited rule.

The second argument relies on good faith in a very different manner. The starting point would be the principle of effectiveness, implied in good faith and in the object and purpose of the treaty,[33] which requires the adoption of an interpretation enabling 'the treaty to have appropriate effects'.[34] This principle is helpful in negative terms, calling for a rejection of the interpretation outlined in the previous paragraph as one that 'does not enable the treaty to have appropriate effects'.[35] Can the principle of effectiveness also assist in positively identifying what effect of fair and equitable treatment is appropriate? To some extent, it might, in framing the reasonableness of the overall interpretative exercise, to which context of the treaty, its object and purpose, and perhaps the purposes of the broader investment protection system contribute. The interpreter might note, inter alia, that: fair and equitable treatment is

[31] *Case concerning the Audit of Accounts between the Netherlands and France in Application of the Protocol of 25 September 1991 Additional to the Convention for the Protection of the Rhine from Pollution by Chlorides of 3 December 1976* (2004) 25 UNRIAA 267 paras 74–75; Kolb (n 1) 266–72, particularly 271; Gardiner (n 27) 154–57. An uncharitable reading of some arguments that place particular importance on the knowledge and perception of negotiators from developed states, particularly the United States (US) (Todd Weiler, *The Interpretation of International Investment Law* (Martinus Nijhoff 2013) 211–21) may also be problematic in this sense: if an appreciation of the significance of a term neither rises to the level of ordinary meaning nor is communicated through preparatory materials, its introduction into the interpretative process with significant effect may be contrary to good faith.

[32] *Certain Questions of Mutual Assistance in Criminal Matters (Djibouti v France) (Judgment)* [2008] ICJ Rep 177, para 113; *Oil Platforms* (n 2) para 31.

[33] Kolb (n 1) 276; Isabelle Van Damme, *Treaty Interpretation by the WTO Appellate Body* (OUP 2009) ch 7; Gardiner (n 27) 159–61.

[34] International Law Commission, 'Draft Articles on the Law of Treaties with Commentaries' [1966] II Yearbook ILC 112, 219 para 6, UN Doc A/CN.4/SER.A/1966/Add.1.

[35] ibid.

formulated in terms of an obligation, as are other obligations in investment treaties; fair and equitable treatment is not limited and qualified in the manner in which other obligations are; one might seek to identify its content by backwards induction from the preambular recitals, to the extent that issues have not been addressed by other rules, and the stability and transparency of the legal system may be read in from the purpose of development of the host state;[36] and, finally, the ordinary significance of vagueness in language is to allocate to adjudicators the power to resolve disputes submitted to them.[37] From this point, good faith might take the interpreter on slightly different routes. She might build on the authority granted by vagueness to decide on what the appropriate effect of the treaty rule is, without excessive elaboration of its content.[38] Or she might emphasize the reasonableness and predictability elements of good faith in turning to the broader system of investment dispute settlement, seeking to contribute to the development of the law by relying on the interpretation of fair and equitable treatment in other treaties.[39] Or, as the *TECMED* tribunal appears to have done,[40] she could articulate the content of the obligation by directly drawing upon good faith and its chief component of respect for legitimate expectations.[41] Overall, in one way or another, good faith would assist in informing a far-reaching obligation.

The third way of approaching fair and equitable treatment in light of good faith is both similar to and dissimilar from those outlined above. The principle of good faith in interpretation would guide the interpreter through the process of interpretation of the vague terms and into the virtually inseparable process of their application within the structure of international dispute settlement.[42] Reasonableness in interpretation would focus on two elements: function of the rule and function of the tribunal. The function of the broad and general rule enunciated in advance is to be capable of application to a wide and infinitely variable set of future cases and circumstances, which

[36] *CMS Gas Transmission Company v Argentina (Final Award)* (ICSID Arbitral Tribunal, Case No ARB 01/08, 12 May 2005) para 274.

[37] Timothy Endicott, 'The Value of Vagueness' in Andrei Marmor and Scott Soames (eds), *Philosophical Foundations of Language in the Law* (OUP 2013) 14, 26–27.

[38] *Eastern Sugar BV (Netherlands) v Czech Republic (Partial Award)* (Stockholm Chamber of Commerce, Case No 088/2004, 27 March 2007) para 335.

[39] *Saipem SpA v Bangladesh (Jurisdiction and Provisional Measures)* (ICSID Arbitral Tribunal, Case No ARB/05/07, 21 March 2007) para 67; *Chemtura Corp v Canada (Award)* (UNCITRAL, 2 August 2010) para 109; Martins Paparinskis, 'Sources of Law and Arbitral Interpretations of *Pari Materia* Investment Protection Rules' in Ole Kristian Fauchald and André Nollkaemper (eds), *The Practice of International and National Courts and the (De-)Fragmentation of International Law* (Hart 2012) 87, 114–15.

[40] *TECMED* (n 10) paras 154–55.

[41] Kolb (n 1) 143–53.

[42] Frank Berman, 'International Treaties and British Statutes' (2005) 26 Statute L Rev 1, 10.

the negotiating parties could not even begin to enumerate or contemplate at the time of negotiating the treaty. The remedy of investor–state arbitration will discipline the discretion by recognized forensic process, governed by law, offering all of the guarantees of due process and impartiality that that implies[43] (including those derived from general principles and good faith).[44] The somewhat paradoxical implication is that interpretation in good faith should appreciate the modesty of the very exercise in which it is engaged, nudging the intellectual inquiry into the direction of application and associated procedural guarantees, partly derived from other branches of good faith. Even this focus still leaves open a number of methodological approaches, some of which would focus on the peculiarities of the particular case, without obviously engaging with the approaches in other cases,[45] with others drawing upon at least a loose distillation of relevant factors and approaches.[46] Overall, whichever approach or sub-approach one follows, the most important aspects of the debate will lie in the area of particularization of rules or identification of the leading examples of their application.

### 7.2.2 Good faith and general international law

The basic structural elements of the customary minimum standard on the treatment of aliens were established in the inter-war period. In identifying these elements, it is impossible not to engage with the great *Neer* case of the United States–Mexico General Claims Commission and its standard formulated, inter alia, in terms of bad faith,[47] whether one eventually proceeds

[43] These sentences draw upon: Frank Berman, 'The Interpretation and Application of Fair and Equitable Treatment: An Arbitrator's Perspective' (*EJIL: Talk!*, 31 August 2013) <www.ejiltalk.org/the-interpretation-and-application-of-fair-and-equitable-treatment-an-arbitrators-perspective/> accessed 24 September 2014; and, more generally, upon Lauterpacht's call for procedural guarantees in international adjudication as one solution for substantive interpretative challenges, Hersch Lauterpacht, *The Function of Law in the International Community* (OUP 2011) ch X; Martti Koskenniemi, 'The Function of Law in the International Community: Introduction' in Hersch Lauterpacht, *The Function of Law in the International Community* (OUP 2011) xxix, xlii–xliii.

[44] Kolb (n 1) 598–663; Robert Kolb, 'General Principles of Procedural Law' in Andreas Zimmermann, Christian Tomuschat and Karin Oellers-Frahm (eds), *The Statute of the International Court of Justice: A Commentary* (2nd edn, OUP 2012) 871, 903–08; Robert Kolb, *The International Court of Justice* (Hart 2013) 945–52.

[45] *Achmea BV (formerly known as Eureko BV) v Slovakia (Final Award)* (Permanent Court of Arbitration, Case No 2008–13, 7 December 2012) paras 279–84; *Rompetrol v Romania (Award)* (ICSID Arbitral Tribunal, Case No ARB/06/3, 6 May 2013) para 279.

[46] Vaughan Lowe, 'Fair and Equitable Treatment: Remarks' (2006) 100 ASIL Proceedings 73, 73.

[47] *LFH Neer and Pauline Neer (United States v Mexico)* (1926) 4 RIAA 60, 61–62 ('an outrage, ... bad faith, ... wilful neglect of duty, or ... an insufficiency of governmental action so far short of international standards that every reasonable and impartial man will readily recognise its insufficiency').

to dismiss it as an authority of minor relevance[48] or accept it as effectively irrefutable.[49] In a debate where opposing views are put forward with such erudition, there is something to be said for taking a step back, rather than contributing to one of the established positions. From this perspective, and not to put too fine a point on it, both sides may seem wrong: *Neer* is certainly not a semi-peremptory statement of law, but neither is it an accidental irrelevance. *Neer* is an important stage in the development of the international standard by means of analogy, honestly and explicitly deriving criteria of procedural outrage from the better-established rules of denial of justice, and then applying them more generally to all rules on treatment of aliens.[50] Once *Neer* is accepted as what it is—a default rule, open to clarification or replacement by specific rules, when they emerge—the solution lies not in the defence of its shorthand or in finding a new shorthand, but in its application to specific cases and elaboration of more specific rules on particular issues.[51]

Whether one views post-*Neer* developments as falling within its framework by elaborating the standard of outrage and special rules or as rejecting *Neer*, bad faith and good faith do not seem to have played an important role. It may be that 'bad faith' is used here in the sense of fault[52]—a blameworthy psychological attitude of the state[53]—in which case the point made is not very helpful. If the scope and content of the obligation itself is not identified, then to consider whether compliance or incompliance has been in bad faith does not add much legal value. The focus might have made sense regarding the issue that the Commission was tackling, since the obligations relating to the protection and security of aliens in general,

[48] *Mondev v United States (Award)* (ICSID Additional Facility, Case No ARB(AF)/99/2, 11 October 2002) paras 115–16; *Railroad Development Corp v Guatemala (Award)* (ICSID Arbitral Tribunal, Case No ARB/07/23, 29 June 2012) paras 216–19; Jan Paulsson and Georgios Petrochilos, 'Neer-ly Misled' (2007) 22 ICSID Rev 242; Stephen Schwebel, 'Is Neer Far from Fair and Equitable?' (2011) 27 Arb Intl 555.

[49] *Glamis Gold Ltd v United States (Award)* (Ad Hoc Arbitral Tribunal, UNCITRAL, 8 June 2009) paras 21–23; M Sornarajah, *The International Law on Foreign Investment* (3rd edn, CUP 2010) 130, 347.

[50] Paparinskis, *International Minimum Standard* (n 2) 48–54 and generally ch 2.

[51] As the General Claims Commission itself proceeded to do in a subsequent case regarding the taking of life: *Teodoro García and MA Garza (Mexico v United States)* (1926) 4 UNRIAA 119 paras 4–5. See also nn 42–46.

[52] This reading would fit within the long-running debates about the role of fault in the law of state responsibility, at the time of *Neer* viewed as closely connected with the primary rules on the treatment of aliens and investors: James Crawford, *State Responsibility: The General Part* (CUP 2013) 24–36, 60–61.

[53] Giuseppe Palmisano, 'Fault' in Rüdiger Wolfrum (ed), *Max Planck Encyclopedia of Public International Law* (OUP) <www.mpepil.com> accessed 24 September 2014, para 45.

and punishment of crimes against them in particular, were considered to require an obligation of due diligence.[54] However, such an approach would be less useful in other areas for the treatment of aliens, where even the basic structural assumptions could be as yet undeveloped beyond a loose prohibition of outrage.

Another reading of *Neer* would put 'bad faith' alongside 'wilful neglect' as providing a foothold for a primary obligation of non-discrimination. This obligation may or may not be implicit in the contemporary minimum standard, and its presence has to be determined in terms of traditional customary law analysis, rather than by relying on different shorthand statements.[55] Yet another approach, adopted in some decisions, is to explain the international standard more generally as an expression of good faith:[56] a point that may be defensible in the sense of broader historical underpinnings[57] but does not call for the particularization of good faith in the form of an international minimum standard of specific content. To the extent that good faith is pressed to support particular requirements of stability or transparency,[58] a nagging suspicion arises that potential breadth of the general concept is used to sidestep the important question of how it has been particularized and developed into particular rules. Of course, good faith may both play an important structural role and be the basis for particularization of specific rules, but one should not be able to conflate these points so as to identify particular obligations without ticking the boxes for their creation in accordance with the traditional rules regarding sources of international law.

### 7.2.3 Good faith and equity, within and outside the law

States, tribunals, and writers have advocated a great variety of approaches to fair and equitable treatment, but almost all of these are underpinned by the commonality of perspective on fair and equitable treatment as a primary rule of international law. At the same time, if one were to consider the issue without taking into account the practice of the last two decades, a historical

[54] Alwyn Vernon Freeman, *The International Responsibility of States for Denial of Justice* (Longmans, Green & Co 1938) ch XIII.

[55] Paparinskis, *International Minimum Standard* (n 2) 245–47.

[56] *TECO* (n 13) para 456.

[57] Kolb describes the international minimum standard as particularizing the prohibition of abuse of rights in the exercise of discretionary competence of regulating conduct of aliens: Kolb (n 1) 482–85.

[58] *Merril & Ring* (n 11) para 187.

reading of fair and equitable treatment could put it in the stratum of practice that is unified by the looseness and flexibility of the criteria, at its weakest introducing flexibility within the law and at its strongest providing for extra-legal discretion. This is not the place to consider whether fair and equitable treatment indeed falls within the pedigree of applicable law clauses[59] or contains an authorization to decide *ex aequo et bono* in a living language.[60] There are good systemic reasons to prefer an inquiry into equity as part of the law[61] to a seeming departure from the strictures of the judicial function.[62] But it may be instructive to consider the added value of good faith for either inquiry.

If 'equitable' treatment is called for, then a consideration of equity within the law would seem to be required, and the looseness of this concept would be likely to lead to at least a partial overlap with good faith and its particularizations, both of them prioritizing purpose and spirit of the rules and conduct over blind formalism.[63] The manner in which equity operates outside the law is more contested.[64] If *ex aequo et bono* authorizes the tribunal to pronounce completely outside the law, then good faith might have no application in the direct sense, even though it may be given effect indirectly through general procedural principles applicable to international adjudication within which this exercise is conducted[65] (as discussed above in part 7.3). But if the rules of existing law are viewed as providing a convenient starting point for identifying any necessary changes,[66] then good faith would be important both in elaborating this position, and in overlapping with corrective equity in identifying the unreasonable elements that would have to be modified. Indeed, the manner in which an inquiry into fair and equitable treatment is sometimes conducted, focusing on the peculiarity of the factual situation and the weighing and balancing of worthy with unworthy,[67] is not that dissimilar from what one might expect from an inquiry into equity at the vanishing point of law.

[59] Weiler (n 31) ch 5.

[60] Paparinskis, *International Minimum Standard* (n 2) 115–20.

[61] *MTD Equity Sdn Bhv and MTD Chile SA v Chile (Decision on Annulment)* (2007) 13 ICSID Rep 500, para 48.

[62] Hernández (n 6) 67–68.

[63] See generally Kolb (n 1) 107–11. Particularly regarding fair and equitable treatment, see Kläger (n 3) 129–32.

[64] See a summary of different approaches in Thirlway (n 1) 44–45.

[65] Elihu Lauterpacht, *Aspects of the Administration of International Justice* (Grotius 1991) 47.

[66] Lauterpacht, *Function of Law* (n 43) 322–23.

[67] Ioana Tudor, *The Fair and Equitable Treatment Standard in the International Law of Foreign Investment* (OUP 2008) chs 3, 5, 7.

## 7.3 Good Faith and Responsibility for the Breach of Fair and Equitable Treatment

In the contemporary law of state responsibility, the starting point of any analysis is that breaches of all primary rules give rise to the same general secondary rules of state responsibility.[68] Secondary rules, as the ICJ put it, 'do not vary with the nature of the wrongful act in question in the absence of a clearly expressed *lex specialis*'.[69] This section does not seek to challenge the orthodox position that a breach of an obligation of fair and equitable treatment gives rise to general secondary rules of state responsibility, just as with any other primary rule. The possible impact of good faith or principles or rules derived from it is determined by the primary rather than secondary obligation. Still, it may be interesting to consider a narrower point: are there any particular challenges raised by the implementation of state responsibility before investor–state tribunals[70] for the breach of fair and equitable treatment, which may be illuminated by the perspective of good faith? The next paragraphs will consider two examples, each taken from one of the two sufficient and necessary criteria for state responsibility: attribution and breach.[71]

The first example relates to the rules of attribution regarding the conduct of state-owned corporations, where ownership per se is insufficient for attribution, and something more is required, such as the company becoming an empty shell, run simply as a vehicle or extension of the government, or being instructed to

[68] International Law Commission, 'Articles on Responsibility of States for Internationally Wrongful Acts' [2001] II Yearbook ILC pt 2, 31, UN Doc A/CN.4/SER.A/2001/Add.1 (ILC Articles); Anastasios Gourgourinis, 'General/Particular International Law and Primary/Secondary Rules: Unitary Terminology of a Fragmented System' (2011) 22 EJIL 993; Crawford, *State Responsibility* (n 52) ch 2. General rules are, of course, subject to *lex specialis*: ILC Articles art 55 (see also arts 41–42).

[69] *Application of the Convention on the Prevention and Punishment of the Crime of Genocide (Bosnia and Herzegovina v Serbia) (Judgment)* [2007] ICJ Rep 43, para 401.

[70] Crawford, *State Responsibility* (n 52) 587–90; Martins Paparinskis, 'Investment Treaty Arbitration and the (New) Law of State Responsibility' (2013) 24 EJIL 617.

[71] Other aspects of the law of state responsibility are also, of course, informed by good faith: Kolb (n 1) part IV. In the particular context of investment arbitration, good faith may be of importance for issues of injury and admissibility: see chapter 5 of this volume. This section focuses on the narrower points, of particular importance to fair and equitable treatment. Another example that might have been considered here is duress by the state regarding the investor, an issue obviously raising grave concerns about good faith and capable of being considered as both a circumstance precluding wrongfulness and a criterion of compliance with the primary rule: *Desert Line Projects LLC v Yemen (Award)* (ICSID Arbitral Tribunal, Case No ARB/05/17, 6 February 2008) para 188; Paparinskis, 'Investment Treaty Arbitration' (n 70) 629–30.

do a certain thing.[72] The distinction between primary and secondary rules may, of course, be more artificial in some cases than in others,[73] but the particular inquiry into attribution as a matter of secondary rules could simultaneously raise questions about compliance with the primary obligation of fair and equitable treatment. For example, the criteria for determining whether the corporation is run by the government as an empty shell (an issue of attribution) seem similar to those relied on for determining whether the conduct has been engaged 'in good faith and form, and not deliberately to set out to destroy or frustrate the investment by improper means' (an issue of breach of the primary rule).[74] Both inquiries are informed by good faith and its preference for substance over form.[75]

The vagueness of fair and equitable treatment and the occasional brevity of reasoning by tribunals may raise questions about the extent to which the awards follow the basic proposition that state responsibility arises only out of a breach of an obligation under international law.[76] The reliance by some tribunals on the legitimate or reasonable expectations of investors led one annulment committee to note that '[t]he obligations of the host state towards foreign investors derive from the terms of the applicable investment treaty and not from any set of expectations investors may have or claim to have'.[77] To identify breach by reference to an investor's expectations under an undetermined system of law rather than binding international obligations would indeed suggest a radical departure from the traditional model of international responsibility.[78] Of course, this objection may be viewed as

[72] ILC Articles (n 68) 48 (art 8, commentary para 6); Crawford, *State Responsibility* (n 52) 161–65.

[73] Eric David, 'Primary and Secondary Rules' in James Crawford, Alain Pellet and Simon Olesson (eds), *The Law of International Responsibility* (OUP 2010) 27, 29–32.

[74] *Waste Management v US (II) (Final Award)* (ICSID Additional Facility, Case No ARB(AF)/00/3, 30 April 2004) para 138.

[75] An affirmative answer regarding attribution of conduct of state-owned corporations does not necessarily call for an affirmative answer regarding breach of fair and equitable treatment by that conduct. It is perfectly possible that the direction or control that the state has exercised is sufficient for attribution but is not of the improper nature to breach the rule: Crawford, *State Responsibility* (n 52) 164–65. For example, in a recent case where attribution of conduct of a state-owned corporation was discussed in a sophisticated manner, one arbitrator dissented on the issue of attribution, but the tribunal was in agreement that no breach had taken place: *Tulip Real Estate and Development Netherlands BV v Turkey (Award)* (ICSID Arbitral Tribunal, Case No ARB/11/28, 10 March 2014) paras 302–27, 401–14; paras 1–11 (Arbitrator Jaffe).

[76] ILC Articles (n 68) art 12.

[77] *MTD Equity* (n 61) para 67.

[78] Radical, but not unimaginable: see Mona Pinchis, 'The Ancestry of "Equitable Treatment" in Trade' (2014) 15 JWIT 13, 66. For example, in multilateral trade, the concept of 'reasonable expectations' has been used in the (rare) disputes over non-violation complaints: Appellate Body Report, *EC—Measures Affecting Asbestos and Asbestos-Related Products*, WTO Doc WT/DS135/AB/R (adopted 5 April 2001) para 190; Crawford, *State Responsibility* (n 52) 238–39. See also Alan Boyle, 'Liability for Injurious Consequences of Acts not Prohibited by International Law' in Crawford, Pellet and Olesson (n 73) 95.

excessively pedantic and could be responded to by explicitly restating the non-frustration of expectations as a criterion of the primary rule.[79] But the focus on expectations, not tied down to a particular legal system, might also be defended through the lens of good faith, if viewed as a principle expressed through respect for expectations, the latter thus necessarily belonging to each and every legal order.[80]

A different but not entirely unrelated question relates to the criteria of state responsibility under international law regarding the breach of contractual obligations: a long-debated point on which the intermediate position is to be preferred, namely recognizing international responsibility for contractual breaches committed in extra-contractual public capacity.[81] Some tribunals have, however, suggested that a contractual breach by the state may give rise to a breach of fair and equitable treatment if it is in bad faith[82] or disproportionate.[83] There is no reason to assume that international law is incapable of generating primary obligations of international law regarding compliance by states with contracts that focus on the content, rather than the character of the breach—treaty rules on umbrella clauses have sometimes been interpreted as doing precisely that.[84] But there is something to be said for pausing before substituting and rewriting contractual terms and consequences by reference to such general and vague standards derived from good faith as bad faith, legitimate expectations, and proportionality.[85] When such developments do occur, the nagging suspicion again arises that good faith-inspired concepts are pressed to do too many tasks simultaneously: providing another layer of protection over and above the contractual terms on rights, obligations, and consequences of breach within the domestic legal order, and contributing to looseness of standards at the international level.

[79] Paparinskis, *International Minimum Standard* (n 2) 251–59.

[80] Kolb (n 1) 143–53. The response to the argument would be to still require an explanation of the manner in which legitimate expectations are expressed within the framework of sources and responsibility. It is perfectly plausible to conclude that the principle of legitimate expectations is derived from the principle of good faith but does not have an independent justification or a separate role to play. Regarding principles of interpretation, see Van Damme (n 33) 65–68.

[81] *Waste Management II* (n 74) paras 114–116; Paparinskis, *International Minimum Standard* (n 2) 242–43.

[82] *Gemplus SA, SLP SA, Gemplus Industrial SA de CV and Talsud SA v Mexico (Award)* (ICSID Additional Facility, Case No ARB(AF)/04/3 and ARB(AF)/04/3, 16 June 2010) paras 7.70, 7.77–7.78.

[83] *Occidental Petroleum Corp, Occidental Exploration and Production Company v Ecuador (Award)* (ICSID Arbitral Tribunal, Case No ARB/06/11, 5 October 2012) paras 384–452.

[84] See, eg, *SGS Société Générale de Surveillance SA v Paraguay (Decision on Annulment)* (ICSID Ad Hoc Annulment Committee, Case No ARB/07/29, 19 May 2014) paras 133–34.

[85] James Crawford, 'Treaty and Contract in Investment Arbitration' (2008) 24 Arb Intl 351, 372.

If that is an accurate description of the development, then good faith and its particularizations might be pulling the legal process away from its preferable direction. Rather, good faith is injecting looseness back into principles, standards, and rules that have been particularized from it at both domestic and international levels; eroding the precision and predictability of rule-making both domestically and internationally; and perhaps even tinkering with some basic underpinnings of the structure of the international legal order.

## 7.4 Particularization of Good Faith in the Obligation of Fair and Equitable Treatment

Tribunals and legal writers have attempted to capture the elusive essence of fair and equitable treatment on numerous occasions, and in more recent years states and international organizations have also contributed to the search for definition. Reasonable people might disagree which of these efforts has been the most successful, but the award in *Waste Management v Mexico (II)* is certainly one of the most cited on this point, and its description of conduct breaching the fair and equitable treatment standard will be taken as a convenient point of departure:

> conduct [that is] ... arbitrary, grossly unfair, unjust or idiosyncratic, is discriminatory and exposes the claimant to sectional or racial prejudice, or involves a lack of due process leading to an outcome which offends judicial propriety—as might be the case with a manifest failure of natural justice in judicial proceedings or a complete lack of transparency and candor in an administrative process. In applying this standard it is relevant that the treatment is in breach of representations made by the host State which were reasonably relied on by the claimant.[86]

This section will consider the extent to which good faith has informed or been particularized as elements of fair and equitable treatment: non-arbitrariness (7.4.1), non-discrimination (7.4.2), due process (7.4.3), transparency (7.4.4), and protection of expectations (7.4.5).

[86] *Waste Management II* (n 74) para 98; Paparinskis, *International Minimum Standard* (n 2) 238–39. Another much-cited description of conduct in breach of fair and equitable treatment was provided by the *Saluka* tribunal as 'act[ing] in a way that is manifestly inconsistent, non-transparent, unreasonable (ie unrelated to some rational policy), or discriminatory (ie based on unjustifiable distinctions)': *Saluka Investment BV v Czech Republic (Partial Award)* (2006) ICSID Rep 274, para 309. To put both awards within the same pedigree might treat with an excessively light touch the distinction between treaty and custom in the area noted in part 7.2 above, but it may be justified by the position of the *Saluka* tribunal itself, which viewed the distinction as more apparent than real and approvingly cited tribunals applying customary law: paras 291, 302, 305, 443.

### 7.4.1 Non-arbitrariness

The leading modern case on the obligation of non-arbitrariness in the treatment of foreign investment is the ICJ judgment in the case *Elettronica Sicula SpA* case (*ELSI*), where arbitrariness was described as 'not so much opposed to a rule of law, as something opposed to the rule of law... a wilful disregard of due process of law, an act which shocks, or at least surprises, a sense of judicial propriety'.[87] Good faith did not explicitly feature in the judgment, which rather explained arbitrariness by drawing on the concept of rule of law;[88] nor did good faith appear in the separate opinions. While judicial decisions may end up framing and explaining legal issues in a manner and language different from that chosen by the parties, the lack of reference to good faith in the judgment accurately captures the approach taken by both the United States (US) and Italy in the litigation. At least prima facie, good faith in relation to primary obligations of investment protection was mentioned only once, when Keith Highet on behalf of Italy pointed in passing to the presumption of good faith, which cannot be overcome 'by merely labelling the requisition as a bad thing, or saying that it was in bad faith or not in good faith'.[89] What the pleadings do show is that the US and Italy mostly dealt in their discussion with the appropriateness of goals and reasonableness of particular measures,[90] but the test set out and applied in the judgment was quite different. The examination of appropriateness and reasonableness

[87] *Elettronica Sicula SpA (ELSI) (United States v Italy) (Judgment)* [1989] ICJ Rep 15, para 128 and more generally paras 123–30; Paparinskis, *International Minimum Standard* (n 2) 239. The US takes what appears to be a minority view in limiting the relevance of the explanation of arbitrariness of *ELSI* to the particular treaty: *Mondev v US* (ICSID Additional Facility, Case No ARB(AF)/99/2, Pleadings, 22 May 2002) 688 <www.state.gov/documents/organization/15441.pdf> accessed 24 September 2014 (Clodfelter on behalf of the US).

[88] Cf *Draft Convention on the Protection of Foreign Property* of the Organisation for Economic Co-operation and Development, which stated that due process as a criterion of taking was 'akin' to the Anglo-Saxon 'rule of law' or continental *Rechtsstaat*: 'OECD Draft Convention on the Protection of Foreign Property' (1968) 7 ILM 117 (art III commentary 5(a)).

[89] 'Oral Arguments', *ELSI* [1989] III ICJ Pleadings 1, 272.

[90] The US argued that 'where the means employed do not fit the expressed goal, or are legally impermissible, then those means are arbitrary and unreasonable': 'Reply of the United States of America', *ELSI* [1988] II ICJ Pleadings 363, 385; see generally 'Memorial of the United States of America', *ELSI* [1987] I ICJ Pleadings 43, 76–80; 'Reply of the United States of America', *ELSI* [1988] II ICJ Pleadings 363, 384–85; 'Oral Arguments', *ELSI* [1988] III ICJ Pleadings 1, 101 (Gardner). Italy objected that concerns had been sufficiently serious, and that the goal was appropriate in principle but could not be achieved by the particular measures: 'Counter-Memorial of Italy', *ELSI* [1988] II ICJ Pleadings 3, 44–45. Later in the proceedings, Italy shifted the focus from the broader questions of ends and means to the technical aspects of availability of competence in principle and the reasons and legal basis provided in the decisions: 'Rejoinder of Italy', *ELSI* [1988] II ICJ Pleadings 417, 464–65; 'Oral Arguments', *ELSI* [1988] III ICJ Pleadings 1, 229 (Capotorti).

was limited to the very deferential statement that '[i]t cannot be said to have been unreasonable or merely capricious'.[91] The availability of the formal and procedural safeguards invoked by Italy in the rejoinder and oral pleadings—recitation of reasons and legal bases, existence of broader competence, availability of functioning remedies—were decisive in rejecting the US claim.[92] If one takes *ELSI* as a guide to arbitrariness as an element of fair and equitable treatment, then good faith, even if providing the backdrop against which the rules on arbitrariness are formulated,[93] does not directly influence the general structure and content of the rule that has been created.

Good faith may, however, be of more direct relevance to particular aspects of arbitrariness. The award in *Cargill v Mexico* is an example of the rare case where the express intention of the state's conduct was to injure the investment to the greatest extent possible (as part of a series of countermeasures adopted to change the policy of the investor's home state) and was therefore found to be in bad faith.[94] Apart from such explicit measures, the most extreme version of arbitrariness in breach of fair and equitable treatment would be conspiracy, going against, as the *Waste Management II* tribunal put it, the 'basic obligation of the State... to act in good faith and form'.[95] The recent awards in the *Yukos v Russia* arbitration, albeit not using the technical terms of 'conspiracy' and 'good faith', approach the issue in a similar manner, basing the findings on responsibility on the fact that 'the primary objective of the Russian Federation was not to collect taxes but rather to bankrupt Yukos and appropriate its valuable assets'.[96] Even in the absence of conspiracy, good faith may illuminate arbitrariness as an abuse of form, which the tribunal in the *Railroad Development Corporation v Guatemala* described as conduct engaged 'under a cloak of formal correctness in defence of the rule of law, in

[91] *ELSI (Judgment)* (n 87) para 129. [92] ibid. [93] Kolb (n 1) 468–69.

[94] *Cargill v Mexico (Award)* (ICSID Additional Facility, Case No ARB(AF)/05/2, 18 September 2009) paras 296–305. Mexico also relied on countermeasures as a circumstance precluding wrongfulness, but the tribunal found that countermeasures could not be opposed to the rights held by the investor, and therefore wrongfulness for the breach of investment protection obligations could not be precluded in the investor–state legal relations considered by the tribunal: paras 379–430; see generally Martins Paparinskis, 'Investment Arbitration and the Law of Countermeasures' (2008) 79 BYBIL 264, 317–51.

[95] *Waste Management II (Final Award)* (ICSID Additional Facility, Case No ARB(AF)/00/3, 30 April 2004) para 138; Paparinskis, *International Minimum Standard* (n 2) 244; Draguiev (n 16) 291–92.

[96] *Yukos Universal Ltd (Isle of Man) v Russia (Final Award)* (Permanent Court of Arbitration, Case No AA 227, 18 July 2014) paras 756, 1579. The *Yukos* tribunal found that Russia had engaged in unlawful expropriation and therefore did not determine whether fair and equitable treatment had been breached (ibid para 1585), but the reasoning regarding the questionable public interest and breaches of due process of law (ibid paras 1581, 1583) makes it likely that an answer to such a question would have been affirmative.

fact for exacting concessions unrelated to the finding'.[97] Still, the examination of abusive purposes should not lose sight of the backdrop of methodology of *ELSI*. Investment obligations are not directed at disciplining policy debates and choices, but at the manner in which these policies are formulated and applied. This function can be best achieved through the elaboration of requirements that non-arbitrariness imposes on form and procedure.[98]

To summarize what has been said so far: good faith may be providing the backdrop against which the obligation of arbitrariness more generally is formulated, and it may be particularly illuminating for those aspects of arbitrariness that address the abuse of form for an improper purpose. But, arguably, good faith, or at least certain principles associated with good faith, should hesitate to venture into certain areas within the rule of arbitrariness, particularly in relation to state contracts. In the *Ambatielos* case before the ICJ, in which the United Kingdom was a respondent, Gerald Fitzmaurice on its behalf:

> emphatically contest[ed] the proposition... that government is under some *special* obligation of good faith. All parties to a contract are under an obligation to act in good faith. But there is no principle of law that I know of which imposes any *special* obligation or responsibility on a government, and in its capacity as a trader or contractor it cannot be in a worse or more onerous position than its own citizens.[99]

Of course, a pleading in the heat of contentious litigation is not the same thing as a reflective observation from the ivory tower, but the suggested focus on the character of the breach and availability of remedies, rather than the good faith of the state, seems close enough to the majority view on the issue.[100] As noted above, some tribunals have relied on good faith and the associated principles of legitimate expectations and proportionality in the discussion of international responsibility for contractual breaches.[101] To paraphrase Fitzmaurice, does that mean that a principle of law now imposes a special

[97] *Railroad Development* (n 48) para 234; Paparinskis, *International Minimum Standard* (n 2) 241–22, 244; Draguiev (n 16) 292–93. These authorities may be viewed as spelling out the International Court's dictum on conduct 'unreasonable or merely capricious': *ELSI (Judgment)* (n 87) para 129.

[98] *Achmea BV v Slovakia (Final Award)* (Permanent Court of Arbitration, Case No 2008–13, 7 December 2012) para 294: 'The Contracting Parties are free to adopt the policies that they choose. The Treaty focuses on the manner in which policies may be changed and implemented, not on the policies themselves'.

[99] 'Oral Arguments', *Ambatielos (Greece v UK)* [1953] ICJ Pleadings 344, 389 (emphasis in original).

[100] Stephen Schwebel, 'On whether a Breach by a State of a Contract with an Alien is a Breach of International Law' in Stephen Schwebel, *Justice in International Law* (CUP 1994) 425; Paparinskis, *International Minimum Standard* (n 2) 226–27, 242–43.

[101] See above nn 81–85.

obligation or responsibility of good faith on a government? The first point to make in response is that an appropriately drafted umbrella clause could lead to international responsibility for a breach of contract under domestic law, even without further qualifications or adjectives. The second point, perhaps underpinning some of the awards, would distance fair and equitable treatment from the customary law rules on state contracts, instead judging the totality of conduct by the state—including the extent to which the conduct is malicious, unexpected, or far-reaching—against the benchmark of equity and its overlap with good faith. The third argument, being the most challenging, would have to either rethink the traditional position on custom suggested by Fitzmaurice, or demonstrate the evolution of customary law in subsequent practice. To put the argument in the perspective of historical law-making, the position of international law on state contracts was always a contentious subject-matter, but states and tribunals managed to arrive at a rough consensus about the relevant questions and perspectives. Whether or not these were the best questions to ask, one should hesitate before replacing an established (if imperfect) methodology with a new and untested one, and instead focus on elaborating the existing rules and approaches.[102] From this perspective, bringing in the language and concepts of good faith may not necessarily be a commendable contribution.

### 7.4.2 Non-discrimination

Some disagreement exists regarding the role of non-discrimination in fair and equitable treatment. Certain treaty rules explicitly provide for non-discrimination; non-discrimination as a criterion of lawfulness of expropriation and as part of the prohibition of 'arbitrariness and discrimination' are two examples of this practice. Fair and equitable treatment is not commonly expressed in explicit terms of non-discrimination, raising therefore the question whether the obligation of non-discrimination is either implicit in fair and equitable

[102] I am not suggesting that the traditional rules on state contracts provide ready-made answers to all questions faced by modern investment protection law. The focus on extra-contractual public powers still leaves a number of issues, on which authorities are not entirely clear, such as: (i) the distinction between the inappropriate publicness of conduct and the inescapably public form of decision-making on any issue by public authorities; (ii) the manner in which powers peculiar to public entities but provided under general rules of the domestic legal order fit within the framework; and (iii) the extent to which the fine distinctions between attribution, primary rules, breach, actors, and privity, elaborated regarding umbrella clauses, are relevant for state contracts more generally. For a sophisticated dissection of various approaches to international responsibility for contractual breaches, viewing the certainty of traditional rules in a more critical vein than this chapter, see Jean Ho, 'Book Review Essay: Unraveling the *Lex Causae* in Investment Claims' (2014) 15 JWIT 757, 763–77.

treatment or, as a slightly different point, a particular part of the obligation of fair and equitable treatment is expressed in terms that require an analysis of non-discrimination. Divergence arises in practice on the former point, particularly regarding the question whether non-discrimination, and of what kind, is implicit in the customary minimum standard. The historical narrative, starting from the prominent prohibitions of discriminatory administration of justice in particular and the discriminatory conduct in general,[103] suggests that when new rules are created, they are formed from and around the core of equality of aliens, that is, obligations of non-discrimination on the basis of nationality. No obvious examples of other customary rules on the treatment of aliens would permit discrimination of aliens qua aliens. At the same time, parties to the *North American Free Trade Agreement* (*NAFTA*)[104] and increasingly tribunals have taken the view that non-discrimination does not constitute a necessary element of obligations regarding the treatment of investors.[105] That is a curious development, which may be explained in various ways.[106] Still, since good faith does not seem to feature significantly in any of the explanations, the next paragraph will instead consider the extent to which good faith may illuminate overlaps between non-discrimination and fair and equitable treatment.

The first example of a possible overlap would be the case of intentional discrimination of investment because of the nationality of the investor. The *Cargill* case of a countermeasure applied to a foreign investor with the purpose of implementing responsibility of its home state was described as being in bad faith vis-à-vis the investor.[107] Of course, such cases are relatively rare, and the usual factual scenario would be likely to involve distinctions between

[103] See generally Paparinskis, *International Minimum Standard* (n 2) ch 2.

[104] *North American Free Trade Agreement*, signed 17 December 1992 [1994] CTS 2 (entered into force 1 January 1994) (*NAFTA*).

[105] Dumberry (n 16) 207–21.

[106] Paparinskis, *International Minimum Standard* (n 2) 246–47. Explanations could include: (i) the substantive and procedural context of *NAFTA*, with explicit treaty rules regarding non-discrimination and the well-known skirmish between the early tribunals and *NAFTA* parties about the principles and guarantees that could be read into fair and equitable treatment; (ii) *NAFTA* parties and tribunals are consistently misreading the law, and therefore contribute (at most) to a rule of special customary law opposable only *inter se*; (iii) *NAFTA* practice accurately captures the development of the corpus of rules on the treatment of aliens in the first careful consideration of the issue in the last decades, appreciating the shift from the loose compendium of different principles and rules to finer distinctions between narrower rules of treaty and customary character; (iv) *NAFTA* practice, despite appearances, is directed not at rejection but at elaboration of the core of non-discrimination, which historically was applied in the context of de jure or purposeful discrimination, and thus would probably be narrower than non-discrimination as a treaty obligation in international economic law.

[107] *Cargill v Mexico* (n 94) paras 296–305. See also n 94.

(certain categories of) foreign investors and investments and (certain categories of) domestic investors and investments, and questions about similarity of situations, dissimilarity of treatment, and reasonableness of justifications would provide the frame of reasoning. Good faith might, perhaps, be relevant in informing the line between reasonableness and arbitrariness in the distinctions drawn.[108] The final question relates to prohibition of discrimination on the basis of criteria other than nationality, expressed in the consolidated *CETA* text as '[t]argeted discrimination on manifestly wrongful grounds, such as gender, race or religious belief'.[109] Some elements in this formula raise further questions,[110] but for the present purpose it is important that the idea of inappropriateness of abusing form for particular purposes is a particularization of good faith through fair and equitable treatment. Whether a legal regime focused on protection of foreign investment can coherently *ex*clude foreignness-based discrimination and *in*clude discrimination not related to foreignness is a different matter altogether and not part of the present discussion.

### 7.4.3 Due process

Due process is the most sophisticated part of fair and equitable treatment, particularly regarding due process in administration of justice.[111] Some but not all of the requirements regarding due process may be viewed as particularizing good faith.[112] For the present purpose, and with a great deal of simplification, one might view the obligations regarding due process as particularizing a number of principles, sometimes in an overlapping manner, which include good faith but are more focused on equality. Due process in administration of justice is traditionally discussed by examining its requirements in different procedural stages: access to justice, delays of justice, due process, substance of the judgment, and execution of the judgment. The next paragraphs will consider the relevance of good faith for each of these issues.

[108] Cf Appellate Body Report, *US—Import Prohibition of Certain Shrimp and Shrimp Products*, WTO Doc WT/DS68/AB/R (adopted 6 November 1998) paras 158–60.

[109] Consolidated *CETA* Text (n 21) art X.9.

[110] Some of the questions might relate to: (i) the criteria for grounds being 'manifestly wrongful': one of the examples is peremptory and the other two are not, and the strength of the argument of them being customary is varied; (ii) whether bringing in grounds of discrimination not related to nationality (or not meant to explain nationality) is an inappropriate conflation of the rationale and scope of investment regime with other regimes for protection of individual rights: see Paparinskis, 'Analogies and Other Regimes of International Law' (n 5) 79–81.

[111] See generally Freeman (n 54); Jan Paulsson, *Denial of Justice in International Law* (CUP 2005); Paparinskis, *International Minimum Standard* (n 2) ch 8.

[112] Kolb (n 1) 131–32.

In the *Barcelona Traction* case, Judge Morelli stated that '[a]ny State which, having attributed certain rights to foreign nationals, prevents them from gaining access to the courts for the purpose of asserting those rights is guilty, in international law, of a denial of justice'.[113] If expressed in these terms, denial of access to justice may be viewed as an expression of good faith in precluding inappropriate inconsistency: the state may have considerable freedom in defining the existence of rights within its legal order, but it would be arbitrary to simultaneously recognize rights and preclude foreigners from the facility of protecting them. State practice and arbitral decisions regarding effectiveness of the right to access also reflect considerations of good faith, protesting the inconsistent or malicious conduct of states to preclude access to justice (including conduct as extreme in one case as an alleged murder of the claimant),[114] but accepting reasonable restrictions.[115] Delays of justice could be viewed as a particular example of refusal to have access to justice in the first place,[116] and in that sense would further elaborate the arbitrary inconsistency between presence of rights and lack of remedies. In particular instances, the inconsistency would be heightened by inappropriate conduct of courts or the executive.[117] Execution of judgments may similarly be viewed as an elaboration of the obligation to provide effective access to protect existing rights, and in particular instances may raise questions of inappropriate interference by other authorities of the state.[118]

The broader rubric of procedural guarantees within judicial proceedings was formulated in a somewhat different manner, evaluating the overall propriety of conduct against the benchmark of various principles. One strand of procedural improprieties related to equality of arms.[119] The other strand, which one might view as elaborating the elements of good faith regarding abuse of form for an inappropriate purpose, focused on integrity of judicial conduct, dealing with situations where judges lacked impartiality, followed

[113] *Barcelona Traction, Light and Power Company, Ltd (Belgium v Spain)* [1970] ICJ Rep 3, 222, 233 (Morelli J).

[114] 'France et Saint-Dominique' (1900) 7 RGDIP 274, 274–76.

[115] Paparinskis, *International Minimum Standard* (n 2) 190–92, 210–11, as cited in *Flughafen Zürich AG and Gestión e Ingenería SA v Venezuela (Award)* (ICSID Arbitral Tribunal, Case No ARB/10/19, 18 November 2014) para 638.

[116] In the 1930 Conference for the Codification of International Law, the texts adopted by the committee in first reading as revised by the drafting committee included among the grounds of responsibility the cases where 'the foreigner… has encountered in the proceedings unjustifiable… delays implying a refusal to do justice': 'Texts of Articles Adopted in First Reading by the Third Committee of the Conference for the Codification of International Law' League of Nations publication, *V Legal, 1930 V 17* art 9(2).

[117] Paparinskis, *International Minimum Standard* (n 2) 192–93, 211–12, as cited in *Flughafen Zürich* (n 115) para 638.

[118] ibid 197, 216. [119] ibid 193–95, 212–14.

strong public feeling on the particular issue, or were subject to impermissible influence by the executive or corruption by the parties.[120] The quintessential case of bad faith in traditional law was *Cotesworth and Powell*, where the judge hid and destroyed court papers, colluded with other parties, and finally disappeared, but not before selling the claimant's tobacco in dispute to his own secretary.[121] In the recent *Yukos* cases, the finding 'that Russian courts bent to the will of Russian executive authorities to bankrupt Yukos' could be viewed as spelling out the abuse of form in the particular instance.[122]

The most contested aspect of obligations regarding due process is the so-called 'substantive denial of justice': the primary obligation regarding the content of judgments. Practice, both traditional and modern, has not generated consensus regarding criteria and methodology, and some approaches draw upon good faith. According to one approach common in traditional practice, content of the judgment could not provide grounds of responsibility, unless it was inspired by manifest ill-will towards foreigners.[123] An intermediate position would not require proof of bad faith, but rather infer it from the inferior quality of judgments. In such cases, 'it should be shown that the decision was so palpably unjust that the good faith of the court is open to suspicion',[124] and the substantive analysis would be reframed in terms of a presumption of procedural impropriety. Another way of making a similar point would be to reformulate the obligation as requiring the existence of courts properly constituted and run by competent judges (rather than delivery of a judgment of particular content), basing the responsibility for unjust judgments on the failure to provide a competent judge.[125] Finally, at the other end of the spectrum, some authorities explicitly rejected any direct relevance of clear or inferred bad faith, focusing instead on the quality and internal consistency of the reasoning and the evaluation of evidence.[126] Modern developments have echoed traditional practice both in

[120] ibid 194, 214–15.

[121] *Cotesworth and Powell (Great Britain v Colombia)* (1875) 2 Moore Intl Arbitrations 2050, 2064–85.

[122] *Yukos* (n 96) para 1583.

[123] The Preparatory Committee of the Hague Conference suggested that international responsibility would arise when '[t]he substance of a judicial decision has manifestly been prompted by ill-will toward foreigners as such or as subjects of particular States': Bases of Discussion Drawn up in 1929 by the Preparatory Committee of the Conference for the Codification of International Law (The Hague 1930), FV García-Amador, 'Report on International Responsibility' [1956] II Yearbook ILC 173, 223 Basis of Discussion 5(4), UN Doc A/CN.4/SER.A/1956/Add.1.

[124] 'Responsibility of States for Damage Done in Their Territory to the Person or Property of Foreigners' (1929) 23 AJIL Special Supp 133, 186; Paulsson, *Denial of Justice* (n 111) 82–84.

[125] Paulsson, *Denial of Justice* (n 111) 200–02.

[126] Paparinskis, *International Minimum Standard* (n 2) 195–97.

their hesitation to base responsibility on the content of the judgment, and in the conciseness and inconsistency of methodology suggested or implied in reasoning. The best approach, in line with some authority in traditional practice and trends in human rights law, may be to focus on internal consistency and comprehensibility of reasoning, leaving inferences of bad faith entirely aside.[127]

### 7.4.4 Transparency

Unlike the wealth of practice underpinning rules on due process, transparency is based on relatively few authorities of direct relevance for treaty and customary rules of investment protection. Arbitral decisions on the issue seem to be addressing the issue with rather different approaches in mind. At least prima facie, the 'complete lack of transparency and candour in an administrative process' of *Waste Management II*,[128] and the expectation that a state acts 'totally transparently in its relations with the foreign investor' of *TECMED*[129] are not quite the same thing. Viewing transparency through the lens of good faith—as the *TECMED* tribunal suggested that it was doing—might perhaps provide a certain framework for developing greater methodological coherence.

A convenient starting point, even if somewhat removed from modern investment protection law, is the 1921 award in *Jesse Lewis*, an inter-state arbitration that had to address a claim by the US that a condemnation of a fishing vessel was wrongful because it was a 'sudden change of course' by the United Kingdom in the application of its laws.[130] The claim was rejected, the arbitral commission emphasizing 'the public proclamations by the Canadian Government as well as by the United States Government', which made it unlikely that this change was sudden and had surprised the foreigner.[131] In *Jesse Lewis*, the inquiry into availability of information was conducted so as to determine whether the state's conduct was internally consistent, or whether it was requiring compliance with rules and simultaneously withholding information about their content. That is a question about the good faith of the state, in the sense of arbitrary inconsistency. The perspective of sufficient transparency to enable the investor to appreciate and respond to the position taken by the state—if necessary by appropriate technical and professional assistance—would elaborate this requirement of non-arbitrariness, quite possibly alongside other principles derived from good faith. The arbitral award in

[127] ibid 215–16. [128] *Waste Management II* (n 74) para 98.
[129] *TECMED* (n 10) para 154.
[130] *Jesse Lewis (United States v Great Britain)* (1921) 6 UNRIAA 85, 92. [131] ibid.

the *Saluka v Czech Republic* case provides one example of the role that transparency might play within the broader context, finding insufficient transparency in the exchange of views that did not enable the investor to understand the government's preconditions for an acceptable solution, and contributing to overall breach of fair and equitable treatment by other substantive and procedural improprieties.[132]

### 7.4.5 Expectations

Expectations of the investor, often qualified as 'legitimate' or 'reasonable', play a very important role in interpretation and application of fair and equitable treatment. This is not the place to consider in detail the process of legal reasoning by which legitimate expectations may be justified as an element of the primary obligation; suffice to say that the process is not straightforward or obvious.[133] The next paragraphs will therefore focus on the contribution that good faith might make to the discussion.

The process of interpreting and applying such a vague term as fair and equitable treatment might, of course, be informed by peculiarities of particular disputes, which might sharpen the issues left open by a more abstract interpretative exercise. Still, at the very least, the *VCLT* principles of interpretation do not obviously nudge the interpreter to formulate the inquiry in terms of expectations. For example, the ordinary meaning of 'fair' and 'equitable' can provide the starting point for criteria of reasonableness and impartiality, but less obviously of respect for expectations.[134] The choice of 'investment', rather than 'investor', as the usual object of protection suggests a certain systemic oddness in approaching the object of protection of substantive obligations through the lens of a loosely connected procedural actor.

When one moves to customary law, the position of the traditional rules on the expectations of aliens is difficult to identify with certainty because protests and arguments rarely focused solely on the suddenness of the change. The broader principle seems to have been focused on the preclusion of retroactive developments, requiring 'important changes [to be] usually prospective in their operation, so that they might have no injurious effect on previous transactions'.[135] In structural terms, the traditional position seems best reflected in authorities such as *Jesse Lewis*, where the tribunal primarily

[132] *Saluka* (n 28) paras 420–25.

[133] Paparinskis, *International Minimum Standard* (n 2) 251–56.

[134] Michael Proffitt (ed) *Oxford English Dictionary* (OUP) <www.oed.com> accessed 24 September 2014, 'Equitable' para 1, 'fair' para 4.

[135] 'Mr Fisch, Secretary of State, to Mr Lopez Roberts, Spanish Minister' (1869) 6 Moore Digest 752, 752.

focused on the propriety of form and process and the availability of judicial remedies, identifying suddenness of change only as a possibly supporting consideration of wrongfulness.[136] Overall, this practice on protection of expectations is better read as an elaboration of a particular aspect of arbitrariness than as a separate perspective.

Good faith may be pressed to justify the protection of investors' expectations in several ways. First, the *Nuclear Tests* judgment of the ICJ is a leading authority regarding the ability of the state to bind itself by a unilateral act, the binding character of such an obligation being based in turn on good faith.[137] Could one justify legitimate expectations as describing the same legal concept, if from the perspective of the addressee rather than the state? The starting point for thinking about the issue is that no reason of principle precludes states from binding themselves vis-à-vis investors by a unilateral act under international law.[138] The objections are rather of a mundane and technical character: a state may be bound only by a unilateral statement of an authority that can represent the state in international affairs for this purpose (as most mid/low-level officials often alleged to have been giving representations would not be);[139] the act has to be given 'with the intention of being bound' under international law,[140] which is not a matter to be easily presumed;[141] and even if all those concerns are overcome, one would be faced with a separate international obligation for the breach of which responsibility would arise, rather than an element of fair and equitable treatment.

Secondly, legitimate expectations could be structured along the lines of estoppel, a principle derived from good faith, either applying estoppel directly to the relationship between the state and the investor, or drawing criteria

[136] *Jesse Lewis* (n 130) 92. In a different sense, the description of the US argument about sudden change of course as 'a principle based upon the bona fide of foreigners' (ibid 92) provides the starting point for an examination of conduct of investors and investment: Peter Muchlinski, '"Caveat Investor"? The Relevance of the Conduct of the Investor under the Fair and Equitable Treatment Standard' (2006) 55 ICLQ 55; see also chapter 5 of this volume.

[137] *Nuclear Tests Case* (n 1) paras 46–49.

[138] W Michael Reisman and Mahnoush Arsanjani, 'The Questions of Unilateral Governmental Statements as Applicable Law in Investment Disputes' in Pierre-Marie Dupuy et al (eds), *Common Values in International Law: Essays in Honour of Christian Tomuschat* (Engel Verlag 2006) 409.

[139] Reisman and Arsanjani point to the *Congo v Rwanda* case (*Armed Activities on the Territory of the Congo (New Application: 2002) (Congo v Rwanda) (Jurisdiction and Admissibility)* [2006] ICJ Rep 6, para 47) to suggest that contemporary practice has moved beyond the authority of the 'big three': ibid 418–19. But in any event the authority would be limited, justifiable on a case-by-case basis, and not a suitable basis for a general principle around which to structure fair and equitable treatment.

[140] *Nuclear Tests Case* (n 1) para 47.

[141] The *Nuclear Tests* judgment, perhaps somewhat unusual in its own terms, is the only case where such an intention has been found to have been present: Thirlway (n 1) 11–12, 14–20.

from it by analogy. The second version of the argument assumes its own correctness, that is the existence of a vague rule on the protection of expectations, which can be clarified by analogy. The first argument is defensible.[142] But it may be understating the importance of assumptions of structural equality, which underlie estoppel in domestic law and inter-state relations under international law, but are not present in investor–state legal relations under international law. In other words, good faith would justify estoppel in circumstances where rights and obligations may be generated in normal interaction by parties to prevent unfair advantage taken by one party, but good faith would not be appropriate for the diagonal structure of investment protection law, where conduct of the investor is distinct from the formulation of rights and obligations.

Finally, legitimate expectations have been derived from domestic legal systems through the modicum of general principles. This is not the place to engage in a review of domestic approaches. It may be, however, that a closer look would reveal that, once the net of inquiry is thrown sufficiently broadly (to include for example China, Russia, and India) and the structural differences duly noted (particularly between substantive and procedural elements), the degree of acceptance of the concept and its formulations are found to be insufficient to justify a formulation and transposition of a general principle to the international level.[143] In all of these arguments, good faith seems less useful than one might have expected.

## 7.5 Conclusion

This chapter has examined the relationship of good faith and fair and equitable treatment. It is not at all surprising that a general principle—*the* most general principle—and a particular primary obligation interrelate in a variety of ways. That is precisely the conclusion that one would expect from an inquiry structured in these terms. The analysis of particular aspects of the relationship has not led to any particular insights into the nature of the international legal order in general or investment protection law in particular—except, perhaps, the most basic of all points that ordinary methods of small-print legal analysis, uninspiring and tedious as they might be, are on most occasions

[142] James Crawford, *Brownlie's Principles of Public International Law* (8th edn, OUP 2012) 420 n 26, 611 n 27.

[143] Michele Potestà, 'Legitimate Expectations in Investment Treaty Law: Understanding the Roots and the Limits of a Controversial Concept' (2013) 28 ICSID Rev 88, 93–98.

capable of dissolving the banks of fog that stand between the observer and the solution to the problem.[144] Good faith plays various roles in legal reasoning about fair and equitable treatment. Sometimes it informs structures of reasoning and interpretation (as with any other rule of international law); sometimes it provides the broader background and hints at the systemic logic of a particular part of the rule; sometimes it is useful in oiling a particular bit of machinery of fair and equitable treatment; and sometimes it would be distinctly unhelpful, pulling the interpreter away from its own particularizations or even rules built on different premises. Overall, there is nothing more to this than the colloquial point about square pegs and round holes, and the sensible precaution that the systemic importance of a peg does not mean that it should be pushed down every hole.

Is there perhaps a broader point to good faith and fair and equitable treatment that this chapter has missed? Good faith is, of course, of great systemic importance in international law, but that does not mean that assertions about the existence of principles or rules derived from it have to be accepted without satisfying the usual law-making criteria, or that such assertions have to be preferred over principles or rules that have satisfied those criteria. For example, legitimate expectations may be a particularly prominent element of good faith, and might provide a useful perspective for thinking about treaty interpretation or customary law-making,[145] but one still needs to satisfy the usual law-making criteria to conclude that a primary obligation of respect for legitimate expectations is imposed. One might also pull together different elements of decisions dealing with bad faith as part of fair and equitable treatment to suggest that not engaging in conduct in bad faith is a separate element of fair and equitable treatment.[146] But is there genuine added value in doing that? At most, good faith (and particularly reasonableness) might caution against excessive taxonomy of the weight of particular elements in constituting or contributing to a breach of fair and equitable treatment;[147] the contextual and integrated examination of all relevant considerations would then be a more appropriate solution.

Overall, the development of fair and equitable treatment is much better served by the elaboration of particular elements of good or bad faith in arbitrariness and its particular applications—discrimination, due process, and

[144] Ian Brownlie, 'Recognition in Theory and Practice' (1982) 53 BYBIL 197, 197.

[145] *See* Maurice Mendelson, 'The Formation of Customary International Law' (1998) 272 RCADI 155, 184–89, 292, 394, 399; Michael Byers, *Custom, Power and the Power of Rules* (CUP 1999) ch 7.

[146] Draguiev (n 16).

[147] Dumberry (n 16) 262–70, generally ch 3.

transparency—than by redirecting the focus to the most general of principles. At the end of the day, what is now required in fair and equitable treatment is the development not so much of very general principles and standards as of detailed rules of technical law—without forgetting the systemic value of the general principles, but not exclusively focusing on them either.

# 8

# Conclusion

*Andrew D Mitchell and Tania Voon*

This volume weaves its way through a number of intersecting fields: chief among them public international law, international investment law, and international trade law. The focus of the analysis is on international investment law, and in particular the significance of the principle of good faith in identifying a protected investment or protected investor, the nationality of a given entity, the jurisdiction of an investment tribunal in resolving a given dispute, and compliance with the fair and equitable treatment standard. Yet the role of good faith in the context of international investment law can be fully understood only having regard to other legal issues, including: the sources of international law; the interpretation of treaties; the law of treaties, in terms of their creation, modification and termination; and the relationship between overlapping disputes in different national, regional and international fora. Accordingly, the volume brings together authors with varied and complementary expertise to tackle good faith from these various angles.

Good faith must be recognized, at the outset, as a 'general principle of law' within the meaning of article 38(1)(c) of the *Statute of the International Court of Justice* and, perhaps, as a principle of international law in the form of customary international law. This status of good faith is confirmed by learned scholars[1] and reflected in jurisprudence of the International Court of Justice (ICJ)[2] as well as numerous treaties.[3] Yet, as Ziegler and Baumgartner explain in chapter 2, the relative absence of controversy regarding the status of the principle of good faith contrasts with the significant uncertainty concerning

[1] See Bin Cheng, *General Principles of Law as Applied by International Courts and Tribunals* (Stevens & Sons 1953) 105. See also John O'Connor, *Good Faith in International Law* (Dartsmouth 1991) 2.

[2] See, eg, *Nuclear Tests (Australia v France) (Merits)* [1974] ICJ Rep 253, 268.

[3] See, eg, *Charter of the United Nations* art 2(2); *Charter of the Organization of American States* art 3(c); *United Nations Convention on the Law of the Sea*, opened for signature 10 December 1982, 1833 UNTS 3 (entered into force 16 November 1994) arts 105, 157, 300.

its precise parameters and content. Moreover, even individual particularizations of the principle of good faith (such as abuse of rights or estoppel) tend to be plagued by some vagueness and dispute about their significance and application to particular circumstances. This characteristic appears to be borne out by an examination of relevant cases across public international law (the jurisprudence of the ICJ), international trade law (the jurisprudence of the World Trade Organization (WTO) in particular), and international investment law (the known awards of investment treaty tribunals).

The requirement of 'good faith' treaty interpretation is even more settled as a matter of international law than is the status of good faith as a general principle of law. Pursuant to article 31(1) of the *Vienna Convention on the Law of Treaties* (*VCLT*),[4] a 'treaty shall be interpreted in good faith in accordance with the ordinary meaning to be given to the terms of the treaty in their context and in the light of its object and purpose'. Moreover, article 31 of the *VCLT* is widely recognized as one of this treaty's provisions that codify or have attained the status of customary international law.[5] Yet again, despite the clear significance of good faith in treaty interpretation, as De Brabandere and Van Damme point out in chapter 3, 'the function of the principle and its relationship with other principles of treaty interpretation remain the subject of debate'. They conclude that good faith operates both in directing the proper interpretation of treaties and in imposing standards on treaty interpreters.

The various complications arising from the principle of good faith arguably become clearest in attempting to apply good faith to particular factual and legal circumstances in the context of international investment law. The last three substantive chapters of this book provide illustrations of these complications in relation to different aspects of international investment law, drawing in particular on the statements of arbitral tribunals in investment treaty awards. However, before moving to those substantive questions of good faith in investment protection, we explore with Munro in chapter 4 the role of good faith in resolving situations of 'parallel' or simultaneous disputes. This form of dispute can arise not only within international investment law or within international trade law but also across these two fields, for example where a home state or other WTO member brings a complaint against a host state within the WTO dispute settlement system at the same time as

[4] *Vienna Convention on the Law of Treaties*, opened for signature 23 May 1969, 1155 UNTS 331 (entered into force 27 January 1980) (*VCLT*).

[5] See, eg, *Arbitral Award of 31 July 1989 (Guinea-Bissau v Senegal) (Judgment)* [1991] ICJ Rep 53, para 48; Ian Sinclair, *The Vienna Convention on the Law of Treaties* (2nd ed, Manchester University Press 1984) 19.

an investor brings a claim against the host state under a bilateral investment treaty (BIT) or other form of international investment agreement (such as a preferential trade agreement including an investment chapter). This type of scenario has been witnessed most recently in response to Australia's standardized tobacco packaging laws, with the WTO and BIT claims continuing at the time of writing and likely to continue for some years.[6]

Chapter 4 identifies 'only limited scope for managing parallel litigation under WTO law and investment law on the basis of principles of good faith'. That is, for example, *lis pendens* and abuse of rights could not typically be used to prevent an investor from bringing a BIT claim at the same time as a host state or other WTO member brings a WTO claim. However, while good faith may not generally provide a solution to difficulties arising from simultaneous claims brought across the two fields, the principle of good faith does offer appropriate tools for restraining inappropriate claims taking place simultaneously within international trade law or within international investment law. Given the conclusions of the earlier chapters regarding the precise meaning of good faith and its relationship to other aspects of international law, it is unsurprising that different tribunals have different approaches to good faith in managing these kinds of 'intra-field' parallel disputes, and that the requirements of good faith are rarely straightforward in these circumstances.

Offering a detailed illustration of the ambiguous role of good faith in international investment law, Schill and Bray in chapter 5 examine good faith 'as a discipline on whether certain foreign investments or their corporate structure benefit from investment treaty protection'. These authors caution that the unbridled use of a 'vague' form of good faith creates risks including unpredictability, personal bias, arbitrariness, and departure from the intentions of states parties to the relevant treaty. Yet the principle of good faith need not be used in such a destructive way. Instead, Schill and Bray conclude that good faith can be appropriately limited to have precise effects only in specific circumstances. In particular, domestic law should be relied on—in preference to a broad principle of good faith—in addressing misuse of corporate structures to obtain investment protection. The role of good faith is thus restricted as follows:

> Good faith … could be legitimately used as a public law tool to limit host state reliance on its own laws, in particular in estoppel cases. The second avenue for good

[6] See, eg, *Australia—Certain Measures Concerning Trademarks and Other Plain Packaging Requirements Applicable to Tobacco Products and Packaging: Communication from the Chairperson of the Panel*, WTO Doc WT/DS434/14 (14 October 2014); *Philip Morris Asia Limited v Australia (Procedural Order No 9)* (Ad Hoc Arbitral Tribunal, UNCITRAL, 16 May 2014).

faith to play a role occurs when the acquisition of the investment or the investment activity is contrary to transnational public policy, albeit compliant with domestic law. In these cases, good faith is properly used as a mechanism to limit the protection of foreign investments or access to investment arbitration.

In chapter 6, Sornarajah tackles a related area also concerning corporate nationality, but with a focus on the use of 'denial of benefits' provisions in international investment agreements. He identifies the two typical situations of corporate restructuring to attain the benefit of a particular BIT as 'round-tripping' and the 'Dutch sandwich', both of which techniques tribunals have permitted even though they evidently 'subvert the aim of the investment treaty in promoting the flow of foreign investment for purposes of economic development'. Sornarajah emphasizes that round-tripping and the Dutch sandwich cannot further this treaty objective because 'they give rise to no fresh investment flows'. Thus, an investor that bases an investment claim on the use of these techniques exercises its right to arbitration other than in good faith; a supportive home state may be complicit in this abuse of right; and a tribunal that permits these techniques does so contrary to a good faith interpretation of the relevant treaties. Sornarajah points to states' use of a denial of benefits provision in reaction to arbitrators' acceptance of techniques such as round-tripping and the Dutch sandwich. However, given that tribunals have narrowly interpreted denial of benefits provisions so as to expand investment protection, he suggests that an alternative would be wider adoption within BITs of the *siege social* theory, 'which emphasizes the place of actual management of the company in determining corporate nationality, with the specific objective of avoiding fraudulent claims to nationality'.

Chapters 5 and 6 present quite different perspectives on the role and significance of good faith in relation to matters of corporate structuring. Sornarajah regards good faith as a legitimate means of dealing with the identified corporate manoeuvres (of round-tripping and the Dutch sandwich) to demonstrate an absence of jurisdiction, yet he acknowledges that such a means is unlikely to be embraced by investment treaty arbitrators. In contrast, Schill and Bray propose greater reliance on 'compliance with domestic law… as a general duty incumbent on foreign investors as a general principle of law'—rather than reliance on the general principle of good faith—whether or not the relevant treaty includes an express provision requiring investments to be made in accordance with the law of the host state. Whereas Sornarajah highlights the potential absence of good faith of a *home state* in supporting an investor's use of dubious corporate restructuring techniques to obtain protection under a particular international investment agreement, Schill and Bray maintain that elements of good faith such as estoppel may prevent a *host state* from 'invoking domestic illegality in situations where the host state breached its own laws or…knew about the investor's illegality and accepted it'. All three authors might agree that the principle of good faith requires foreign investors to comply with international law (or 'transnational public policy', to use the preferred term of Schill and Bray), where that law extends beyond domestic law, for example in relation to the protection of human rights or the prevention of corruption.

Chapter 7 moves beyond the definition of a protected investment and related jurisdictional questions to the core substantive obligation of 'fair and equitable treatment' in international investment law. This chapter returns to the theme of caution in applying the principle of good faith. Paparinskis emphasizes the need for the development and application of 'detailed rules of technical law' in place of an amorphous, open-ended principle of good faith. Good faith could conceivably be relevant in assessing compliance with various elements of fair and equitable treatment. However, Paparinskis explains that good faith may not always provide a useful clarification of these different elements, some of which are better established than others. For example, the existence of arbitrariness or non-arbitrariness may not be more easily determined by reference to the concept of good faith. Good faith may be seen as more closely related to certain aspects of due process, which Paparinskis describes as 'the most sophisticated part of fair and equitable treatment'. As an example, he explains that 'denial of access to justice may be viewed as an expression of good faith in precluding inappropriate inconsistency'. In relation to substantive denial of justice, Paparinskis nevertheless suggests that a focus on 'internal consistency and comprehensibility of reasoning' may be preferable to reliance on the principle of good faith.

Chapter 7 also refers to good faith in relation to the 'legitimate expectations' of investors. A violation of fair and equitable treatment is sometimes alleged on the basis that the host state has breached an investor's legitimate expectations, particularly to the extent that the state induced these expectations through specific investor-directed representations or conduct. Paparinskis makes clear that fair and equitable treatment does not necessarily have to include an assessment of the investor's expectations. Although the relevance of those expectations 'might…be defended through the lens of good faith', he also finds on closer examination that good faith is not particularly useful in justifying the protection of investors' expectations through the fair and equitable treatment standard. Paparinskis argues that investors' expectations are best protected and analysed as a part of the existing rules against arbitrariness than as a part of good faith or through a stand-alone concept of legitimate expectations.

The notion of legitimate expectations may also arise in the context of expropriation in international investment law, an area in which further examination of good faith might be fruitful. The notion of legitimate expectations also brings us back to the relationship between international trade law and international investment law. In the WTO, legitimate expectations may be relevant to the rarely used option of a 'non-violation' claim, pursuant to which a WTO member may contend that another member has applied a measure that nullifies or impairs the attainment of WTO objectives, whether or not it also breaches WTO rules.[7] The WTO panel in *Japan—Film* explained that the purpose of allowing such a claim:

> is to protect the balance of concessions under GATT by providing a means to redress government actions not otherwise regulated by GATT rules that nonetheless nullify or impair a Member's *legitimate expectations* of benefits from tariff negotiations.[8]

The expectations of WTO members have also been referred to as regards the conditions of competition between various products in the more standard WTO claims of violation of the agreements.[9] Here, then, legitimate expectations of WTO members under WTO law may be compared to legitimate expectations of foreign investors under international investment law. Further research into the understanding of these concepts in these two related fields might be fruitful, particularly as regards the role of good faith in justifying reliance on legitimate expectations, in assessing the legitimacy of expectations, and in identifying adherence to or departure from legitimate expectations.

WTO law may also offer further insights into legitimate expectations outside the realm of non-violation complaints. The WTO Appellate Body has long held that adopted Panel and Appellate Body Reports 'create legitimate expectations among WTO Members, and, therefore, should be taken into account where they are relevant to any dispute'.[10] Yet the Appellate Body has twice rejected attempts by WTO panels to adopt 'legitimate expectations' (of exporting members, members or private right holders) as a principle of treaty interpretation.[11] To better understand and question these distinctions,

[7] *Marrakesh Agreement Establishing the World Trade Organization*, opened for signature 15 April 1994, 1867 UNTS 3 (entered into force 1 January 1995), annex 1A (*General Agreement on Tariffs and Trade*) art XXIII:1(b).

[8] Panel Report, *Japan—Measures Affecting Consumer Photographic Film and Paper*, WTO Doc WT/DS44/R (adopted 22 April 1998) para 10.50 (emphasis added).

[9] See Appellate Body Report, *India—Patent Protection for Pharmaceutical and Agricultural Chemical Products*, WTO Doc WT/DS50/AB/R (adopted 16 January 1998) para 40.

[10] Appellate Body Report, *Japan—Taxes on Alcoholic Beverages*, WTO Docs WT/DS8/AB/R, WT/DS10/AB/R, WT/DS11/AB/R (adopted 1 November 1996) 14.

[11] Appellate Body Report, *European Communities—Customs Classification of Certain Computer Equipment*, WTO Docs WT/DS62/AB/R, WT/DS67/AB/R, WT/DS68/AB/R (adopted 22 June 1998) paras 80–82; Appellate Body Report, *India—Patents (US)* (n 9) paras 42, 45, 48.

further research into the relationship between good faith and legitimate expectations in the context of treaty interpretation in public international law, international trade law, and international investment law might prove beneficial.

In all, this book demonstrates an underlying tension between the accepted significance of good faith as an overarching principle in international law and the difficult process of applying good faith in a defensible and consistent manner in particular circumstances. If overused, good faith may be used to hide and protect subjective bias and judgment, diminishing predictability and accountability in decision-making. If ignored, conduct that is evidently contrary to good faith may be shielded through reliance on narrow textual interpretation or technical loopholes. Although this book has attempted to shed light on the various roles that good faith may play in international investment law, the authors have also identified areas in which further refinement is needed to clarify the scope and meaning of the particular forms in which good faith exists. That refinement may take place through scholarly debate and public engagement as well as judicial and arbitral pronouncements. Through greater concretization of the principle of good faith, a balance may be better struck between the importance of this principle in restraining conduct of states and investors and the need for clear guidance in applying standards and rules regarding the protection of investments.

# *Bibliography*

## BOOKS


Aust A, *Modern Treaty Law and Practice* (CUP 2000)

Aust A, *Review of the Convention on Contracts for the International Sale of Goods (CISG) 2002–2003* (Kluwer Law International 2004)

Badia A, *Piercing the Veil of State Enterprises in International Arbitration* (Kluwer Law International 2014)

Bartels L and Ortino F (eds), *Regional Trade Agreements and the WTO Legal System* (OUP 2006)

Bernhardt R (ed), *Encyclopedia of Public International Law*, vol 1 (North-Holland Publishing Company 1992)

Binder C, Kriebaum U, Reinisch A and Wittich S (eds), *International Investment Law for the 21st Century: Essays in Honour of Christoph Schreuer* (OUP 2009)

Brown C, *A Common Law of International Adjudication* (OUP 2007)

Brownlie I, *Principles of Public International Law* (6th edn, OUP 2003)

Brownlie I, *Principles of Public International Law* (7th edn, OUP 2008)

Byers M, *Custom, Power and the Power of Rules* (CUP 1999)

Cheng B, *General Principles of Law as Applied by International Courts and Tribunals* (Stevens and Sons 1953)

Cheng B, *General Principles of Law as Applied by International Courts and Tribunals* (Grotius Publications 1987)

Corten E and Klein P (eds), *The Vienna Convention on the Law of Treaties: A Commentary*, vol I (OUP 2011)

Crawford J, *Brownlie's Principles of Public International Law* (8th edn, OUP 2012)

Crawford J, *State Responsibility: The General Part* (CUP 2013)

Crawford J, Pellet A and Olesson S (eds), *The Law of International Responsibility* (OUP 2010)

Davies P, *Gower and Davies: The Principles of Modern Company Law* (8th edn, Sweet & Maxwell 2008)

Dolzer R and Schreuer C, *Principles of International Investment Law* (2nd edn, OUP 2012)

Dolzer R and Stevens M, *Bilateral Investment Treaties* (Martinus Nijhoff 1995)

Douglas Z, *The International Law of Investment Claims* (CUP 2009)

Douglas Z, Pauwelyn J, and Viñuales J (eds), *The Foundations of International Investment Law* (OUP 2014)

Dumberry P, *The Fair and Equitable Treatment Standard: A Guide to NAFTA Case Law under Article 1105* (Kluwer Law International 2013)

Dupuy P-M et al (eds), *Common Values in International Law: Essays in Honour of Christian Tomuschat* (Engel Verlag 2006)

Fauchald OK and Nollkaemper A (eds), *The Practice of International and National Courts and the (De-)Fragmentation of International Law* (Hart 2012)

Freeman AV, *The International Responsibility of States for Denial of Justice* (Longmans, Green & Co 1938)

Gardiner R, *Treaty Interpretation* (OUP 2008)

Gazzini T and De Brabandere E (eds), *International Investment Law: The Sources of Rights and Obligations* (Martinus Nijhoff 2012)

Hartkamp A et al (eds), *Towards a European Civil Code* (4th rev edn, Kluwer Law International 2010)

Hernández C, *The International Court of Justice and the Judicial Function* (OUP 2014)

Hofmann R and Tams C (eds), *From Clinical Isolation to Systemic Integration* (Nomos 2011)

Horn H and Mavroidis P (eds), *The WTO Case Law of 2002* (CUP 2005)

Huerta-Goldman J, Romanetti A and Stirnimann F (eds), *WTO Litigation, Investment Arbitration, and Commercial Arbitration* (Kluwer Law International 2013)

Jennings R and Watts A (eds), *Oppenheim's International Law*, vol 1 (9th edn, Longman Group 1992)

Kläger R, *'Fair and Equitable Treatment' in International Investment Law* (CUP 2011)

Kolb R, *La Bonne Foi en Droit International Public* (Presses Universitaires de France 2000)

Kolb R, *The International Court of Justice* (Hart 2013)

Lauterpacht E, *Aspects of the Administration of International Justice* (Grotius 1991)

Lauterpacht H, *The Function of Law in the International Community* (Clarendon Press 1933)

Lauterpacht H, *The Development of International Law by the International Court* (Stevens and Sons 1958)

Lauterpacht H, *The Function of Law in the International Community* (OUP 2011)

Lowe V and Warbrick C (eds), *The United Nations and the Principles of International Law: Essays in Memory of Michael Akehurst* (Routledge 1994)

Lowe V and Fitzmaurice M (eds), *Fifty Years of the International Court of Justice: Essays in Honour of Sir Robert Jennings* (CUP 1996)

Marmor A and Soames S (eds), *Philosophical Foundations of Language in the Law* (OUP 2013)

Mattli W and Dietz T (eds), *International Arbitration and Global Governance* (OUP 2014)

McLachlan C, *Lis Pendens in International Litigation* (Martinus Nijhoff 2009)

Mercurio B and Lim C (eds), *International Economic Law After the Crisis: A Tale of Fragmented Disciplines* (CUP forthcoming 2015)

Molinuevo M, *Protecting Investment in Services: Investor–State Arbitration versus WTO Dispute Settlement* (Kluwer Law International 2011)

Newcombe N and Paradell L, *Law and Practice of Investment Treaties: Standards of Treatment* (Kluwer Law International 2009)

O'Connor J, *Good Faith in International Law* (Dartsmouth 1991)

Panizzon M, *Good Faith in the Jurisprudence of the WTO: The Protection of Legitimate Expectations, Good Faith Interpretation and Fair Dispute Settlement* (Hart 2006)

Paparinskis M, *The International Minimum Standard and Fair and Equitable Treatment* (OUP 2013)
Parra A, *The History of ICSID* (OUP 2012)
Rosenne S, *Developments in the Law of Treaties 1945–1986* (CUP 1989)
Rovine A (ed), *Contemporary Issues in International Arbitration and Mediation* (Martinus Nijhoff 2013)
Sauvant K (ed), *Appeals Mechanism in International Investment Disputes* (OUP 2008)
Sauvant K (ed), *Yearbook on International Investment Law & Policy 2011–2012* (OUP 2013)
Sayed A, *Corruption in International Trade and Commercial Arbitration* (Kluwer 2004)
Schill SW (ed), *International Investment Law and Comparative Public Law* (OUP 2010)
Schreuer C, *The ICSID Convention: A Commentary* (2nd edn, CUP 2009)
Schwebel S, *Justice in International Law* (CUP 1994)
Shany Y, *The Competing Jurisdictions of International Courts and Tribunals* (OUP 2003)
Sornarajah M, *The International Law on Foreign Investment* (3rd edn, CUP 2010)
Teubner G, *Standards und Direktiven in Generalklauseln: Möglichkeiten und Grenzen der empirischen Sozialforschung bei der Präzisierung der Gute-Sitte-Klauseln im Privatrecht* (Athenäum 1971)
Thirlway H, *The Law and Procedure of the International Court of Justice* (OUP 2013)
Thirlway H, *The Sources of International Law* (OUP 2014)
Tudor I, *The Fair and Equitable Treatment Standard in the International Law of Foreign Investment* (OUP 2008)
Van Damme I, *Treaty Interpretation by the WTO Appellate Body* (OUP 2009)
Van Harten G, *Investment Treaty Arbitration and Public Law* (OUP 2007)
Wehland H, *The Coordination of Multiple Proceedings in Investment Treaty Arbitration* (OUP 2013)
Waibel M et al (eds), *The Backlash against Investment Arbitration* (Kluwer Law International 2010)
Weiler T, *The Interpretation of International Investment Law* (Martinus Nijhoff 2013)
Werner J and Hyder Ali A (eds), *A Liber Amicorum: Thomas Wälde—Law Beyond Conventional Thought* (Cameron May 2009)
Yannaca-Small C, *International Investment Law: Understanding Concepts and Tracking Innovations* (OECD 2008)
Zimmermann A, Tomuschat C and Oellers-Frahm K (eds), *The Statute of the International Court of Justice: A Commentary* (2nd edn, OUP 2012)
Zoller E, *La Bonne Foi en Droit International Public* (Editions Pedone 1977)

## JOURNAL ARTICLES

Amaza IP, 'Multiplicity of International Dispute Settlement Forums: Avoiding the Risk of Parallel Proceedings' (2012) 6 DRI 149
Berman F, 'International Treaties and British Statutes' (2005) 26 Statute L Rev 1

Brown C, 'The Relevance of the Doctrine of Abuse of Process in International Arbitration' (2011) 8(2) TDM 1 <transnational-dispute-management.com>

Brownlie I, 'Recognition in Theory and Practice' (1982) 53 BYBIL 197

Byers M, 'Abuse of Rights: An Old Principle, A New Age' (2002) 47 McGill LJ 389

Cairns D, 'Transnational Public Policy and the Internal Law of State Parties' (2009) 6(1) TDM 27 <transnational-dispute-management.com>

Crawford J, 'Treaty and Contract in Investment Arbitration' (2008) 24 Arb Intl 351

Cremades B, 'Good Faith in International Arbitration' (2012) 27(4) Am U Intl L Rev 761

Dajic S, 'Mapping the Good Faith Principle in International Investment Arbitration: Assessment of Its Substantive and Procedural Value' (2012) 46 Zbornik Radova 207

Dawidowicz M, 'The Effect of the Passage of Time on the Interpretation of Treaties: Some Reflections on *Costa Rica v Nicaragua*' (2011) 24(1) LJIL 201

De Brabandere E, ' "Good Faith", "Abuse of Process" and the Initiation of Investment Treaty Claims' (2012) 3 JIDS 609

De Ly F and Sheppard A, 'ILA Final Report on Lis Pendens and Arbitration' (2009) 24 Arb Intl 1

Douglas Z, 'The Hybrid Foundations of Investment Treaty Arbitration' (2003) 74 BYBIL 151

Douglas Z, 'Nothing if Not Critical for Investment Arbitration: *Occidental, Eureko* and *Methanex*' (2006) 22 Arb Intl 27

Douglas Z, 'The Plea of Illegality in Investment Treaty Arbitration' (2014) 29 ICSID Rev 155

Draguiev D, 'Bad Faith Conduct of States in Violation of "Fair and Equitable Treatment" Standard in International Investment Law and Arbitration' (2014) 5 JIDS 273

Dumberry P, 'The Protection of Investors' Legitimate Expectations and the Fair and Equitable Treatment Standard under NAFTA Article' (2014) 31 J Intl Arb 47

Fauchald OK, 'The Legal Reasoning of ICSID Tribunals—An Empirical Analysis' (2008) 19(2) EJIL 301

Favre A, 'L'interpretation objectiviste des traits internationaux' (1960) XVII *Annuaire suisse de droit international* 75

Feldman M, 'Setting Limits on Corporate Nationality Planning in Investment Treaty Arbitration' (2012) 27(2) ICSID Rev 281

Fitzmaurice G, 'The General Principles of International Law, Considered from the Standpoint of the Rule of Law' (1957) 92(2) RdC 119

Franck S, 'The Legitimacy Crisis in Investment Treaty Arbitration: Privatizing Public International Law Through Inconsistent Decisions' (2005) 73 Fordham L Rev 1521

Gaffney J, ' "Abuse of Process" in Investment Treaty Arbitration' (2010) 11 JWIT 515

Guglya L, 'The Dispute Settlement Architecture of the Softwood Lumber Agreement 2006: the Interplay of Dispute Resolution Mechanisms in the Late Phases of Softwood Lumber Controversy' (2011) 8(3) TDM 1 <transnational-dispute-management.com>

Hansen R, 'Parallel Proceedings in Investor–State Treaty' (2010) 73 MLR 523

Ho J, 'Book Review Essay: Unraveling the *Lex Causae* in Investment Claims' (2014) 15 JWIT 757

Hudec R, 'The New WTO Dispute Settlement Procedure: An Overview of the First Three Years' (1999) 8(1) Minn J Global Trade 1

Hunter M and Silva GCE, 'Transnational Public Policy and Its Application in Investment Arbitrations' (2003) 4(3) JWIT 367

Jennings R, 'State Contracts in International Law' (1961) 37 BYBIL 156

Kolb R, 'Principles as Sources of International Law (with Special Reference to Good Faith)' (2006) 53 Nether Intl L Rev 1

Kurtz J, 'A General Investment Agreement in the WTO? Lessons from Chapter 11 of NAFTA and the OECD Multilateral Agreement on Investment' (2002) 23 U Pa J Intl Econ L 713

Kurtz J, 'The Use and Abuse of WTO Law in Investor–State Arbitration: Competition and Its Discontents' (2009) 20 EJIL 749

Lauterpacht H, 'Restrictive Interpretation and the Principle of Effectiveness in the Interpretation of Treaties' (1949) 26 BYBIL 48

Lowe V, 'The Role of Equity' (1988–1989) 12 Aust YBIL 54

Lowe V, 'Fair and Equitable Treatment: Remarks' (2006) 100 ASIL Proceedings 73

Martinez-Fraga P and Samra HJ, 'The Role of Precedent in Defining Res Judicata in Investor–State Arbitration' (2012) 32 Northwest J Intl L & Bus 419

Mavroidis P, 'Highway XVI Re-visited: The Road from Non-Discrimination to Market Access in GATS' (2007) 6(1) World TR 1

McLachlan C, 'The Principle of Systemic Integration and Article 31(3)(c) of the Vienna Convention' (2005) 54(2) ICLQ 279

Mendelson M, 'The Formation of Customary International Law' (1998) 272 RCADI 155

Mitchell A, 'Good Faith in WTO Dispute Settlement' (2006) 7 Melb J Intl L 339

Mitchell A and Heaton D, 'Book Review: Good Faith in the Jurisprudence of the WTO, by Marion Panizzon' (2009) 36(3) L Issues Eco Integration 273

Mitchell A and Heaton D, 'The Inherent Jurisdiction of WTO Tribunals: The Select Application of Public International Law Required by the Judicial Function' (2010) 31 Mich J Intl L 561

Moloo R and Khachaturian A, 'The Compliance with the Law Requirement in International Investment Law' (2011) 34 Fordham Intl LJ 1473

Muchlinski P, '"Caveat Investor"? The Relevance of the Conduct of the Investor under the Fair and Equitable Treatment Standard' (2006) 55 ICLQ 55

Paparinskis M, 'Investment Treaty Arbitration and the (New) Law of State Responsibility' (2013) 24 EJIL 617

Paulsson J and Petrochilos G, 'Neer-ly Misled' (2007) 22 ICSID Rev 242

Pauwelyn J, 'Adding Sweeteners to Softwood Lumber: The WTO–NAFTA "Spaghetti Bowl" Is Cooking' (2006) 9(1) JIEL 197

Pauwelyn J, 'At the Edge of Chaos?' (2014) 29 ICSID Rev 372

Pauwelyn J and Salles LE, 'Forum Shopping Before International Tribunals: (Real) Concerns (Im)Possible Solutions' (2009) 42 Cornell Intl LJ 77
Pinchis M, 'The Ancestry of "Equitable Treatment" in Trade' (2014) 15 JWIT 13
Potestà M, 'Legitimate Expectations in Investment Treaty Law: Understanding the Roots and the Limits of a Controversial Concept' (2013) 28 ICSID Rev 88
Powers P, 'Defining the Undefinable: Good Faith and the United Nations Convention on the Contracts for the International Sale of Goods' (1999) 18(2) J L & Commerce 336
Pryles M, 'Reflections on Transnational Public Policy' (2007) 24(1) J Intl Arb 1
Puig S, 'Social Capital in the Arbitration Market' (2014) 25 EJIL 387
Reinhold S, 'Good Faith in International Law' (2013) 2 UCL JL & Jur 40
Reinisch A, 'The Use and Limits of Res Judicata and Lis Pendens as Procedural Tools to Avoid Conflicting Dispute Settlement Outcomes' (2004) 3 LPICT 37
Reisman WM, '"Case-Specific Mandates" v "Systemic Implications": How Should Investment Tribunals Decide?' (2013) 29 Arb Intl 131
Roberts A, 'Power and Persuasion in Investment Treaty Arbitration: The Dual Role of States' (2010) 104 AJIL 179
Roberts A, 'Clash of Paradigms: Actors and Analogies Shaping the Investment Treaty System' (2013) 107 AJIL 45
Schill SW, 'W(h)ither Fragmentation? On the Literature and Sociology of International Investment Law' (2011) 22 EJIL 875
Schill SW, 'Illegal Investments in Investment Treaty Arbitration' (2012) 11 LPICT 281
Schwebel S, 'Is Neer Far from Fair and Equitable?' (2011) 27 Arb Intl 555
Shookman J, 'Too Many Forums for Investment Disputes? ICSID Illustrations of Parallel Proceedings and Analysis' (2010) 27 J Intl Arb 361
Sinclair A, 'The Substance of Nationality Requirements in Investment Treaty Arbitration' (2005) 20 ICSID Rev 368
Sornarajah M, 'Mutations of Neo-Liberalism in International Investment Law' (2011) 3 Trade L & Dev 204
Spoorenberg F and Vinuales J, 'Conflicting Decisions in International Arbitration' (2009) 8 LPICT 91
Steinberg R, 'Judicial Lawmaking at the WTO: Discursive, Constitutional, and Political Restraints' (2004) 98(2) AJIL 247
van Aaken A, 'Defragmentation of Public International Law Through Interpretation: A Methodological Proposal' (2009) 16(2) Ind J Global Legal Studies 483
Van Alstine M, 'The Death of Good Faith in Treaty Jurisprudence and a Call for Resurrection' (2005) 93 Georgetown LJ 1885
Virally M, 'Notes and Comments: Review Essay: Good Faith in Public International Law' (1983) 77 AJIL 130
Voon T, Mitchell A and Munro J, 'Legal Responses to Corporate Manoeuvring in International Investment Arbitration' (2014) JIDS 41

Voon T, Mitchell A and Munro J, 'Parting Ways: The Impact of Mutual Termination of Investment Treaties on Investor Rights' (2014) 29(2) ICSID Rev 451

Yee WP, '"Protecting Parties" Reasonable Expectations: A General Principle of Good Faith' (2001) 1 OUCLJ 195

Zeitler HE, '"Good faith" in the WTO Jurisprudence, Necessary Balancing Element or an Open Door to Judicial Activism?' JIEL 8(3) 721

# Index

The manufacturer's authorised representative in the EU for product safety is Oxford University Press España S.A. of el Parque Empresarial San Fernando de Henares, Avenida de Castilla, 2 – 28830 Madrid (www.oup.es/en or product.safety@oup.com). OUP España S.A. also acts as importer into Spain of products made by the manufacturer.

www.ingramcontent.com/pod-product-compliance
Lightning Source LLC
LaVergne TN
LVHW011801200926
848484LV00003B/756
* 9 7 8 0 1 9 8 7 3 9 7 9 1 *